Witnessing Whiteness

The Need to Talk about Race and How to Do It

Second Edition

Shelly Tochluk

ROWMAN & LITTLEFIELD EDUCATION

A division of

ROWMAN & LITTLEFIELD PUBLISHERS, INC.
Lanham • New York • Toronto • Plymouth, UK

Published by Rowman & Littlefield Education
A division of Rowman & Littlefield Publishers, Inc.
A wholly owned subsidary of The Rowman & Littlefield Publishing Group, Inc.
4501 Forbes Boulevard, Suite 200, Lanham, Maryland 20706
http://www.rowmaneducation.com

Estover Road
Plymouth PL6 7PY
United Kingdom

British Library Cataloguing in Publication Information Available

Library of Congress Cataloging-in-Publication Data

Tochluk, Shelly, 1971–
    Witnessing whiteness : the need to talk about race and how to do it / Shelly Tochluk.
— 2nd ed.
        p. cm.
    Includes bibliographical references and index.
    ISBN 978-1-60709-256-8 (cloth : alk. paper) — ISBN 978-1-60709-257-5 (pbk. : alk.
paper) — ISBN 978-1-60709-258-2 (electronic)
    1. Whites—United States—Attitudes.   2. Whites—Race identity—United States.
3. Race awareness—United States.   4. Racism—United States.   5. Interpersonal
relations—United States.   6. Responsibility—United States.   7. Educators—United
States—Attitudes.   8. Community education—United States.   9. United States—Race
relations.   I. Title.
    E184.A1 T63 2010
    305.800973—dc22   2009034237

Printed in the United States of America

⊗ ™ The paper used in this publication meets the minimum requirements of American
National Standard for Information Sciences—Permanence of Paper for Printed Library
Materials, ANSI/NISO Z39.48-1992.

Contents

Preface: A Work in Progress   v

Acknowledgments   ix

Introduction   xi

Part I   **Dis-Ease in the White Community**

Chapter One   Naming the Problem   3

Chapter Two   Facing the Dis-ease   35

Chapter Three   Uncovering a Hidden History   53

Part II   **The Journey into Witnessing**

Chapter Four   Fellow Travelers: Engaging the Journey   85

Chapter Five   Clearing the Way: Whiteness in Sight   113

Chapter Six   Blindness at the Crossroads: Leaps of Faith 141

Chapter Seven   Interior Shadows: Lingering Racism   171

Part III   **The Work of Witnessing Whiteness**

Chapter Eight   How Do We Witness?   199

Chapter Nine   How Can We Create a Witnessing Culture?   241

Bibliography   267

Index   273

About the Author   277

Preface

A Work in Progress

This book requires a preface—a caveat, if you will. When matched against the tremendous need to confront issues of racism and white privilege, this book does not go far enough. If you are one who already sees the fullness of the problem and its links to our various educational, social, and economic systems, the model of *witnessing* proposed here might ask for too little. For some people of color and white antiracist activists, the contents may appear soft and too warmly conveyed for the urgency of the situation. For these reasons, an explanation is warranted.

Fundamentally, the intention is to start a dialogue and offer a first step for those just beginning to see whiteness, its effects on relationships, and its connection to our social and economic systems. As such, the book speaks to a particular group of people. Readers of this book are likely to be people who seek to do good work in the world, who want to be of service to social justice efforts, and who care enough to pick up a book on whiteness in the first place. Within this group, there is much diversity of experience and perspective. Yet one thing is generally common: we white people do not interrogate ourselves on what it means to be white on a regular basis. This often results in a lack of both (1) the desire to see ourselves as part of a racial dynamic and (2) the skills to navigate racial terrain successfully.

Since admonishing and shaming people is not likely to inspire either personal or political change, this book uses a different approach. It offers an invitation that hopefully piques interest and inspires thought. I also hope this book convinces readers that perceiving whiteness and developing active responses is imperative personally, socially, and politically if we are going to transform our society into a more equitable and just place.

Because a primary intention of this book is to reach out to my home community, I use the pronouns "us" and "we" when referring to white people in general. However, this book is for people of color and multiracial people as well. (For those unfamiliar with the term "people of color," it refers to persons of any racial background who are not considered, or do not self-identity, as white.) There are many people of color who want to understand better the history of whiteness, how people experience whiteness, and how people continue to struggle against lingering racism after years of work, as well as some action steps we can take as a response.

To people of color, I apologize for the potentially distancing effect my use of the pronouns "us" and "we" might have. Hopefully, readers of color will understand that my word choice intentionally places myself within the white group as a way to self-identify with the continued work necessary on this topic and to reduce the defensiveness that so often surrounds discussions of race.

Additionally, I would like to offer a couple of explanations regarding my use of language. Like Frances Kendall, I too have struggled over whether or not to capitalize the term "white" in order to be consistent with my capitalization of "Black."[1] I capitalize "Black" because most Black people I know can talk about their identity as Black people. They know what it means for them to be Black, and it is important. They capitalize it and, therefore, I do as well.

On the other hand, most "white" people I know have no idea what it means that they are white. There is little racial awareness formed around this term, and for this reason, it seems inappropriate to offer "white" the same weight. This is in no way intended to diminish white people's humanity but simply to highlight that our society has not asked us to do the work required to form an identity around being white. Readers will note that when I speak of Radical White Identity, a consciously-formed antiracist white identity constructed within a group of which I am a part, the term is capitalized. I therefore offer my inconsistency as a challenge to white readers. We should sit with the discomfort of our whiteness being left in the lower case until we work toward an antiracist white identity of which we can be proud.

My thanks also goes to Frances Kendall for alerting me to the way my use of terms related to vision—*blurry, blind,* and so forth—as a metaphor related to our needed awareness around race issues might offend.[2] I had never considered that my use of these words betrays my privileged status as an able-bodied person who takes sightedness for granted, yet I too have been unable to find alternate language to convey the points I raise. For this I apologize and remain open to suggestion.

Also, I must confess that absolutely nowhere in this book do I treat the complex issues that face biracial and multiracial people who are part white.

Admittedly, I focus on the easy split: those who are seen as "white" and those who are not. I do this primarily because much of the book draws from my search to develop a stronger and healthier sense of my racial self as a white person. Although I know several biracial people who are working to integrate their whiteness into a healthy racial identity, I do not feel sufficiently qualified to speak of that process.

In addition to the above, the dichotomy offered between "white" and "people of color" can also be seen as a vestige of my either/or thinking so reflective of modern society. Even the term "people of color" troubles plenty of my colleagues, as it does myself, and yet I find no other way to move forward except to use these imperfect categorizing terms until some new language or approach arises.

Ultimately, the model of *witnessing* invites a process, a journey that offers possibilities for an altered way of being that can lead to an effective antiracist practice but without defining an exact goal or destination. The nature of the path requires this open-ended beginning. This racial identity journey involves challenging terrain . . . for everyone. The tone, therefore, reflects the need for each individual to determine how, and to what degree, this information should be utilized and incorporated. This may also be where my own faith enters. We must leave room for spirit to move, to guide, and to lead people toward their next steps.

Also important to note, however, is that writing with this tone required me to move through a deep personal process. Had I attempted to write this book in previous years, the message would have been altogether different. The writing would have been less giving, more expectant, demanding, and judgmental. Both the tone and content would have reflected the fact that I was not resolved within myself about who I am as a white person.

For me, part of my journey involved a wholesale rejection of my home community, my culture, and my sense of self. I fell into a troubling pattern that many distressed whites demonstrate. Part of that included unwittingly objectifying people of color as I turned to them in escape from my "white" life. I retreated into a world of color, what many describe as "colorful" garb, "colorful" music, and "colorful" people. At that time, I had strong, negative feelings for anything that reminded me of my former, less aware, white self. I found conversations with most white people on matters of race fruitless. I now see that those conversations failed, in part, because they were not in the spirit of two people sharing dialogue. They were arguments, meant to bolster my view of the world and break theirs down.

I now feel more at home, at home. I remain unsatisfied with the level of understanding of my white community in terms of race, but I accept my home community as flawed and in need of healing, like most communities. I now find conversations to be spirited moments of engagement and learning. Reaching deeply into myself, I find connecting points. Remnants of former ways of thinking help me to build bridges with those as yet unfamiliar with the strange language I speak. I find myself in conversations in which the terms *white privilege, systemic and institutional racism,* and *white supremacist system* are defined and explored.

Those conversations now inspire this writing. If I can write from a place of empathetic understanding, utilizing my own process to help encourage others like myself to take those first few steps along the path toward deeper racial awareness, then perhaps a larger group might just hold out their hands and join me in that undefined future where well-intentioned people become perceptive, then angry, then empowered, and finally active against racism. Coming to grips with race is a process. It takes too long and there is no time to wait. I know. That is why we must get as many people started as soon as possible.

My suggestion is that the potential benefits of this experience will expand if readers approach the book actively, jotting down notes while each chapter is read, taking note of questions that arise, and journaling as inspired. Reading this book as part of a group process is certainly the best approach. To help in that effort, free resources are available for download at www .witnessingwhiteness.com, including chapter-by-chapter discussion and workshop guides.

NOTES

1. F. Kendall, *Understanding White Privilege.* (New York: Routledge, 2006), xiii.
2. Kendall, *Understanding White Privilege,* xiv.

Acknowledgments

Numerous individuals offered insight, support, time, and encouragement during initial stages of this work. Particular thanks go to my formal guides, who opened themselves for full view and whose stories shaped my perspective: Jennifer Obidah, Luis Rodriguez, Michael Meade, Katie Gottfred, Karen Teel, Lorraine Cole, Amanda Perez, Cayce Calloway, Lee Mun Wah, Spencer Brewer, Bob Roberts, Perry Bernard, Shirley Better, Lincoln W., Dave Adelson, and William King. Thanks also to the colleagues who supported this work during its dissertation stage: Helene Lorenz, Elizabeth Nelson, Nelson Rodriguez, and Heidi Gailor-Loflin.

Among those who graciously read, critiqued, and contributed to this work are Traci Dorf, Mary McBride, Nora and Keith Powell, Holly Mosher, Judy Moussa, Katrina Hamilton, Michelle McPeek, Michele Dumont, Anne Wilcoxen, Jackie Fisher, Robin Gordon, Michael Wagner, Pam Muniz, and Ken and Debbie Winters. Without their questions, feedback, and suggestions, this work would not be what it is. To those whose professional advice I turned to in the later stages, a significant debt is owed: thanks to Melanie Bush, Christine Sleeter, Francie Kendall, and Paul Kivel. Their encouragement and example were instrumental in the editing and publishing process.

My deepest gratitude goes to the family and friends who supported me in various ways throughout this endeavor by reading, critiquing, and engaging in continuing dialogues, thereby shaping my life, perceptions, understandings, and this work: Cathy and Larry Tochluk, Julie Chavez, Jennifer Selig, Salina Gray, Aisha Blanchard-Young, Jorge Zeballos, Vance Aniebo, Alex Keeve, Matt Sawaya, Cameron Levin, Sarah Glasband, Hillary Stephenson, Jason David, Clare Robbins, the members of AWARE-LA, and Orland Bishop.

Introduction

It was a crowd of primarily Black spectators that first brought my racial being to consciousness. I will never forget the pointing, laughter, and yells: "Look at the white girl!" As a sophomore in high school in the mid-1980s, I was the different one for the first time, the minority within a group. Eight Black girls and I competed to go to the California State track meet in the 400-meter race. Even though my Orange County high school was very racially mixed (large percentages of Asian and Latino/a Americans), my classes were predominantly white. Selecting mostly white friends and avoiding any direct challenges concerning larger issues of racial identity or justice was easy. For me, racial awareness only existed when I was on the track competing against high-caliber high school athletes, and this was a rare event.

Continued participation in the world of NCAA Division I sprinting brought new issues surrounding race to the foreground. My first collegiate cross-race friendships at UC Irvine were fun, familial, and often flirtatious on the track. The struggles of my Black teammates were acknowledged, but only jokingly and often under the breath. For example, the very real racial profiling struggles they faced were often masked beneath laughing refusals to run behind the white girls on cross-training runs off campus.

"You just can't chase white girls out on the street!" some of the men would yell, half-opposing the distance workout itself, but half-opposing the prejudice they knew went unchecked just a few steps off campus. It was funny, and it was not funny. All in all, the friendships felt real, comfortable, and nurturing. Although we did socialize off the track, these interactions were rather limited and did not continue significantly once the season concluded. Essentially, the parties we enjoyed together were "kum-ba-ya" moments, multiracial experiences that celebrated our diversity while simultaneously ignoring serious issues lying just under the surface.

When I later competed for UCLA, the responses to race issues were dealt with very differently. Discriminatory experiences at UCLA were not discussed softly on the track. Although not a daily focus of attention, when issues did surface, my Black teammates' pain and anger were evident and far from hidden or covered over. There were times when I felt personally implicated just hearing about their experiences. These moments made building relationships with them a bit strained. But in the end, relaxed friendships formed as the powerful bonds created through mutual experiences of physical trials and competition proved strong. But, again, the relationships off the track were limited and short-lived.

After these collegiate experiences, I existed with a continuous recognition of myself as a racial being and a disavowal of prejudice and racism. But there was still something missing. Why was I unable to maintain these friendships off the track? I still hold deep affection for these men and women who were such an instrumental part of my life. What allowed these relationships to remain superficial enough that they could fall away so quickly once the season ended and we graduated? I still remain close with several of my white former teammates, so the answer has little or nothing to do with a phase-of-life change. Why was it so hard to translate close interracial experiences into sustained relationships?

Ultimately, within several months of my retirement from competitive athletics, I existed once more in an almost exclusively white social world. If the single most important factor in developing friendships is proximity, that we become friends with those who are available, perhaps we can decide that my post-collegiate lack of interracial friendships was just natural.[1] But after all of the interracial experiences that I had had, it felt decidedly *un*natural. Besides, one of my Black teammates and I later taught in the same school district for several years and never made efforts to renew our connection. In the end, after living a *de*segregated life, the return to a segregated life felt like a failure of some kind.

What this speaks to is pervasive. According to the Civil Rights Project report, segregation still marks education, housing, and employment in our society, all of which lead us into segregated social lives.[2] Even when programs exist to integrate these environments forcibly, they are usually competitive and the cross-race individuals often do not have equal status, helping to explain why deep friendships do not frequently develop.[3]

But this cannot account for my experience. My teammates and I had equal status on the track. While we were in competition somewhat, we were teammates first. Overt racism or prejudice did not undermine our friendships. I have to be honest enough to reflect and admit that we simply were not that close to begin with. Something stopped us from fully entering each other's lives so that connections even broke down with those I was around most often. Whatever this something was, it affected my interest and ability to collaborate with people of color within my own school district.

Looking at it now, I know that part of the problem was my incomplete understanding of myself as a racial being, affected by my own whiteness in ways I did not perceive. At that time, I was unable to hear my Black peers' complaints of racism without requiring them to prove the validity of their experiences. I could not recognize the unequal ground we traveled to achieve the same positions. Nor was I able to see our difficult moments together as openings for deepening friendship as opposed to causes for rejection. All of this and more caused me to pull away.

My relationship to my whiteness finally became meaningful to me when a significant friendship formed with a Black man I worked with at an urban elementary school. He articulated the ways that my thoughts, feelings, and actions were thoroughly influenced by white privilege. However grateful I may now be for his insight, I assure you that I fought him at every turn. It is highly disconcerting and offensive to be told that you are unconscious of what influences your attitudes and beliefs about the world. The insinuation that unrecognized socialization was largely responsible for my thinking and actions struck at the heart of my sense of individuality and freedom. But, unfortunately, as offensive as an idea might sound, it still may be true.

This friend brought me face to face with how the social and economic benefits of whiteness shaped my value system, use of language, and perception of the world. For example, I was horrified to realize the offensive and false nature of the judgments I had grown up hearing. I had been influenced by statements like "If I were them I would . . ." when discussing people continuing to reside in gang-infested neighborhoods.

The privilege inherent in judging those struggling while sitting in comfort became clear. I had to face the fact that my speech unknowingly reflected judgments against those with whom I worked at the school site. As I questioned those in that community, I left no confusion regarding my ignorance of the struggles they faced. Adding to that, when I did begin to recognize my errors, my worldview and learned judgments then caused me to respond with pity more often than empathy. A sense of superiority still pervaded my communication style and behavior.

None of this was intentional. Being confronted with my continued failure to eliminate my own patronizing approach, no matter what I did, made me feel either guilty or resistant, depending on the day. Ultimately, accepting that the way I acted was a problem felt like a rug being pulled out from under me.

I had to reevaluate everything. For quite some time I felt rather lost in the world and clung to those who appeared knowledgeable about race. I became a student of my Black colleague, sometimes unhealthily subservient, sometimes fiercely defensive.

After several years of discussions, challenges, and tears, I now see my racial self as incredibly significant and meaningful. I also see how being white means more than what I determine it to mean. Its historic significance lives on within me whether I perceive it or not. My whiteness affects my teaching, my relationships, and my ability to collaborate with community partners in more ways than I could have imagined. But through questioning that experience, I also have developed a healthier sense of self and recognition of what takes place.

During those years I came face to face with a variety of discomforts and pains related to being a white person in the United States, a dis-ease I now believe to be reflective of a collective white experience. I spent several years trying to find solace in teaching students of color in an urban school district and doing community work with people of color until one day, while attending a meeting at the Community Self-Determination Institute in Watts, one of the staff members turned to me and said something like this: "You know, we're really glad you're here, and we like you and all. But we are working with our own people. We can do this. What we really need is for you to go and work with the white people."

She went on, but my mind was already spinning in several directions, understanding deep down what that really meant for me. Her suggestion essentially asked me to face my biggest fear, talking to white people about race. To be truthful, that was most likely not the first time somebody said that to me. I would wager that it was simply the first time I was ready to hear what it implied, that I needed to take another step on my journey, one that would lead me home to really heal the inner pain I was avoiding and ignoring.

So, finding myself incompletely recovered from my initiation into seeing whiteness, I began to ask some questions. What should the next phase of my racial identity development look like? I realized that for quite some time I had been seeking validation from people of color to help me see myself as a worthy person in the world. My sense of self had relied upon the Black teachers at my school site, who said I was not a "regular" white person. I recalled the satisfaction I felt when the Black counselors and administrators called me an "angel" for my work. When some of the Latino parents and I spent time together, I felt valuable because of the "service" I could provide.

Recognizing how much of my so-called service was tied to my need to feel good about myself, I began to wonder how many other white people were living a similar experience. Further, how can whites like me leave the guilt behind and exemplify a healthier way of being? How can we dedicate ourselves to working towards equity without letting go of our sense of self? These questions became a formal project.

I looked for models, deciding that I would do in-depth interviews to locate answers. I interviewed pairs of cross-race friends because I wanted to hear how race, particularly whiteness, played a role within a sustained, long-term relationship. Ultimately, I wanted to talk to people who had done significant personal work with each other and had experienced both deep conflict and transformation.

Rightly imagining that these people's experience might translate into wisdom, I hoped to learn what it would take to better form and sustain relationships with the people of color in my life. I also hoped their experience would help me understand how to create a positive sense of my racial self so that my work did not involve seeking validation from people of color. Admittedly, the concept of *witnessing* offered in this book had not yet occurred to me. Rather, this model emerged out of the process of analyzing and interpreting the conversations. Because of that, I do not know what the people I spoke with would have said about the ideas I put forth.

This book includes pieces of dialogue from the larger project, highlighting white people who have begun to see their own whiteness. These people share their struggles and the way race issues continue to affect their cross-race friendships. They talk about how they see whiteness and where they continue to find white privilege and racism lingering within their psyche. The stories of their struggles demonstrate a variety of paths with varying levels of challenge. But, collectively, they illustrate a process that can lead toward healing for people who care about equity, improved cross-race relationships, and a life that subverts dominating whiteness.

To find the white people, I searched where whites often do not go successfully: within friendships with people of color who are intensely aware of race issues, people of color who actively work to educate people regarding issues of race and their community's healing. I asked for a lot. Both the white person and the person of color talked to me about personal racial identity, perceptions of whiteness, enduring cross-race friendships, and continuing struggles with race issues.

Although wanting most to hear from whites because they would be models for me, I had long ago learned that people of color are usually more keenly aware of white privilege and its effects. Therefore, the original research highlights the perceptions of both the white people and their friends of color as equally as possible. In this book, however, the white people receive increased space in terms of their introductions and backgrounds, as their particular journeys can help white people like myself see our possible paths.

Among others, this book includes community activists and educators, such as Chicano poet Luis Rodriguez and his friend, mythologist Michael Meade, as well as diversity trainer, Lee Mun Wah, producer of *The Color of Fear,* and Spencer Brewer, his white friend who helped make the film possible. The book also includes antibias teacher-trainers Jennifer Obidah and Karen Teel, coauthors of *Because of the Kids,* as well as Lorraine Cole, the CEO of the YWCA USA, and her white friend Katie Gottfred, founder of LEAP Learning Systems, a nonprofit organization advancing language development within the Cabrini Green housing project in Chicago.

During the years spent interviewing, researching, and analyzing data related to the questions I had generated, I also participated regularly with a growing movement of people in Los Angeles called AWARE-LA, Alliance of White Anti-Racists Everywhere. The dialogue space provided by this group was essential in clarifying my thinking and strengthening my resolve that I am not the only one experiencing distress over what it means to be white in the United States. I am not the only one searching for a way of being that promotes a healthy sense of self while simultaneously working to increase the capacity to be effectively active in equity efforts.

AWARE-LA promotes the development of a *Radical White Identity,* an identity I have been working to create for myself.[4] We recognize that working toward a solid, effective antiracist practice must include the creation of a healthy white identity. Working toward this also involves training ourselves to better recognize and respond to the racism and white privilege that are enacted in our daily lives . . . essentially, *witnessing.*

My first crying fit in the parking lot of an elementary school campus where I refused to acknowledge that my being white had anything to do with anything occurred more than a decade ago. After much consideration, I now stand convinced that the future of our country depends on white people being able to turn within, into the depths of our being, focus on our whiteness for a time, and perceive its effects on our deepest psyche and our collaborative relationships. We must face our deepest shadow, our country's historical legacy of white supremacy. While uncomfortable to admit, its memory lies within us, embedded.

Ours is a collective history so deeply ingrained that it cannot be wished away, consciously put aside, or dismissed. Healing lies in the courageous move to interrogate our racial legacy and understand its continued manifestations. Only when we develop the capacity to name the effects of white privilege can we begin the work of investigating to what degree our relationship with our whiteness requires alteration. Basically, white people must be able to bear witness to the overt and subtle ways that issues of race and dominating whiteness continue to emerge in our daily lives if we are going to be able to do anything about it.

One purpose of this book is to encourage white people—those who identify as European Americans living in North America, specifically—to investigate our sense of self from a racial point of view in order to create more intimate and honest relationships with ourselves, others, and the world in general. As uncomfortable as it may become, we have to keep our eyes focused on ourselves. We have to keep whiteness squarely in sight.

One thing white people are really good at is shifting a conversation on race to focus on other groups. As soon as a finger gets pointed at us, many of us point somewhere else and expect the conversation to move in that direction. We shield ourselves reflexively, often without real awareness of what we are doing. This is precisely the type of dominating whiteness that we need to start noticing. Our tendency to shift focus away from ourselves is very strong. We have been getting away with it for so long that it appears normal. For that reason, this book will keep the finger pointed at white people.

The history of race in the United States is so tragic that each group requires its own healing process. Although true that there are many similar consequences of oppression for groups of color in general, each group also has its distinct needs based upon its differential history. Some call it ethno-specific healing work. Fortunately, there are many people out there working to uplift and heal their specific communities. Joy DeGruy Leary is but one example. Her work on *Post-traumatic Slave Syndrome* discusses the ways that African Americans require healing from their trauma, both past and present.[5]

Dr. DeGruy Leary's work is thought-provoking and inspiring. An African American woman deeply committed to the healing of her community, her insight is precise. Although targeting her Black community, all readers can benefit from her work. I know I am grateful that my Black teacher-colleagues introduced me to her work. Dr. DeGruy Leary's work not only expanded my vision regarding the trauma experienced by the African American community, but it reinforced my conviction that white people also need to focus on our own healing, not only for our own sake but for our country as a whole.

I recognize that white people have developed ways of being due to our history in this country from which we need to heal and that we play an important role in shaping the beliefs and attitudes of those in our surroundings. There is no reason to believe that different groups require the same healing process. That would make about as much sense as a doctor giving the same medicine for all maladies.

The white experience has been different, and therefore the process through which we must pass must also be different. For white people, as the group that has held dominant status, we are less in touch with how race affects us. For this reason, our first step is to identify the ways our whiteness emerges. Our first step is to become witnesses to our whiteness.

NOTES

1. Festinger, L., S. Schacter, and K. Black, *Social Pressures in Informal Groups; A Study of Human Factors in Housing* (Oxford: Harper, 1950).

2. "Race, Place, and Segregation: Redrawing the Color Line in Our Nation's Metros," *Civil Rights Project,* 2002, http://www.civilrightsproject.ucla.edu/research/metro_housing.php.

3. Jackman, M. R., and M. C. Crane, "'Some of My Best Friends Are Black . . .': Interracial Friendship and Whites' Racial Attitudes," *Public Opinion Quarterly* 50 (1986): 459–486.

4. Goldberg, S. & Levin, C., AWARE-LA, *Toward a Radical White Identity,* http://awarela.wordpress.com/toolbox/.

5. DeGruy Leary, J., *PostTraumatic Slave Syndrome* (Milwaukie, OR: Uptone Press, 2005).

Part I

Dis-Ease in the White Community

Chapter 1

Naming the Problem

Racism has become unacceptable in our society. We outlawed discrimination and we are becoming a post-racial society. In fact, race has no biological reality. Focusing on our ethnicity is therefore a much better way for us to talk about, and appreciate, our cultural differences. Self-identifying as being white simply reinforces old problems of division, so I make sure to let people know that I am colorblind since I see us all as part of the human race.

There was a time when I spoke using this language. I have plenty of friends and colleagues who continue to describe their approach to race using these terms. Admittedly, this sounds like the right and healthy approach to most white people and some people of color. The trouble is what many of these statements ignore and deny. The trouble is what is left unexplored and unsaid. The reality is this: There is a deep dis-ease regarding race residing within much of the white community.

White people in general are ill-at-ease over issues of race, and we are not very skilled at naming the true nature of the problem. We are confused by its complexity and our discomfort arises in our multiracial schools, organizations, companies, and collaborative relationships whenever race becomes the focus of a conversation. Unfortunately, many of us choose a colorblind, transcendence-seeking optimism that ends up stifling the honestly difficult dialogue we need to have in order to deal with the very real racial dynamics that continue to play out in our interactions. The strategies we use to avoid dealing with race, sadly, then allow us to behave offensively without awareness. What we need are witnesses who can help sound the bells of alarm and raise a voice in the interest of improving our ability to create healthier, more successful, and more productive relationships and institutions.

CAN I GET A WITNESS?

Have you ever been a witness? Witnesses see a situation clearly and speak out about wounding events. Can you recall a time when you found yourself in the midst of a situation where you needed to speak out? Was someone's safety or emotional well-being hanging in the balance? What did you do? If I were in a serious traffic accident, I hope a witness would be present to call for help. Without a witness, my injuries might prove unnecessarily fatal. If assaulted, I hope a witness would be present to disrupt the event and describe my attacker. Without a witness, my search for justice might go unrealized. Events that take place in the shadows might require concerted effort to witness. A scream in the night hopefully can bring someone running, someone close enough to see and interrupt the problem.

If I am ever in a situation requiring me to witness a trauma-filled situation, I hope I will have the courage to be present and speak the truth of what I perceived. Depending on the circumstances, I might be frightened myself—but I can only imagine what turning and running would do to my sense of self. My own soul would suffer if I attempted to justify turning away. Ultimately, choosing to disconnect from the situation at hand would damage my own spirit.

Depth psychology, the study of the unconscious, shapes my perspective. In a class on trauma, one of my mentors spoke of "percepticide" to describe the ways that we kill off our own perceptions when we feel that we are in a dangerous situation.[1] Although it is easy to imagine that we would shut down in the face of a lethal threat, we can do this even if the situation is not life-threatening. When we fear that we will be socially punished because people in our immediate surroundings cannot tolerate hearing about what we see, we often silence ourselves and shut down parts of our psyche.

Like a child who runs to tell a parent something only to be dismissed, we only say "Yeah, but . . ." in protest so many times before we turn away and stop trying. We become numb and disconnect from aspects of ourselves. What we know becomes exiled, and over time that information becomes unavailable as we move through life.[2] This idea is not new. Frances Kendall offers a somewhat related idea in her book *Understanding White Privilege*. She speaks of white people "anesthetizing" themselves to avoid guilt and other confusing feelings and refers to Charles Mills' explanation of "structured blindness and opacities."[3]

Regardless of what terms we use, this type of dissociation can also stop us from creating or maintaining emotional connection with others. If I am not fully seen, why should I see you? If my injury and perception does not receive attention, why should yours? If I have shut myself off from my own pain, shouldn't you do the same? In other words, when we are not able to witness or be witnessed, we end up with splits in our psyche that keep us disconnected from both ourselves and other people. Of course, our attempts to avoid painful emotional states are understandable. Unfortunately, once we split off from the aspects of our lives that bring us pain, we disown and reject them, casting them into the shadows of our psyche.[4]

This book argues that there is a scream to which we must respond, a traumatic situation that remains obscured in the shadows. We need people to come running because there is a deep distress to which we must bear witness. Repeatedly turning away has created deep injury. Undoing this damage requires us to face the painful situation and become clear-seeing witnesses.

RACIAL IDENTITY IN THE SHADOWS

I talk about race quite a bit these days, with family, colleagues, students, friends, and new acquaintances. One of the most common responses I receive when beginning this dialogue with white people for the first time is a sigh, a deep breath, and some type of statement indicating that they are not really comfortable naming "white" as part of their personal identity.

Bearing witness to this discomfort is important in order to determine corrective action. Unfortunately, racial identity for white people is a very blurry topic and we are not very good witnesses of our own whiteness. Our relationship with race involves a great deal of anxiety, and we ignore our racial identity for some very understandable reasons. But this neglect allows the ways race affects us to remain within the shadows of our unconscious.

As we leave our relationship to race unexplored, unquestioned, and untreated, our whiteness becomes analogous to the far side of the moon. We never see the mysterious far side that scientists tell us appears far more battered and beaten than the visible side facing the Earth. White people often act out of our unexplored whiteness and then feel injured when our attempts at overcoming racial issues fail. Witnessing whiteness involves not only shining a light into our shadows and facing the damage our history of race continues to do to our psyche but also clarifying our individual relationship to race and our racial identity.

Fortunately, mythology can offer us something to take with us as we journey into our racial shadow. A primary figure linked with the dark moon is Hecate. For those unfamiliar with this figure, Hecate, a Greek goddess who shared powers with Zeus over the heavens, Earth, and underworld, could give humanity anything she wished. Shown frequently as having three heads, she could see in all directions. Symbolically, she holds the torch of illumination that reveals the treasures of the unconscious and she represents the dark within us that we do not wish to acknowledge.

Each of her multiple aspects offer guidance as we move forward. On one hand, Hecate is often seen as the hag, a witch practicing evil. As a bearer of uncomfortable truths, she offers unwelcome light emanating from the shadows. This book assuredly offers uncomfortable truths regarding our relationship to race. So, in the minds of some readers struggling against descending into what remains hidden, the image of the hag—a harping woman continuously poking and prodding—might arise.

On the other hand, Hecate is also the fairy godmother stirring up brews for magical transformation. She represents the wise mother holding deep wisdom. She is the ruler of the crossroads, asking us to consider that the messiness of our lives is also the raw material used to create soul. For those of us willing to descend into the depths of our own unconscious, these images remind us that becoming more attuned to the hidden sides of ourselves increases our wisdom and can help us make better choices as we reach new crossroads in our journeys. Inviting the image of Hecate to join us can be helpful because the uncomfortable truth is that white people have neglected the consequences of race for such a long time that we can hardly define our own discomfort.

CLARIFYING OUR VIEW: DEFINING OUR TERMS

Let us start by naming our distress. Speaking generally, white people are uncomfortable being called white, naming ourselves white. But, admittedly, we are not at ease with anything having to do with race. So we have to start there, acknowledging that this mess called "race" is problematic at its core. Without time to sort through the overwhelming collection of evidence, I will simply say what many already know: It is true that race has no natural, biological reality.[5]

Of course we see physical differences among people from different environments. Yes, we turn to science to help us understand these differences—but science cannot find any coherent and absolute way to locate race. Yes, many of us have been taught that certain physical characteristics go together with a certain race. But when we look closely at the subject, we end up confused if we try to pinpoint where many people fit within racial categories. Variety outweighs consistency. Ultimately, we made up the concept of race as we tried to increase both our understanding and manipulation of our world. In other words, race is *socially* constructed. Because of this, our experience of racial identity follows no absolutely consistent physical markers or experiences.

That said, regardless of the false nature of racial categories, the concept of race holds great social force. Our society uses race in spite of some people's disavowal and often treats us differentially as a result. Race has truly gotten under our skin, into our psyche, and lingers within the layers of our unconscious. To begin honestly, we must discuss what may be the most challenging aspect of any discussion of race. We must deal with the terms *racist, racism,* and *systemic white supremacy.* We must also confront the fact that some people might ask us to associate those words with our speech and actions.

Understandably, these words can appear inflammatory and many of us shut down as soon as they are spoken. We see ourselves as essentially good-hearted people doing the best we can within a society deeply impacted by the wounds of our country's past. Our resistance arises, in part, because individually we avoid behaviors historically considered racist. To be a racist, to be associated with racism and a system of white supremacy, is tantamount to saying that we represent the worst of what the United States has to offer. Being a racist means that we are mean-spirited, closed-minded, and lack essential goodness.

Imagine a list of negative attributes one might use to criticize, a set of characteristics that inspire a defensive reaction. Consider the emotional reaction you might have if labeled that way. For most whites, the label *racist* will spark a more defensive reaction than almost any other slight. I would certainly rather be called narcissistic, greedy, or insensitive than be called racist. For this reason, we have great difficulty withstanding any conversation that asks us to consider ourselves related to that term.

But if we do not at least investigate and understand how we have developed opinions about what the term does or does not mean, we do ourselves a disservice. For example, close your eyes for a moment and imagine a racist. What is the image that forms in your mind? Take a moment and write down a few descriptors. Some might have a picture that looks something like a Southern or Midwestern rural or small-town person who drives a truck and wears a baseball hat. This was the stereotypical image I grew up ingesting.

Others might imagine a conservative lawmaker who enacts policies that disproportionately benefit whites. Still others might imagine a social liberal who advocates for differential treatment of people based on race. These are just a few of a thousand possible images that different people might have. The big question is, how many of us imagine ourselves when we think of a racist? If I were a betting person, I would wager that few of us see ourselves in that category.

The problem with this is that our images can amount to psychic finger-pointing that results in a personal distancing from the issue. Imagining only a neo-Nazi or member of the KKK as racist psychologically cuts us out of the problem. This book argues that we *all* are part of the problem of race in the United States and we *all* can be part of the solution. This includes well-educated people who already see themselves working toward social equity. This also can include many people of color since we *all* have been negatively affected by the social conditions of our country.

Although it is certainly true that social and economic benefits and privileges have been heavily bestowed upon white people throughout our nation's history, playing our various roles within an inherently inequitable system has exacted a heavy psychological toll on us all. What this means is that everyone who lives in this country has a personal stake in healing our relationship to race if we are ever going to be able to move past it. *Everyone.*

However, we still need to define what is meant by the term *racism.* For the sake of brevity, this chapter offers an abbreviated analysis from a couple of more thorough sources. In short, racial prejudice and racism are not interchangeable concepts. The first few pages of Beverly Daniel Tatum's bestseller *Why Are All the Black Kids Sitting Together in the Cafeteria?* discusses the difference between the two ideas.[6]

According to Tatum, *racial prejudice* is a preconceived judgment or opinion based on insufficient knowledge. Tatum argues that we all have prejudices by virtue of living in a society offering a preponderance of misinformation about different groups. We might consciously reject overt prejudices, but very often prejudices remain due to misunderstandings, an incomplete knowledge base, or isolated experiences.

Racism, on the other hand, involves a system that offers advantage based on race. White people might consciously reject prejudice, yet we are often completely unaware of how the structure of our society continues to advantage whites over other groups. In this view, racism is not necessarily about the belief system one holds as much as racism involves the systemic inequity maintained through both individual and institutional means.

In *Institutional Racism,* Shirley Better defines and compares *individual racism* and *institutional racism* and illustrates how each relates to beliefs, attitudes, practices, and structures.[7] To offer just a few of the ideas presented, on the individual side of racism a person might believe social and economic inequality are acceptable, hold an attitude of blindness to racism, say negative statements based on race, and follow both conscious and unconscious behavior patterns that reinforce inequity. Although this is just a sample of what Dr. Better offers, the list illustrates that not all aspects of individual racism are necessarily conscious. Individual racism can involve following customs and patterns that people consider race-neutral but actually uphold social and economic inequity.

On the other hand, institutional racism includes the maintenance of white-skin privilege, segregation, and formal and/or informal politics, practices, and procedures. Overall, this is what some people are talking about when they refer to *systematic dominating whiteness* or *systemic white supremacy*. Essentially, these terms calls us to notice the basic fact that white people, and our social norms and patterns, continue to wield controlling power within our social, economic, political, and educational structures in ways that maintain inequity. (The overwhelming power held by whites remains in effect even when we have isolated figures holding high positions of power, such as President Barack Obama, and when increasing numbers of people of color are beginning to influence public policy.)

And yet it is also true that as individuals we may not have created these structures. True, we might even disagree with how racial inequity continues. But the fact is that systems of inequity largely remain unchanged and we are related to these systems of inequity because our continued existence within them usually supports the status quo.

Our ability to notice *systemic, institutional* racism expands with our consciousness regarding unintended *individual* racism. The model of witnessing described in this book depends on increasing our ability to notice both individual and systemic forms of racism and dominating whiteness. But in order to even begin to do that, we must be willing to fathom that our lives are not as far removed from the concept of racism as we hope.

WHAT DOES IT MEAN TO BE WHITE?

Just as the term *race* poses difficulty, the term *whiteness* is similarly troublesome. As part of the social construction of race, whiteness suffers from all of the same confusions as race in general. The concept is not clear. What do we mean when we say that someone is white? Are we simply talking about skin color? Skin color is actually a poor predictor of whether or not someone is considered white and anthropologists now generally agree that race itself has no biological reality.

In fact, the American Anthropological Association put out a "Statement on Race" to reflect the thinking of most contemporary scholars.[8] Within the statement they note:

> In the United States both scholars and the general public have been conditioned to viewing human races as natural and separate divisions within the human species based on visible physical differences. With the vast expansion of scientific knowledge in this century, however, it has become clear that human populations are

not unambiguous, clearly demarcated, biologically distinct groups. . . . Historical research has shown that the idea of "race" has always carried more meanings than mere physical differences; indeed, physical variations in the human species have no meaning except the social ones that humans put on them.

So, what is whiteness? In my experience, when interacting with people living relatively segregated lives, the question provokes a tilt of the head and a furrowing of the brow. "What do you mean?" comes with a queried look. Upon further prompting, a great many respond that being white means nothing. If anything at all, being white may be described as being either just normal or neutral.[9] On the other hand, when speaking with people living in areas with a high degree of diversity *and* whose lives are marked and shaped by that diversity, a common response is that being white is something bad, that it is connected to an unjust history.

If some whites consider whiteness as being normal, then the question becomes normal how? Is whiteness a way of being in the world? Is there a white culture? Some say yes, some say no. If yes, what does that culture look like? For many, white culture is an amalgamation of a variety of variables that any particular person may or may not exemplify. Some of these include skin color, a position of racial dominance, the ability to avoid issues of race, the primacy of individualism, the achievement of middle-class economic success, and often a residentially, socially, and/or socioeconomically segregated life.[10]

And yet we occupy so many social positions that each individual's experience necessarily varies. My conception of whiteness is surely different from that of someone coming from a different region or socioeconomic class. My experience, having grown up in a middle-class suburb with white-collar, college-educated parents, is undoubtedly far different from that of someone from either a rural town or a working-class, urban area. Even so, the general concept of "white culture" remains widely used. The term "white culture" means something to a lot of people. Taking a step back and considering to what degree each of us fits into that picture is helpful. Later chapters will investigate both how our country's history shapes these meanings and how they continue to be enacted and perceived.

Viewing whiteness as a process, as suggested by Ruth Frankenberg, can be helpful. Whiteness is not a thing that can ever be fully captured and nailed down.[11] Whiteness is irregularly experienced and dynamic, always shifting and changing. This perspective helps me understand why there are moments when I see whiteness so clearly that I am ready to dedicate years of my life to making it visible for other people and then only a day later the meanings of whiteness practically disintegrate in front of me, seemingly too fragmented

and illusory to grasp. Now that I have been party to this dissolution a sufficient number of times, I know that it will only be a matter of time before my
perception of whiteness reconstitutes.

An important aspect of our blurriness over our whiteness is the fact that
whiteness is simply invisible to many of us. Some authors use the analogy of
a fish in a fish bowl in an effort to help us understand. Does a fish notice the
water in which it lives? The idea is that white people are accustomed to living in a world dominated by whiteness. We are saturated with the whiteness
in our social world. Our position has sustained us in ways that we do not
perceive.

Another approach is to use the analogy of handedness.[12] In a world dominated by right-handed people, we of the dominant group rarely perceive that
our world has been created for our benefit. I recall arriving late one day to
a college class and sliding as quickly as I could into the first available seat,
which happened to be along the left aisle. I was a bit put out as I tried to pull
up the collapsed writing desk, finding it on what I considered the wrong side!
I had unwittingly sat in the few seats that catered to left-handed people and I
sat rather uncomfortably for the rest of the class period. My perception of the
writing desk as on the *wrong* side illustrates how white people often experience situations that are not designed specifically for us as problematic.

When our normal, daily experience includes items and services oriented
toward our needs, it is a real surprise to be in spaces that do not cater to our pref-
erences. In this way, many white people take things for granted that people of
color recognize as benefits of being white. Peggy McIntosh's well-known article
"White Privilege: Unpacking the Invisible Knapsack" offers a list of advantages,
both significant and minor, that she receives because she is white.[13]

At a conference I attended a number of years ago, Dr. McIntosh described
how she developed the list. After making a prayer asking for guidance in
her ability to understand racial disconnections more clearly, the examples
came to her in the middle of the night. She awoke and hurriedly wrote them
down, convinced that in the light of day they would be irretrievably lost to
unconsciousness. Even she, noted for her ability to perceive the privileges of
whiteness, admits that she struggled to keep them in mind. One might suggest
that Hecate, that mythological carrier of wisdom related to the moon, was
accessed during the unconsciousness of sleep.

We all can use some help in perceiving what has been left unspoken, and
therefore unnoticed, for most of our lives. Thankfully, many others have
been doing this work for some time and offer their realizations as helpful
aids. There are even those who have used Dr. McIntosh's work as inspiration to highlight how white privilege emerges in their own fields, such as in
schools.[14]

Unlike those living in fairly segregated areas, for white people in diverse environments the water in the fish bowl can become visible fairly quickly. We are faced with mirrors that remind us that we are perceived as part of a white group. In these circumstances, the dis-ease of naming our whiteness can take on a different feeling. This is where the majority of my white colleagues and students fit in.

We live in a multiracial environment in which the political and historical associations with whiteness are readily understood. In our context, being white means being an oppressor. Whiteness symbolizes our history of slavery, the genocide of the Native American populations, racism, and the Ku Klux Klan. Whiteness is bad. To claim whiteness is to associate oneself with irreconcilable damage to humanity. Being white is shameful.

No wonder that the white community, in general, is not at ease with its own whiteness. At best, being white is just normal or neutral. At worst, whiteness aligns us with a shameful history to which we do not want to be connected. Sometimes both occur at the same time in the same person. We might feel that being white has no effect on our thoughts and behaviors, but we recognize that others associate us with negative aspects of U.S. history.

When I felt this way, my reaction was to be both saddened and angered at feeling simultaneously misunderstood and under fire. Top that off with the proposal that we are part of a white culture. Seeing our white selves as part of a culture of whiteness automatically throws us into a collective that may offer little of which to feel proud. I understand why our resistances go up at this point. Not only is our individuality at stake, so is our fundamental ability to see ourselves aligned with goodness. Used to seeing ourselves as decent, good, hard-working people, this whole idea can catapult us into a fight-or-flight reaction. For this reason, focusing on our whiteness can feel like an attack on our sense of self.

White people in general have several common responses to this perceived threat to self. Each of these can involve an effort to reframe our understanding to avoid alignment with racism. Each of these can also allow us to deflect our need to give meaning to our whiteness. Each of these can also create difficulty in our relationships with friends, colleagues, and community partners. Collectively, these responses involve turning away and leaving our racial identity very blurry, which renders us incapable of truly witnessing the dis-ease we face.

RESPONDING TO OUR DIS-EASE: LOOKING AWAY

Avoidance of our whiteness can manifest in several different forms. We can deny the continuing effects of race and its categorizations, move toward ethnicity, become colorblind, or believe we are post-racial and transcend race altogether. Important to acknowledge is that we can take up one or all of these approaches with the best of intentions. Some of us were taught these strategies as the best way forward, and therefore naming the approaches *avoidant* might feel wrong. For others of us, the flight from the discomforting meanings of whiteness is not made consciously. We are not aware that we are distancing ourselves from the problem of our whiteness instead of working toward a solution.

The following approaches can sound good, feel good, and follow a thread of logic that we believe will move us closer to equity and justice. It is precisely the feel-good nature of them, however, that disguises causes for concern. The nettle of race we are in is not so easily disentangled. Even if adopted as a way to move forward, these approaches disguise the ways that race continues to affect us all. Only if we allow ourselves to see the shadow side of each of these avenues might we begin to see a different path that will not simply cover over our symptoms but lead us toward the type of long-lasting, substantial healing that can transform our collaborative relationships and institutions.

Equal Protection under the Law

One way we allow our view to remain blurry and evade the need to look at whiteness is to point out that our country has outlawed racial discrimination. For whites who live in relatively segregated areas or who have little intimate, social contact with people of color (especially those from different class backgrounds), it is not that hard to assume that racism has been eliminated from most people's lives. Discrimination is against the law, right? After all, we elected a Black President. Racism must be over, right?

I was fortunate to grow up in a home completely absent of racial slurs. In fact, I do not recall my parents ever bringing up the subject of race. My friends and I never talked about race. My friends' parents never used race language. When my Black teammates began calling my parents "Mom" and "Dad," to include them in the larger family of sprinters during my freshman year in college, I think my parents smiled more broadly than when I performed well in a race.

My teachers did not seem particularly discriminatory either, except if you count Mr. C., my high school government teacher who bellowed at our newly-arrived Vietnamese English learners when they could not comprehend his directions. I remember his classroom vividly because it was perhaps the only time that I truly acted out in a class setting, challenging him on his cruelty. Truthfully, though, I did not interpret his behavior as being racist; I just thought he was mean. He had been mean to me too, calling me "tough luck, Tochluk." Besides, he was only one person, and he was the exception to the rule. At least that is how I perceived his behavior.

All in all, I experienced very little that I would have termed discriminatory and I did not know anyone who espoused racist beliefs. I grew up learning about equality and the Civil Rights movement. Every adult in my world advocated equal treatment for all. Because of this, I walked in the world thinking that racism was not much of a problem.

The trouble is that when we focus on legal race neutrality and are not open to the possibility that both personal and institutional racism still exist, we cannot even hope to be able to identify existing racism. We thus give up our chance of making any additional positive change. In *Colored White: Transcending the Racial Past,* David Roediger explains that one of the greatest barriers to the continued fight against racism is the view that issues of race are in the past.[15] Those who bring up the issue of race are now often considered the trouble since so-called race-neutral policies are now widely in effect. Many argue that if we would just stop talking about race that people would be able to move past our racial history.

One problem with concentrating on race-neutral language is that we often do not perceive how race is a factor in the way we look at social and economic issues and policies. For example, Roediger explains that when a governmental program benefits a predominantly white, middle-class population, such as home-mortgage tax deductions or subsidies for highway construction that benefit white suburbs, those policies are seen as race-neutral. On the other hand, when a program significantly benefits people of color, such as public assistance, those programs are often seen as race-specific even if they are universal in policy. Those programs are then seen in racial, often pejorative, terms.[16] This habit of mind does not simply disappear when select people of color attain high positions in our society.

Roediger goes on to describe how although some might explicitly avoid speaking of race, there are those who make wordless racial appeals and offer coded messages by linking nonracially identified ideas with visually racial representations. This effectively denigrates people of color and links them with issues such as welfare reform, job-training programs, criminality, and sexual promiscuity.[17] For example, a *US News & World Report* cover once used a picture of seven women to illustrate its article on welfare. Six of the seven women were women of color, most were Black, and only one was white.[18]

It is through this type of linkage of image with issue that the stereotypical image of a welfare recipient has become a Black woman in many minds, even though approximately one-third, or more, of all welfare recipients were white throughout the past two decades.[19] A more in-depth discussion of this issue can be found in Michael Brown's *Race, Money, and the American Welfare State*.[20]

We swim within this swell of media images and social and political messages on a daily basis. When we ingest images and perceptions uncritically, we can unwittingly act out of them when engaged with those we encounter. Our relational patterns can easily betray the prejudices that our social conditioning engenders, and to imagine that they have no effect because we have outlawed discrimination is to seriously underestimate the power of the unconscious mind.

Essentially, our seemingly race-neutral policies continue to betray clear signs of racism, and we often unconsciously accept skewed and selective information from our media outlets. We would do well to realize that there are many factors that play into which stories are told in the media and how images and words are associated. The important point is that when we are unconscious to the differential attention paid to different groups and racist portrayals, then we are unable to do anything to stop the problem. That is just one way that we become party to racism's continuation. If we cannot even see racism in action, then we cannot be witnesses who call for change.

Let us take a few examples from the media to check our ability to witness racism in action. Do we take notice that African American women who go missing receive scant media coverage while a veritable media blitz takes place when white women are in danger?[21] Sure, rich or famous women of color might have the social and political power to receive attention—but what of those without money or power? Most of the white women receiving coverage are neither rich nor powerful, yet they receive plenty of attention.

Once we notice this pattern, we have to ask ourselves, are we outraged? If not, why? Does this issue appear insignificant? If it does, imagine that it is your daughter, sister, or partner missing and you cannot get the media interested in running the story. This disparity of coverage is no small matter. The degree to which the media pick up a story can have life-and-death consequences. Local media attention can generate important leads in a time-sensitive situation. National media attention might also influence the degree to which local authorities call for additional aid.[22] Only if we are aware of these racist practices can we raise our voices and call attention to the matter, letting news sources know that we see this as a problem.

Another example of how racism emerges in subtle and often unnoticed ways is the now-famous differential language used to describe victims of Hurricane Katrina. One aspect of differential coverage became widely known after Yahoo's image pages put news photos and captions near enough to each other for a comparison to be impossible to miss.

In case you did miss it, though, the Associated Press published a photo of a young Black boy wading through floodwaters with food. The caption read, "A young man walks through chest-deep flood water after looting a grocery store in New Orleans on Tuesday, Aug. 30, 2005." Within a similar time period, Agence France Press published a photo of a white couple similarly wading through floodwaters with food. The caption read, "Two residents wade through chest-deep water after finding bread and soda from a local grocery store after Hurricane Katrina came through the area in New Orleans, Louisiana."

We have to question ourselves here. Do we more easily identify with other white people and therefore offer a more understanding view when white people are in a dire situation? Are we more inclined to consider a Black person as acting criminally even in similarly dire circumstances? Is it possible that we fail to question when people of color are characterized negatively because we are emotionally removed from their lives? How often does this happen unfairly without our recognition?

How many of us were offended at the onslaught of negative and racist portrayals of Barack Obama during the months preceding the presidential election in 2008? The group with which I work, AWARE-LA, created a blog to track the eruption of inflammatory and racist speech and images targeting him.[23] The barrage was unbelievable to witness, even for someone like myself who has become increasingly observant of these patterns.

Much of the differential media coverage that occurred was fairly subtle in nature though. To help us perceive more clearly, a widely distributed online article written by Tim Wise, a nationally-recognized speaker on issues of white privilege, named a long list of ways that racism and privilege shaped the portrayals and coverage of the candidates and their families.[24]

Finally, consider the lack of sensitivity and unconsciousness required for the editorial board of the New York Post to allow a cartoon portraying a chimpanzee shot by police officers with a statement saying that someone else would need to write the next stimulus bill to run in its paper in February 2009. As this cartoon ran literally on the same day when a photo showed President Obama signing the stimulus bill he wrote into law, it is near impossible for race-conscious individuals to imagine that the chimp was not intended to represent the President. Although only a few discrete examples are offered here, we need to recognize that these eruptions of racism occur regularly without most white people's recognition or admission.

Although many forces combine to create these discriminatory practices and patterns, it is likely that many white people involved in their creation do not play their role consciously. I would venture to say that the majority do not perceive themselves as acting on prejudices. Those of us who passively receive the media images and messages many times are not even aware that differential treatments are taking place.

But this does not excuse us from seeing the problem and recognizing that we play a role in its continuation. It is exactly because of our lack of consciousness that we need to train ourselves to become witnesses to discrimination. Our sensitivity must increase, because only when we can see racism and name it can we put voice to our internal sense of justice and begin to call people to account when they highlight subjects differentially, consciously or not.

Let us keep in mind that these issues go largely unnoticed by white people because of our dominant racial position. We do not see our lives impacted by racism, and therefore we are usually less sensitive. By and large, however, people of color see these injustices, recognize their linkage to a long history of maltreatment, abuse, and neglect, and are justifiably angered. Several years ago, I sat with Dr. Shirley Better and invited her to participate in my investigation of cross-race friendships. We talked at length about what I wanted to do and my approach.

One of the things Shirley said that day that particularly struck me went something like this: "Do not be fooled. The majority of middle-class Black folks are angry too. We might have learned how to be successful in the white world and we might be very pleasant in our interactions with you. But we are angry about how racism continues, and you don't even see it." Hearing her made me stop and think. How many times have people of color tried to let me know what they experience? How do I respond in those moments? Might this have something to do with whether or not they feel close to me, able to really tell me the truth of their experience?

I have to admit that I still struggle with my almost knee-jerk reaction to hearing a person of color claim that he or she has suffered discrimination. For example, one of my friends of color might say, "You know, I went to the store and that white woman ignored me because I am . . ." My mind almost immediately begins racing and I begin to ask questions. One of the first questions is, "How do you know it was because of race?" A close second is, "How do you know it was not because of . . . ?" I start to imagine all of the possibilities of what might have happened in that white person's head that have nothing to do with race. I am quite sure I am not the only white person who does this, judging from what I have heard from people of color on this issue.

There are a couple of reasons why we do this that deserve attention. First, many of us are raised with the idea of being the "devil's advocate." We often respect the role of "the questioner" who pokes holes in someone's argument. I know that I do this same thing to my white friends and colleagues about all sorts of issues. Questioning is something I do. I question. I know some people of color who have also been raised to do the same thing. But there is also another factor.

When a person of color suggests that a white person has acted in a discriminatory fashion, I start imagining myself in that white person's place. Very subtly, when I ask questions about the situation, I am looking for how I might have acted if I had been that white person, how I might have been misperceived had I been there. Admitting that the white person in question might have been prejudiced somehow seems to implicate me.

Without realizing it, I put myself in the psychological position of defending myself as I defend the white person in the situation. Not so subtly to the person of color, I engage in a battle to make sure that any discriminatory act experienced be provable in order to protect my sense of self and the world. Regardless of intent, these two combined characteristics—the devil's advocate position and the psychological defense of myself—create an infuriating experience for the people of color trying to share their story.

We can better recognize the problem with this if we take an example from our own experience. Whenever I start speaking about our need to work against racism, I invariably find a white person just itching to tell me the story of the one time when he or she was subject to a prejudicial act. I remember one moment especially clearly. A gentleman who had heard of my work approached me to make sure I was aware that racism is a problem that affects every group and that we should not just concentrate on white-against-people-of-color racism. He went on to narrate the one time, *the one time,* a person acted discriminately against him. An African American coach would not let him play the position he wanted on the football field and he recalled that this was because he was white. This experience had to have happened at least twenty years prior to our conversation.

This is not to diminish the pain of this individual who felt so slighted by his coach. Losing an opportunity because of your racial placement is understandably distressing. Many of us might be able to reflect on some moments where our whiteness was used against us in some way. But we would do well to think about how often this has happened.

True, just one instance of racial discrimination can be so impacting that feelings of hurt and anger still emerge quickly within conversations twenty years later. But imagine enduring consistent racist acts over a lifetime and throughout one's family history. Living in a world fraught with discrimination can shape a person and define perspectives about the world. Racism is painful in a way that time does not always heal.

That many people have worked hard to bring an end to racist policies and practices must be acknowledged. Unfortunately, we cannot take it for granted that seemingly race-neutral legislation translates into social equity in either our wider society or in our individual institutions or companies. In our large social context, media outlets often offer us discriminatory views of people and their approach can have life-or-death consequences. We are also not immune from the various ways our experiences with race embed themselves in our unconscious and emerge in our relationships.

Race is not Real

Another way we try to solve the problem of race while unwittingly falling victim to its effects is by reminding ourselves that race is a social construction. We can then take the position that we simply are not white. I admit the logic here appears flawless and goes something like this: Race is an idea constructed by humans. Race is not biologically real. The whole concept of race is false. Anyone can see that my skin is not actually white. Rather, I can more accurately describe my skin tone as olive, tan, or some shade of pink. Therefore, I am not white.

I remember using this logic myself on numerous occasions. I have had graduate-school professors use this approach, one who proudly held out his arm one afternoon to show me that, yes, in fact, his skin truly is olive colored. A dear friend of mine proudly tells the tale of her preschool-aged son grappling with language one day and coming up with the word "toink" to describe her skin tone, interpreted as a combination of tan and pink. My friend uses this story to highlight that she understands the false nature of race language. She is not alone.

Many of us reject racial whiteness as a personal identifier when we are ready to say that we disagree with the divisions that race perpetuates, the false categorizations that do not offer exact, accurate self-reflection. We do this believing that we are striking back against prejudice and racism. Through this argument, we hope to demonstrate that we will not be fooled into continuing a fundamentally flawed system of naming.

Deciding that we are not white also, however, allows us to scratch racial identity off of our already crowded to-do list. We can move on with our lives, imagining that issues of race are taken care of as far as it relates to us. Sure, there are plenty of people who identify with race and prejudiced viewpoints—but we are no longer part of the "race problem" because we are not part of the race. Those of us taking on this approach generally are philosophically opposed to prejudice, so we do not see ourselves doing anything that would cause distress in anyone from another group.

Unfortunately, there is also a subtle implication in this approach that often goes unnoticed by white people, but it is hardly lost on a good number of people of color. The implication is this: If we reject being called white, we also reject the idea that we are connected to a broader, white culture. Let me say it again in a few different ways.

If we are not white, then whiteness is meaningless for us. If we are not white, then there is absolutely no reason why we should concern ourselves with what people of color have been saying for generations about the features of white culture. If we are not white, then we have nothing to gain by investigating how our country's history of racism shapes us. If we are not white, then conversations about our unwitting participation in perceived racism is irrelevant. All of these statements become possible when we take whiteness off the table.

Our claim that we are not white is true, but only as long as we are talking specifically about skin color in its most literal form. The problem is that whiteness is related to a lot more than fair skin and we cannot deconstruct its effects by simply walking away from race. True, the idea of deconstruction might strike fear in anyone familiar with academic, postmodernist thought. For many, this approach leads one down a never-ending rabbit hole where nothing is real, no value judgment can be made, and existential trauma ensues. I am familiar with this hole. Just like Alice, I have been captivated at the wonders. I have also found the critique. Navel gazing ourselves to death is possible, and we could spend time analyzing our whiteness but never linking new understandings with real movement or action. That is not helpful.

Distancing ourselves from our discomfort with racial identity by claiming that we are not white betrays our hopes. Although we hope that the distance excuses us from being a part of the problem of race, our denials do not stop us from being treated as white. Philosophically rejecting whiteness does not stop us from escaping racial profiling. We will never have to deal with the frustration of being passed over by cab drivers due to our race. We will never be mistaken for gardeners when working in our front yards.

Worse, in our lack of investigation, we cannot recognize that social and economic benefits often come with our whiteness. We remain blind to the myriad ways that whiteness opens doors. We also do not stop enacting the whiteness that has embedded itself within us through years of social conditioning. Expectations of respect, attention, and courteous service from all people we encounter are experienced as normal. Then, as we remain unconscious of the ways we receive unearned benefits, we act in ways that are thoroughly infuriating to people of color in our surroundings.

Ethnicity Replaces Race

Another response to the challenges presented by the concept of race, and whiteness in particular, is to shift our attention toward ethnicity. There is something really important about returning to our roots. Our assimilation story has left many of us without a rooted sense of self. The loss of our ethnic heritage and culture plagues many within the white population in this country. For that reason, we do need to attend to our ethnicity. Knowing more about the cultures we come from, the traditions that supported our forebears, and the lineage they represent can offer us a grounding that we not only deserve but also psychologically require. Ethnicity offers us a way to identify with something other than whiteness, which can seem rather hollow, false, and negative.

One of my African American friends first encouraged me to explore this side of myself during a period when I was struggling against my whiteness. I asked my parents questions concerning where, exactly, my great-grandparents came from in Germany, Italy, and Russia. Since I look very much like my mother, have held her up as a role model for years, and she is full German, I looked most closely for areas where I could connect to my Germanic heritage.

I went through all of my grandparents' old items, searching for remnants of cultural artifacts that might connect me to my ethnic heritage. A strange thing happened as I searched through my maternal grandparents' old trunk. I found that all of the artifacts were Chinese. My grandparents had spent a few years living in China prior to World War II and these were my grandmother's prized possessions. A hand-carved Chinese trunk I have at the foot of my bed was one that she brought back with her in the 1930s. There was nothing German to be found.

I had to get creative with the search, and less concrete. As I questioned my mother, I learned that it is a cultural tradition in Germany to eat salad at the end of the meal, as opposed to at the start, which is the norm in the United States. There is my German tradition. My family eats salad last! Looking deeper, I can recognize a certain discipline and order in the way I live my life, a particular rigidity I associate with Germanic culture. As anyone who has traveled in Germany knows, the trains there leave on time. Now, there is something that fits. I suppose I can call that my cultural heritage.

On the Italian side, there is far less, unless you count that I make good lasagna. Admittedly, however, it is meatless and I made up the recipe myself. I imagine my far distant great-great-grandmother would be less than impressed. During this period of time, I also came extremely close to changing my last name, Tochluk, back to its original Russian form, Tochilanko.

I benefit when feeling connected to something ancient, like when I read old Germanic fairytales and feel somehow related to them. I will continue exploring my ethnicity as I move forward, searching for fragments of a culture long lost to my family. For the truth is that my cultural connection is lost; I am not

German. That culture is too disconnected. My Germanness was traded in long ago for the benefits available in this country for European immigrants able to fit into the white group. Feeling connected with my ancestry is essential, but I cannot kid myself into believing that I share the same culture as contemporary Germans. I do not.

At the same time that this process of reconnecting with our heritage is essential, there simultaneously is a problem. The downside is not that we search for rootedness; the downside is that whites' uncritical movement toward ethnicity can act as a disguise that masks multiple issues. For example, Omi and Winant's *Racial Formation in the United States* explores the valuable contributions that an acknowledgment of ethnicity can offer. But, the book also expresses concern that ethnicity language often functions as a new form of race language. [25]

Essentially, they remind us that there are many different ethnic groups, such as Japanese Americans, Korean Americans, and Chinese Americans, who are simply called Asian American by most people in the United States. Omi and Winant suggest that even though we would like to think that these specific ethnic categories allow people to retain their ethnic identities, the use of the broad category, Asian American, is "clearly a racially based process" because "the majority of Americans cannot tell the difference between members of the various groups." [26]

In other words, the idea that we are avoiding the vestiges of race through a turn toward ethnicity is illusory. We have simply replaced the old, objectionable race terms for new terms such as European American, African American, Asian American, Latin American, or Native American. In our effort to deal with our country's diversity, we continue to collapse people into groups that closely mirror the parameters of the old race categories.

One problem with this disguise is that the language of ethnicity allows us to escape the negative associations with race without acknowledging the very real effects that our history with race continues to have on our perceptions. A focus on ethnicity allows us to more readily ignore our country's history of racism and its continuing effects. For example, seeing various groups within the country as ethnicities allows us to evaluate each group's assimilation into American society against that of the early European groups.

Oftentimes, white people will recall our own family history in efforts to understand and evaluate the experience and "progress" of other groups. We often justify the oppressions of some groups as we recount tales of discrimination suffered by our immigrant family years ago. White people often say something like this: "All of our ancestors went through the process of coming to the United States and figuring out how to fit in. All groups struggled when they first arrived and gave up aspects of their heritage, and most had to learn a new language. So, why can't this group move past it like mine did?"

We see this emerge when we discuss the achievement gap between different ethnic/racial groups in regards to standardized testing, high-school graduation rates, college admissions, and employment statistics. We also tend to start pitting one group against the other, such as the well-known problem of holding up Asian Americans as "the model minority," without attending to groups' differential histories. This also allows us to ignore the very different experiences among various Asian Pacific Islander groups, some of which continue to struggle markedly.

Another deep problem with this is that however long European Americans search within our family histories, we will never find an appropriate comparison with those who remain hyphenated Americans in our social consciousness. European immigrants become Americans when they blend in. People who have long been considered members of races other than white based on physical features do not blend in. They remain racially typed and the fact that this alters their assimilation experience is pushed to the side with a narrow concentration on ethnicity. White people find some groups blameworthy for not assimilating while the different position they hold in the public's psyche and institutions goes ignored. Essentially, we blame those who have been most victimized by racism.

Admittedly, this is challenging in no small part due to our efforts to answer to the wishes of the various groups who prefer terms of ethnicity to the language of race. For many of us, the shift to ethnicity language is made in concert with requests from people of color. It might therefore feel inappropriate to criticize a focus on ethnicity. Because race is a fabrication, there are plenty of people who simply cannot locate themselves within race's ill-defined categories. Ethnicity simply makes more sense.

Since each racial or ethnic group living within the United States has a substantially different historical experience, we all have different needs. For example, many of my Latino/a students struggle to place themselves racially, and statistics from a past U.S. census report suggests that an important factor associated with whether or not Latinos/as consider themselves to be white is socioeconomic status.[27] This question of what it means to be white is a complicated one with which each group that has been able to claim the privileges of whiteness has to grapple.

White people who cannot fully recapture a lost cultural heritage, like myself, often experience a real sense of loss. Sure, there might be subcultures of whites that feel attached to what they see as a particularly American culture, like those who would claim a "Southern" culture. However, many of us find ourselves looking at other groups and longing for the connection we imagine they feel with their roots, their homeland, their culture. Many white people can be heard saying, "We don't have culture. They have culture."

Even if African Americans do not choose to reconnect with their African ancestral culture, many white people generally assume that Black culture in the United States is rich with meaning. Many of us also travel and bring other group's cultural artifacts home with us. In my familial home, for example, we have puppets from Indonesia, figurines and baskets from Africa, a rug and bedspread from Guatemala, and carvings from Mexico. For a long time, I saw my inclinations toward tourism as evidence of my openness and respect for other cultures, having no idea how much it also betrayed my inner sense of loss.

In the mid-1990s, I attended a performance put on by the UCLA Drama Department. In one main hall, individual artists each had a roped-off section of space. Each enacted a cultural way of being. There was someone representing Santeria, another portraying a Middle-Eastern culture I cannot remember. And then I saw her, the white woman. I stood transfixed in front of the white female artist. She sat on a chair on a square stage four feet above the crowd in a glass case. She wore a delicate white dress and was holding a bag from Pier 1 Imports. She admired the exotic artifacts from lands abroad one after the other.

I stood transfixed for several minutes, trying to sort out the emotion rising in me. There was something very discomforting about seeing her that way. I recognized that woman. She was myself. Or at least, she had been me. She was my mother. She was my grandmother, perhaps to some lesser degree. I felt that, that blandness, that plainness, that whiteness. I felt her whiteness as a lack, a loss. I felt this loss in my bones. I could barely move as I was reminded of how I loved what other cultures have precisely because I know the inner emptiness that results when tradition is traded in for whiteness.

I know I am not alone. I hear the same sentiments too much from other white people. If anything, this is one of the truest hallmarks of whiteness I have yet encountered. There is a hole within many of us, created when our families gave up our culture in order to be successful in the United States. Of course, there are plenty of people from other groups and cultures who also travel, collect artifacts, and shop at Pier 1 Imports. However, the collection of objects is not the focus here. What struck me most was the deep underlying pain emerging from many white people as they discuss what it means for them to feel disconnected from their ancestral culture.

At this time, with what I now see, there is nothing about that setting that feels coincidental: the glass separating the woman from the audience, the stage that put her on a pedestal, the center, privileged position within the room, and the way her presence commanded attention. Even given that secure foundation, she exuded a sense of loss, of being lost, adrift in the larger world . . . captured by the glass case.

The various meanings of this type of whiteness are very real for me. When I am able to witness these features of my whiteness and acknowledge them I gain the power to alter my relationship to them, to alter my relationship with myself. In this way, I am better able to navigate the world. I am better able to relate to people of color. I can admit to what they already know about whiteness. We can share in a conversation of complexity that seeks not to make it all okay, but grounds us in the understanding that we exist together without those particular barriers to our communication.

But most whites are not able to have those conversations if we hide within our focus on ethnicity. Instead, there are coping strategies many whites use, either consciously or unconsciously, in order to deal with the feeling of ethnic loss. (Please note that coping strategies are not necessarily healthy.) Although not an exhaustive list, some of the most frequent forms include:

- Identifying ourselves with our lost heritage to whatever degree possible (such as claiming that we are German even when we have little to no relationship to Germanic culture)
- Emphasizing other identities (such as our gender, religion, joining a subculture, etc.) as a more defining aspect of our lives
- Identifying with other cultures, taking on beliefs and/or practices from other groups
- Focusing on relationships with people of color
- Embracing mainstream American culture and its value systems

Each of these coping strategies can feel like it enhances our sense of self and helps us find grounding and connection. But each has a downside if we use the coping strategy to escape confronting our identity. Further, unfortunately, depending on how enacted, these strategies are often offensive to traditionally oppressed groups. Unhealthy manifestations of the above coping strategies can include:

- Denying our relationship with collective white America
- Uncritically appropriating cultural practices and behaviors from other groups with little consciousness regarding their deeper meanings
- Using people of color for the "culture" they bring into our lives
- Creating needy relationships with people of color wherein we seek validation and/or escape from the white community
- Holding up American culture as a product of diverse contributions without acknowledging the role of exploitation and the ways in which groups benefited differentially

Unfortunately, so many whites have trampled people of color as we ran away from our whiteness that many people of color are highly suspect when whites demonstrate an interest in their culture and participate in traditional ceremonies and practices or wear their cultural symbols and dress.

If we can understand that our cultural exploration or adoption is often warily perceived as related to appropriation, the exploitation of another group's culture for another's benefit, and a history of oppressive behaviors, then we can more effectively explain our intention to people of color. If we can avoid becoming defensive, we might be able to hear the concerns of people of color, then be offered the opportunity to explain the respect we have for the cultural tradition or faith. Further, we can enter a discussion about how our interest in a particular culture is related to our own sense of cultural loss. Even more helpful is an ability to discuss how we understand our approach in terms of our relationship with our own whiteness and the benefits that have traditionally come with membership in that group.

Overall, the more we understand ourselves, the reasons for our actions, and how our cultural explorations might be perceived in relationship to an oppressive history, the more we are able to navigate our way through challenging conversations, build authentic relationships, and break down the wounds built up over years of injury. Perhaps even more important, we might be able to avoid enacting a disrespectful form of appropriation.

To sum up, we benefit greatly from a healthy investigation of our ethnic heritage. Researching and reconnecting can help us deal with the loss many of us feel because of our assimilation into whiteness. We run into trouble, however, when we focus narrowly on ethnicity as a way to escape grappling with race identity. If we remain unclear about our own whiteness, then we do not perceive the negative, unhealthy aspects of the coping strategies that we use to help us manage the cultural loss we feel. We then both ignore the effects of historical and contemporary racism and offend people of color.

We Don't See Color

Being colorblind is a fourth way we distance ourselves from our discomfort with whiteness. This is not to say we *intentionally* use the term as a distancing technique. Most of us say we are colorblind as an assurance to others that we are *not* prejudiced. I learned this type of language as a child when my teachers would say, "I don't care if you are yellow, purple, blue, or green." I know when I used the term *colorblind,* my intentions were positive. I wanted to let people know I treated everyone equally. Many people told me being colorblind moved us away from our history of racism and toward a future of equity, so I felt being colorblind was an attitude that aligned me with progress and humanity's evolution.

My understanding of this term completely changed after reading Ruth Frankenberg's book *The Social Construction of Whiteness: White Women, Race Matters.*[28] Reading her analysis of the use of the term, I recognized myself in some areas and saw differences in others. But the subtle implications she described altered my perspective. I was so shaken I asked people of color in my social and work circles if they, too, saw in that language what Dr. Frankenberg outlined. Indeed they did, and I have not used the term *colorblind* to describe my perspective since.

There are three basic problems with using the term *colorblind*. First, the entire idea of colorblindness is a lie. Of course we see color. Of course we perceive different skin tones and the physical features most commonly associated with racial categories. To tell ourselves differently denies reality. Colorblindness is a complete fabrication. Alone, this argument might appear unimportant, calling up a response such as, "Sure, I *see* color, but what I mean is that a person's color doesn't *mean* anything." This moves us into the second area of trouble with colorblindness.

When we say that we do not see another person's color, what we essentially are saying is that we do not see a person's racial placement as meaningful. Basically, we are saying that we do not see the ways that a person of color experiences the world differently than does a white-appearing person. Worse, being colorblind usually means that since we do not see differential experiences, people of color will have to convince us that race continues to matter in their lives.

In essence, when we say we are colorblind, we end up saying, "Race doesn't matter to me, and therefore it should not matter to you." That being the case, the alignment with colorblindness builds a shield to protect us from considering how lingering, unconscious prejudices might play out. Essentially, claiming that we are colorblind can stop us from being open to dialogues with people who experience and/or perceive racial injustice.

Finally, white people tend not to speak of being colorblind when speaking of interactions with other whites. Colorblindness really only comes up when we speak of how we see, or do not see, people of color. We are essentially saying that there is something about people "of color" that should not be seen. This implies that there is something negative about being associated with color and that there is no value in being recognized as a person of color. In essence, we are saying, "I don't hold this part of who you are against you." Although there are many people of color who use this term to indicate they do not hold our whiteness against us, there are far more who reject the colorblindness approach for the above reasons.

In addition to offending people of color and denying and dismissing their experiences, choosing colorblindness also has one glaringly negative ramification for white people. Being colorblind truly keeps us blind, blind to ourselves. Our whiteness, already a rather blurry topic, moves from being uncomfortable and out of focus to being purposefully hidden from ourselves. As we refuse to see the color in someone else's life, we refuse to see the whiteness in our own.

Our philosophic refusals to see our racial identity as significant do not translate into a psychological overcoming, and issues of race continue to affect us. We do have an option, however. To use Ruth Frankenberg's words, we can become race cognizant, or race conscious. We can develop a clear vision of how race impacts our lives and the lives of others so that we can move toward honestly witnessing the ways our whiteness plays a role in our daily lives.

We Transcend Race

A final way we turn away from our whiteness is when we say we are post-racial and have transcended race. This approach was often heard expressed during the months surrounding Barack Obama's election as President of the United States. Those claiming that he, and we, have transcended race sought to mark the profound and real progress we have made as a country. Yet, on the other hand, holding up this singular moment as proof that racism is no longer a deeply affecting aspect of people's experience in our country was also wishful thinking.

Of the various approaches described in this chapter, this is perhaps the most deeply felt because when we see ourselves as "beyond race," we often align our belief system with our sense of spiritual being and a more hopeful future. It does not really matter to which faith community we belong. From this perspective, we focus on what is most inherently meaningful about our lives. We very often search for what "resonates" with us, that which rings true and feels right, that which fits with our individual experience of the world. Race, as a fabricated concept itself, understandably does not fit with our deep sense of self. And racism is something that strikes such painful chords that we wish for it to disappear altogether.

I know my core—my spiritual self, my soul—transcends race. The deepest and most essential aspect of who I am in the world is not related to race. Personally, I can still hold this to be true and simultaneously recognize that my current manifestation, my current physical form, exists this way for a purpose. To my way of thinking, the learning that my spirit/soul requires on this planet, in this time/space pattern, is related to me being a white woman.

For me, my spiritual self is connected to my physical form. I see my job as needing to learn as much about existence in this context as possible. For that reason, although I completely understand the personal nature of the transcendence approach and the intricate role spirituality plays in our sense of self, it is worthwhile to offer our idea of transcending race up for questioning. Just because our deepest spiritual nature is not related to race does not mean our socialized behaviors in the world are not. Similarly, just because our deepest desires and hopes are to be post-racial, does not mean our socialized behaviors in the world are.

For many white people, our belief that our experience of the world transcends race also comes with additional values. For example, many of us who are dedicated to transcendence as a broader ideal also have a sense of spirituality that manifests as a deeply felt connection with all people and things. This sense of connection can translate into a desire and push toward creating community, wholeness, togetherness, or oneness. Spiritually-oriented people are oftentimes committed to expanding consciousness, continued growth, and becoming more compassionate people in the world as well.

Although paradoxical, our efforts toward racial transcendence can sometimes thwart our ability to truly live out those spiritual goals. For instance, in some ways similar to the earlier mentioned approaches, transcending race can sometimes mean remaining unaware of how racial identity affects our way of being in the world. But if part of life's effort is to be more connected to others, then being less aware of how our whiteness plays out seriously jeopardizes our chances of truly coming together with other individuals. How can people tell us about how racial dynamics affect them if we refuse to acknowledge that race remains significant in people's lives?

Additionally, in an odd sort of way, transcending race can become a tool for reinforcing individualism more than a way to find deeper connection with others. Let me offer an example to illustrate this. A good number of years ago, I fell in love with a Black man. Although this gentleman considered dating me, he ultimately decided it was not a good match. Much went into that decision, but what I remember most was how race played a role. He argued that being with me would be painful for the Black women in his life due to the way white women had been represented as the epitome of womanhood throughout our country's history. Added to that was the history of Black men being persecuted for even looking at, or speaking to, a white woman, which eventually turned white women into prizes to be won—trophies, if you will—in the minds of some Black men.

The man knew many women who regularly talked among themselves about how this history lived on and he refused to add to their hurt. He recognized that the effects of our history are not over, and he was careful to recognize how his behavior in the world would impact others. From what was reported, this same consideration is what prompted Denzel Washington to refuse to kiss Julia Roberts in the film *Pelican Brief,* if I recall the magazine story accurately.

At that time, I could not see why the injury to Black women was important, or more correctly, I did not want to care about what this man saw and what Black women would feel. I could not grasp why what someone else thought about our potential relationship made a difference. I recall saying things like, "We can't be responsible for their feelings." "Why should we be punished for something we were not a part of?" "Why can't we just be beyond race?" Even though I thought I transcended race and was ready to be in relationship with anyone, that very belief caused me to become insensitive to the effects my actions would have on others. I was only concerned about myself.

The point of this is not to say interracial dating is wrong. People will always follow love when truly deep and powerful. Love does not and should not know racial boundaries. However, sensitivity is in order. Transcending race should not mean refusing to acknowledge how our actions affect others. The very least required of us is to expand our awareness and understand the issues and perspectives involved. Besides, if we are going to function well in a diverse world, the ability to sensitively explain why we make the choices we do, in full awareness of the complexity of the situation, the better able we will be to really connect with those who might otherwise feel betrayed.

A last aspect of the transcendence approach that can prove troubling is how the effort to raise one's consciousness can sometimes become twisted into a view of oneself as more evolved than another. In reference to the above situation with my failed attempt at building an interracial relationship, I can imagine having said something like this: "We should not have to worry about those who are still stuck in race thinking. We are more conscious than that." The belief that those who see race and racism and feel its injury are less evolved, less conscious, and therefore less worthy of consideration completely contradicts efforts toward community, oneness, and compassion.

Still worse, within white people this approach can unwittingly reinforce the historically racist views of evolution that held that whites are the most evolved manifestation of humanity. This can affect how we interact with our world. If the majority of whites choose transcendence and claim we are living in a post-racial society, and the majority of people of color call out for an increased focus on race in efforts to hold whites accountable for continuing racism, then who is the more evolved? Whose perspective receives attention? Essentially, in white people, the idea of transcending race can unintentionally perpetuate a sense of superiority that can prove exceptionally damaging when people of color and whites come together in dialogue and community building.

This is not to say moments of transcendence do not occur. My participation over the past decade in multicultural and multiracial groups, conferences, and events leaves me grateful for the many incredible people who offer their hearts to nurture others, regardless of differing backgrounds. Certainly, I have witnessed countless moments of true acceptance and understanding, ceremonies and dialogues where race fell away and only the human spirit remained.

That being said, those moments become possible when people have a deep resolve to ensure that their way of being in the world takes care not to injure another. In my circles, that has meant that those producing the events and conferences explicitly treat issues of race, placing their effects in the center of the room and asking participants both to acknowledge the trauma and the perpetuation of racial wounding and to hold themselves accountable for their actions, be they conscious or unconscious.

Similar to the other ways that we evade the discomfort of our whiteness, transcending race fails us in our efforts to demonstrate rejection of racism and prejudice. As with the previous four approaches, transcending race also asks us to remain ignorant as to how our whiteness plays a role in how we think and behave. Holding ourselves as beyond race can cause us to ignore the pain of others and see ourselves as more evolved than those who talk about the continuing effects of race on our lives. Lastly, the idea of being beyond race can have negative effects within efforts toward community-building unless we build the capacity to bring race into the dialogue and work it through on the way to deeper connection.

FROM BYSTANDER TO WITNESS

The methods most white people use to avoid facing our dis-ease about being white do not work terribly well. Yes, our various approaches can satisfy us on the surface, make us feel as though we are on the side of right, and offer us some good-sounding arguments for why we no longer need to focus on race. Unfortunately, the shadows emerge the moment race enters the situation and we find ourselves disconnected from those who speak of continuing problems. We quickly become defensive and resistant, unable to withstand the critique that we continue to be related to the problems. But we can do things differently. Instead of turning away from our whiteness, we can turn the other direction. We can face the dis-ease. We can clarify our vision.

Trauma theory can help us understand the needed shift. Within any traumatic situation there are several positions we might inhabit. We know each of the positions fairly well, as we play each role at different times throughout our lives. We can be the perpetrator, victim, bystander, or witness. When we are the perpetrator, the cause of the trauma, justice then generally involves us being held accountable in front of the community. When we are the victim who suffers the brunt of the trauma, then care and attention is required to heal from the situation.

As a bystander, we might stop to look at the situation, but we are not involved in the remedy. This is in contrast to the witness. If we witness, we see the situation clearly enough to speak out. Continuing to turn away from the way race affects us places us either in the perpetrator or bystander position. We cannot interrupt racism, either someone else's or our own, if we cannot see how racism manifests in a systematic fashion. We do not have to remain blind, numb, and dumb to how race affects our relationships and the wider community. Instead, we can begin to witness.

NOTES

1. Lorenz, H. S., and M. Watkins, "Silenced Knowings, Forgotten Springs: Paths to Healing in the Wake of Colonialism," *Radical Psychology* 2, no. 2 (2001), http://www.radpsynet.org/journal/vol2-2/lorenz-watkins.html.

2. Lorenz, H. S., and M. Watkins, "Depth Psychology and Colonialism: Individuation, Seeing Through, and Liberation," *Quadrant* 33, no. 1 (2003): 14.

3. Kendall, *Understanding White Privilege,* 85.

4. Lorenz and Watkins, "Silenced Knowings."

5. Mahoney, M. R., "Segregation, Whiteness, and Transformation," in *Critical White Studies,* ed. R. Delgado and J. Stefanic (Philadelphia: Temple University Press, 1997), 654.

6. Tatum, B. D., *Why Are All the Black Kids Sitting Together in the Cafeteria?* (New York: Basic Books, 1999).

7. Better, S., *Institutional Racism: A Primer on Theory and Strategies for Social Change* (Chicago: Burnham, 2002).

8. American Anthropological Association, *Statement on "Race,"* May 17, 1998, http://www.aaanet.org/stmts/racepp.htm.

9. Tatum, B. D., "Racial Identity Development and Relational Theory: The Case of a Black Woman in White Communities," in *Women's Growth in Diversity: More Writings from the Stone Center,* ed. J. V. Jordan (New York: Guilford Press, 1997); J. H. M. Vanderryn, "A Qualitative Analysis of the Meaning of Being White American," PhD diss., University of Colorado, Boulder, 1997.

10. Twine, F. W., "Brown-skinned White Girls: Class, Culture, and the Construction of White Identity in Suburban Communities," in *Displacing Whiteness: Essays in Social and Cultural Criticism,* ed. R. Frankenberg (Durham, NC: Duke University Press, 1997), 239.

11. Frankenberg, R., Introduction, "Local Whitenesses, Localizing Whiteness," in *Displacing Whiteness: Essays in Social and Cultural Criticism,* ed. R. Frankenberg (Durham, NC: Duke University Press, 1997).

12. Better, *Institutional Racism,* 16.

13. McIntosh, P., "White Privilege: Unpacking the Invisible Knapsack," in *Peace and Freedom* (Philadelphia, PA: Women's International League for Peace and Freedom, 1989).

14. Olson, R. A., "White Privilege in Schools," in *Beyond Heroes and Holidays: A Practical Guide to Anti-Racist, Multicultural Education and Staff Development,* ed. E. Lee, D. Menkart, and M. Okazawa-Rey (Washington, DC: Network of Educators on the Americas, 1998), 83.

15. Roediger, D. R., *Colored White: Transcending the Racial Past* (Los Angeles: University of California Press, 2002).

16. Roediger, *Colored White,* 60.

17. Roediger, *Colored White,* 40–41.

18. Crass, C., *Beyond Welfare Queens: Developing a Race, Class and Gender Analysis of Welfare and Welfare Reform,* 2004, http://colours.mahost.org/articles/crass6.html

19. Parvez, Z. F., "Women, Poverty, and Welfare Reform," *Sociologists for Women in Society,* 2002, http://www.socwomen.org/socactivism/factwelfare.pdf.

20. Brown, M., *Race, Money, and the American Welfare State* (Ithaca, NY: Cornell University Press, 1991).

21. Eugene Robinson, "(White) Women We Love," *Washington Post,* June 10, 2005, A23.

22. Mark Mennott, "Spotlight Skips Cases of Missing Minorities," *USA Today,* June 12, 2005.

23. AWARE-LA, "Doubletake 08: Taking a Second Look at Race and Racism in the 2008 Presidential Elections." http://doubletakeblog.wordpress.com/

24. Wise, T., "This Is Your Nation On White Privilege." Red Room: Where the Writers Are, http://www.redroom.com/blog/tim-wise/this-your-nation-white-privilege-updated

25. Omi, M, and H. Winant, *Racial Formation in the United States* (New York: Routledge, 1994).

26. Omi and Winant, *Racial Formation in the United States,* 23.

27. Moore, S., and R. Fields, "The Great 'White' Influx." *Los Angeles Times Online,* July 31, 2002, http://www.uwm.edu/%7Egjay/Whiteness/latimesarticle.htm.

28. R. Frankenberg, *The Social Construction of Whiteness: White Women, Race Matters* (Minneapolis: University of Minnesota Press, 1997).

Chapter 2

Facing the Dis-ease

"You are not helping him," said Mrs. Washington. "You come in here and think you're helping. Well, you're actually hurting him. Giving him so many chances with no consequence is only teaching him that he doesn't need to take responsibility for his actions. Allowing him to talk back to authority like that is going to get him killed someday," she continued. Mrs. Washington kept talking, explaining, and instructing me about my insufficient understanding of the ramifications of my approach to her community.

As the newest in a long line of fifth grade teachers, I wanted so much for Dustin to give the graduation speech he had prepared. After the abusive parental relationship he had survived and the difficulties he had experienced in foster homes, I wanted desperately for him to stand in front of the whole school as a leader and to feel successful and loved on graduation day. But he kept breaking rule after rule. He knew that continued infractions meant losing the opportunity. But, I kept giving him extra chances, wanting him to feel the type of unconditional love with which I had grown up.

Being unaware of the subtleties of how my whiteness informed my thinking and actions, what I completely missed was the way that my needs influenced how I saw Dustin and what I thought was best for him. At that time, I was just starting to recognize the way my race and class positions had shaped me. Looking at these issues had aroused some very deep feelings of shame and guilt. Seeing for the first time the way that being white had benefited me, I began to see the relationships with my students as my opportunity to make up for societal inequity.

I saw myself as being in service, dedicated to being there for my students no matter what. This work with my students would be my redemption, the thing that would make my life, and the privileges I had received, absolvable.

This was my payback. My dedication to my students would make my whiteness okay. Seeing Dustin up on stage would have made *me* feel like a good, worthy person.

Implementing the rules and disallowing him from making that speech would have seemed a testament to *my* failure to inspire him. Giving Dustin repeated chances offered *me* additional chances to feel successful. Did I realize that at the time? No. Was I able to see that my lack of a solid racial identity was the underlying cause for my problematic approach? No. Was I willing to hear Mrs. Washington tell me why my overt behavior was damaging? Thankfully, yes.

It is no wonder that white people want to be colorblind, return to our ethnic heritage, and claim we live in a post-racial society. Facing the dis-ease of whiteness does not eliminate confusion. My approach to relationships actually seemed to get *more* difficult when I began to face my whiteness.

My hunch is that this pattern affects people in all sorts of employment and social positions within our society. When we begin to notice how race and racism operate in our daily lives, figuring out how to navigate can be very confusing. The flavor of each particular situation would necessarily differ, but the core trouble might be similar if we seek to work through negative feelings about being white through our actions with people of color.

My initial struggles came about because I no longer knew how to be myself once I recognized how race and class had affected me. A sense of aloneness enveloped me and everything previously known was up for question. Thankfully, one of Hecate's roles is as a protector of those who live on the edge of society's margins. Her guidance as we struggle to figure out a more viable way of living that allows those at the margins to also feel centered in some way can be really helpful. As it turned out, learning to witness my own whiteness, thereby creating a new way of seeing myself, required me to develop my racial identity.

WHAT ARE THE OPTIONS?

Beverly Daniel Tatum describes how none of the well-known models of whiteness inspire white people to invest in a sense of racial identity.[1] There are essentially three models with which large numbers of white people are familiar. The most common model is the *White Racist*. There may still be plenty who fit this category, but few who want to claim it.

Second, we have the *Unconscious White*. This model refers to those of us who are oblivious to the effects of race and say, "Being white doesn't mean anything." This model, by virtue of essentially naming ourselves as ignorant, is hardly attractive, even though this is the category where most of us rightly fit. In our efforts to escape our discomfort, we often do, in fact, remain rather unconscious and ignorant about what it means to be white. We might see social inequity and strive to do good work in the world in response, but we do so without allowing that our racial identity should hold meaning. The unconscious white does not face the dis-ease.

Alternatively, there is the *Guilty White*. This model describes some of us who recognize both our connection to the shameful aspects of United States' history and how that history shapes our current social structures, and we feel badly about our association with it. Although it took me until adulthood to see my relationship to an unequal system, others become aware very early in life. Either way, we often cope by trying to distance ourselves from anything associated with whiteness while we resist seeing ourselves as white people. In this position, it feels good when someone tells us that we're not like regular white people, or that we are a different kind of white person. The idea of the guilty white also closely aligns with the commonly used put-down attacking the "bleeding-heart, liberal do-gooder."

What do we do when our options appear so limited? For those of us who see the effects of past injustices at work in the twenty-first century, we might want to be part of correcting the situation. Keeping an eye on our disastrous history understandably inspires guilt and shame in many of us. The question becomes, what do we do with that feeling? Do we turn around and flee? Many do.

However, many of us also turn to community service efforts so that we can feel good about our work in the world, knowing that we are trying to do at least something to make up for the history from which we benefit. Certainly, this had a lot to do with my dedication to my students. We want to face the effects that privilege has had on people in our country, but our relationship to this work remains strained. Our lack of resolution and our incomplete recovery from the guilt can follow us and create problems even in our efforts to face our dis-ease.

ADVERSE CONSEQUENCES OF AN INCOMPLETE RECOVERY

When we see that racism continues, we often dedicate ourselves to work toward improved race relations and increased social justice. We recognize that current social ills are rooted in an unjust past and present, and we offer ourselves—and the influence we can have in various communities—as part of corrective actions. Yet we often experience difficulty in multiracial situations. Two common challenges are our lack of confidence and our overconfidence.

On one hand, when we enter multiracial spaces, we often take with us our own discomfort with our racial selves. Especially for those of us who have only recently begun to recognize the ways that the more subtle forms of racism emerge, our earlier lack of sensitivity can turn into an awkward oversensitivity. Where once we never noticed race (or at least claimed not to), increased awareness makes issues of race appear ever-present. Race consciousness is at its height and we can often feel paralyzed while trying to figure out how to behave in order to subvert the racism in the room while not appearing racist by concentrating on race in the room! What will the person of color think? What if I say the wrong thing? Our deep sense of guilt over our history and our current ineptness damages our ability to relate.

As I moved through this phase of awareness, my new sensitivity created anxiety that worked against me when trying to develop relationships with people of color. My lack of confidence in myself as "a person who sees race" kept me from feeling comfortable and confident in my behaviors and opinions. I needed a supportive network to help me work through these questions, but there were no white people in my life who understood what I was going through. There were no white people in my social circles who could help me work through these anxieties without asking me to return to my old way of seeing the world and deny the impacts of race.

There were no whites around me who could help me see where my thoughts and behaviors *were,* in fact, problematic. There were no whites who could simultaneously challenge me to keep digging deeper into my behaviors to find trouble spots *and* help me develop skills to better communicate across race. I had no white friends who could both hold me accountable for the ways lingering prejudices emerged in my words and actions *and* hold me up as a valuable person in the world who legitimately struggles. In part due to the absence of white models, I turned to people of color for help.

White people turning to people of color is a long-established and well-known pattern. People of color become the supportive networks we turn to in order to feel better about ourselves and/or be prompted toward further growth. Sometimes this can be really beneficial, with white people learning much and improving their efforts to educate for social justice in ways that people of color also value. On the other hand, helping white people see what has previously been invisible to us usually also involves working through our resistance and denials. This takes a great amount of dedication and effort and can leave our friends of color feeling overburdened and exhausted.

Questions from people of color such as, "Why do I have to be the one to teach you about yourself?" or "Why should I have to fix the problems your people started?" are common. Although people of color will likely continue to regularly offer insight, acceptance, and nurturing, white people need to develop the skills to take on some of this work. White people need to develop the capacity to help each other grow, encourage each other to take next steps, and find a way to become *appropriately* sensitive to race issues.

My belief is that the majority of people in this country are both well-intentioned and disturbed by the inequity in our society. Taught to question, "How can I leave this world better than I found it?" many of us battle against grim forces such as poverty, homelessness, disease, illiteracy, and so forth. We donate resources, volunteer, and/or engage in philanthropy. We visit unfamiliar communities, offering our service. We develop programs in our institutions and companies. But we consistently create trouble when we engage in this work without sufficient awareness of what we bring to the table.

Whereas white people can experience a *lack* of confidence when first coming to awareness of race issues, we can also be *over*confident if we join social causes while seeing racism as existing only outside of ourselves. In other words, we can be *over*confident when it comes to our ability to offer ourselves in service if we do not see how our racial socialization affects us and how it might be associated with adverse effects. Our guilt can translate into a sense of purpose, sometimes a *mission,* that gets us into the door, but our fragile sense of self can keep us resistant to the growth required for effectiveness.

When white people go into communities of color without sufficient awareness, we can fall into three interrelated traps: we take on a savior complex, enact a superiority complex, and feel sorry for those with whom we work. These three tendencies arise together so much of the time that teasing them apart proves challenging. For the sake of clarity, the following sections describe each of the three in isolation, along with some adverse effects. Yet the reader may quite rightly see these elements infused within each other.

The Savior Complex

The savior complex refers to a pattern wherein white people see our participation in a community as essential. Sarah Sentilles speaks of her relationship to this attitude in her book *Taught by America,* in which she describes her two years teaching in Compton as part of the Teach for America program.[2] I experienced something similar when teaching elementary school in Inglewood. Like Sarah, I also began teaching students without sufficient training or materials. I began my first year teaching having never taken a teacher education course and with a set of twenty second-grade reading books for the twenty-seven fifth-grade students in my class. I too learned to scavenge for math books, desks, and chairs. I recognized the systemic problems Ms. Sentilles describes.

I also recall feeling the following sentiments early in my tenure at the school, both as a counselor and then later as a teacher. "I can't leave because then who would they have? They need me. I'm better than anyone else they will get to come work here." Michelle Pfeiffer's character in the movie *Dangerous Minds* could have been my model. More recently, Hillary Swank's real-life character in *Freedom Writers* follows a similar track. I was the white woman who would single-handedly lift up the students and offer them what their community did not. Dedication and perseverance on my part would allow these extremely bright young students to overcome the adversity they faced. I would be their heroic guide to support their own inspiration.

Seeing the racism in those ideas took awhile. I had to recognize that regardless of my efforts, the truth was I was one more well-intentioned white girl who showed up in the community intending to make a difference, knowing virtually nothing about the people who lived there and lacking the skills and commitment necessary to educate the students successfully for the long term. I was well-meaning and hardworking. But I was still part of the problem.

In a moment where Ms. Sentilles describes her sense of belonging within the Compton community, she admits that, "I belonged—and at the same time, I didn't belong. I had been sent to Compton, not invited. I was dropped into that community, a colonialist, a missionary believing I carried something Compton needed, when so many had come before me." She describes the learning that she gained from her time spent in Compton, how it changed the entire trajectory of her life, and how she feels a continuing sense of accountability to those who live there.

These aspects of her story resemble my own in some ways. I, too, must see myself as part of a system that allows the most inexperienced young teachers, usually white, to work in areas with the highest need.[3] We enter these positions believing that our good intentions will make up for our lack of skills and cultural knowledge. They do not. We enter believing that we are essential in the success of those we touch. We fool ourselves. We touch lives, yes. But, if we concentrate on glorifying our areas of success, we neglect the systemic change we rightly should work toward.

Additionally, when our approach incorporates the idea that another group needs us for their betterment, we overestimate the value we bring to the situation. We ignore or justify the effects of our inexperience, saying things like, "At least I am here. Without me, they would be worse off." The list could go on. Our mission can be read as missionary, and like those who descend upon another's land without sufficient cultural knowledge and respect, we can do real damage as we neglect cultural mores and unintentionally offend, thereby rendering our work less effective. This same basic scenario plays out not only in schools, but anywhere we find white people volunteering or hired to "make a difference" in communities other than their own.

The Superiority Complex

The savior complex often goes hand in hand with a sense of superiority. When we approach communities of color with an attitude of internalized superiority (usually not a consciously-held opinion), we often move toward leadership positions before gaining sufficient knowledge of the community's members, concerns, and contexts. Even without this vital information, we sometimes believe that we know what the community or organization's goals should be and what needs to be done to achieve those goals.

We can also be unconscious of our tendency to take over the direction of conversations. In other words, we take up valuable time and space without dedicating enough time to listen, to learn, and to gain the skills required for success within the community. Making matters worse, we are all too often unconscious of how people of color read this lack of humility as enactments of privilege and racism.

When white people begin to display one or more of these tendencies, some people of color might offer a challenge. Depending on the person involved, this might be our only chance to demonstrate our willingness to grow in the situation. If we are unable to explore to what degree our whiteness plays a role in our behavior, we are likely to show resistance and invalidate the concerns raised. When we do this, the people of color involved might, if we are lucky, continue to pester and prod until we respond favorably.

Far more likely, however, is that people of color pull back and turn to each other for support. An often unspoken, yet palpable, tension then usually arises. During moments of informal socializing, people of color will retreat from those who have slighted them and will coalesce, leaving white people to themselves. This sequence of events can happen without anyone even consciously recognizing the dynamics in play, individuals seeking support from those they believe will understand them.

Generally speaking, regardless of which group is in the majority, the white people feel left out and excluded. White people get together and try to figure out why the people of color sit together and avoid in-depth conversations or socialization with us. At this point, we usually resort to blaming the people of color for what we see as "their divisiveness," completely missing that we likely played an essential role in creating the sense of discomfort that put the separation in motion.

We wonder, "Why are we not fully accepted? What did we ever do?" If we dare to ask, we might receive another opportunity to name the oppressive behaviors we continue to enact. But we might not. Either way, something is required of us that unresolved guilt or ignorance sometimes makes difficult for us to offer. We must offer an open mind, open to the possibility that our intentions to "help" have brought with them rather pernicious forms of subtle racism. We might already feel bad enough deep down. Admitting to lingering, albeit unconscious, racism might send us over the edge, so we often avoid that conversation. We keep working together, but the divide between people produces a tension that can become the "elephant in the room." Understandably, this can impede efforts to create community programs and events.

Beyond the tensions among staff and organizers, however, the division is often readily apparent to community members. In this way, the racial dynamics bleed into the work. The people of color involved see white people trying to "help" and "save" them, seeing into our behavior an attitude of "we know best." We also may not appear willing to consider that we might enact racism in the process. There are many ramifications of this process, including the degree to which the community feels drawn to participate in programs developed. Thus, a concrete consequence of this dynamic is poor program attendance and a resulting decrease in a school or organization's effectiveness.

The adverse consequences of a perceived sense of superiority on the part of white people increase exponentially when power differentials exist. The key difference here is the reduced likelihood that white people will be challenged and brought to awareness of their missteps. Drawing again from my experience in schools, let us take as an example the parent-teacher conference. But first, let us admit up front that lousy parents exist everywhere. Some spoil. Some neglect. The list is long. But this is about white teachers who meet with parents of color.

We need to talk about white teachers, like myself, who enter communities of color armed with seemingly solid educational backgrounds, a set of values that serve us well in U.S. middle-class society, and the intent to see our students succeed. When success does not happen, our sense of ourselves as their saviors tarnishes. We anticipate the parent-teacher conference, relishing the idea of getting the parents to support our efforts and becoming a two-timing system to hold the student accountable. We realize that we need help. In fact, we cannot single-handedly propel all of our students to success. The whole "It takes a village" idea feels more real.

Unfortunately, very often this hoped-for collaboration does not happen. Even though I had some lovely relationships with my students' parents, I had very low attendance rates on conference day overall. This frustrated me to no end. In hindsight, I can understand that some of the parents' resistance to meeting with me had to do with me and the teachers they met with previously.

One way I participated in the problem included offering unsolicited parenting advice.

I told parents what they ought to do if their children did not complete homework, and so on. I did this without asking the parents how they felt we could be partners. No visits home occurred. Although I began each year promising myself I would make phone calls for good behavior and send home positive notes, within two months that became a low priority. I became the bearer of bad news and with a slap in the face to go with the message I conveyed.

Admittedly, this topic raises many issues and there are many dynamics that enter that have to do with class, culture, age, educational background, language, and so forth. Each could be discussed extensively. But race also emerges. When I offer parenting advice to a parent *without asking if there is interest in my viewpoint,* I position myself as the powerful holder of knowledge in the situation. Some parents are vocal enough to remind teachers of their boundaries, but many are not.

Similar to the description mentioned previously, parents of color might simply walk away. My students' parents never challenged me concerning behaviors perceived as racist. But, looking back, I certainly exhibited some subtle racism. Not every day, and not with every parent. But my success, or lack thereof, had something to do with me. My first few years of teaching were the most challenging. Had I had the wherewithal to seek counsel and inspect my approach to parents, my sense of aloneness in the struggle would have lessened and I would have improved more quickly.

Since that time, I have learned that at the same time that I experienced a lack of attendance, there were teachers of color *at the same school* who did not experience the same issues I did. These teachers of color went to the homes. They overcame their own fears and anxieties. They created parent-teacher events. The parents came. They reached out respectfully before trouble emerged. Their students achieved more than mine.

Without the appropriate openness to investigating how I carried myself in the situation, my sense of having superior knowledge kept me blind to the ways that I contributed to the further disintegration of the parent-teacher relationship. I am sure that in many cases future teachers suffered the effects. Parents who felt mistreated upon leaving my classroom certainly entered the next teachers' classroom with less enthusiasm. As a pattern, this is devastating, especially considering that 40 percent of public school students in the United States come from communities of color while 90 percent of the teachers are white.[4]

The dynamic described also can be tailored to fit any number of scenarios people face when communicating with community members. The only way to break this pattern, already entrenched in many institutions and organizations, is for us to be able to really be honest and talk about concerns over racism openly, discussing earlier experiences and offering ourselves as ready to receive feedback. As long as power differentials exist, this will remain a struggle, but we have to start somewhere. We would do well to remember that we are the factor upon which we exert the most control.

Sympathy Gone Awry

A third problematic element within our approach involves our deeply-felt sadness in seeing people living in challenging situations, when our sympathy turns into pity. In the absence of intimately knowing the individuals who live in a community—their strengths, joys, and valuable personal resources—we can act in ways that disempower. With intent to become models for others and demonstrate how our way of being offers a road to success, we often:

- Approach communities of color in ways that neglect some valuable, available community resources
- Disparage or ignore beloved aspects of culture present in communities of color that inspire pride and joy
- Continue the process of cultural loss in new generations by using positions of authority to highlight our sense of what it means to be a valuable person, not recognizing that we simultaneously ask people to think less of those they love
- Remain entrenched in a well-researched cycle of low expectations that emerge subtly even when we consciously intend to serve all community members[5]
- Create enmeshed relationships where our sense of value and goodness depends upon the success we inspire in the community of color, leading us to relate in ways that undermine relationships of equality

Each of the above issues presented emerges differently depending upon the context. Honest exploration and self-questioning is the only true way to know to what degree each of us individually enacts these problematic behaviors.

In the interest of offering a concrete example, however, let me tell you about one more rather common error white teachers make when we feel sorry for the members of the multiracial school communities we enter. White liberal teachers in the inner city, even those already trained at top institutions, can be real trouble. There is one thing we do that has become a joke: We completely fail to see that strict discipline and nurturing can go hand in hand, and that each of them is essential for success.

I walked into an inner-city school with a couple of degrees in psychology already under my belt. Beyond academic learning I was extremely concerned for the emotional well-being of my students. My liberal attitude backfired. (Recall my earlier experience with Dustin as a prime example.) The guilt I carried over my own privileged background, mixed with the sadness I felt for the students living in conditions I could not imagine surviving, combined to make me too soft, inconsistent with consequences for misbehavior, and unable to see *my* need to offer students opportunities, even when students failed to meet criteria. In short, my guilty conscious and my pity led me to teach students that they were not accountable to high expectations and personal responsibility.

The book *Because of the Kids,* by Jennifer Obidah and Karen Teel, expands on this discussion, offering many examples of how a well-meaning white teacher can be party to the disengagement of students of color due to a lack of race consciousness.[6] Clearly, my intent was to promote success. But it took African American teachers like Mrs. Washington to point out to me how my approach was very "white" and would actually do the students a disservice. They educated me lovingly. But I struggled.

I struggled, in part, because I approached my work in a community of color with an unhealed sense of self. My work acted as a salve for my deeply-penetrating guilt and shame. My unresolved understanding of who I was as a white person and what that meant for my behavior in the world allowed me to make numerous missteps that undermined my positive intentions. I intended to be of service, be helpful, and to some degree I certainly was. The fact that some of my former students continue to stay in contact with me is a testament to that. But there were also, perhaps even more, moments where things did not go as well.

In order to become more successful, which I believe I did over the course of my years teaching, I had to give up a number of assumptions and look closely at myself. First, I had to stop seeing the image of the racist as some evil bad person out there, disconnected from me. Second, I needed to find supportive people to help me discover the subtle ways that racism continues to live deep within my psyche. Third, I had to admit that my work was as much about myself, and my need to heal, as it was about those with whom I worked. Although that might seem an overstatement, recognizing the way guilt and unresolved anxiety concerning my whiteness sabotaged my work actually released me to become a more *appropriately* confident person engaged in more effective work, able to make more honest and intimate cross-race relationships.

When white people feel guilt and shame in response to the confrontation with our country's relationship with race, we can become unsure of ourselves.

Unless we can create a positive sense of our witnessing selves, our efforts will likely involve neediness, prompting us to seek validation from people of color. I remember taking solace in statements from people of color that I am "a different kind of white person" or "not really white."

But in seeing ourselves as not really white, we see ourselves as outside of the problem and therefore we are often also less able to hear the critical feedback we need in order to enact a more successful way of being. This is where that magical and powerful mythological figure can again prove helpful. Yes, opening ourselves to critique means accepting that we will face shadows and scary places. But, Hecate carries a torch that lights the way so that we might head down a new road and release ourselves from our familiar way of seeing the world.

This new way hopefully involves developing an antiracist white racial identity that offers us a healthy sense of self. For this to occur, however, we need a different model of what it means to be white. Fortunately, many people have been working on these ideas for some time now.

WORKING THROUGH WHITENESS

Two approaches that push people beyond the *Racist, Unconscious,* and *Guilty White* are fairly well known within antiracism circles. The first is the model of the *Abolitionist.* The abolitionist begins with the understanding that race is a social construction and, therefore, racial categories have the potential to be deconstructed, dismantled, and done away with. In some ways, this approach is similar to the "race is not real" approach that we can use to avoid looking at the problem of our whiteness.

The abolitionist position differs, however, because it calls on white people to become "traitors to their race." Abolitionists believe that "the key to solving the social problems of our age is to abolish the white race, which means no more and no less than abolishing the privileges of the white skin." They hold that "the defection of enough of its members to make it unreliable as a predictor of behavior will lead to its collapse." One of its guiding principles is that "treason to whiteness is loyalty to humanity."[7] This model asks us to look at how white skin offers benefits and then refuse to participate by giving up those privileges. We are to find our sense of self in our essential humanity.

Unfortunately, becoming aware of, and resisting, skin privilege is an incomplete strategy. Practically, resisting the benefits of skin privileges does nothing to stop others from perceiving and treating us preferentially in ways we cannot control. We also can only resist something that we consciously recognize. This model can allow powerful unconscious elements to slip by undetected and remain unworked. We require a deeper and more long-lasting look at how whiteness is embedded in the deepest layers of our social and cultural unconscious. This process takes time. With the majority of white people still utilizing the approaches that turn away from our whiteness, a model that asks us to break race down without spending significant time interrogating the subtleties of our whiteness appears premature.

A second alternative is the model of the *White Ally*. Beverly Daniel Tatum describes how this model can offer white people a hopeful alternative and aid in the integration of white identity.[8] The term *white ally* is most often used to describe white people purposefully and actively working in ways that oppose either individual or institutional racism. A white ally traditionally takes responsibility for lingering racism and continues to explore ways to combat white-skin privilege. Commonly, the white ally model is seen as synonymous with an antiracist activist. White allyship also tends to involve an advanced, comprehensive analysis of the interrelated nature of systems of oppression and active efforts to support various movements for social justice.

Certainly, there have been white people working against oppression for hundreds of years in this country. But Tatum indicates that information about how to become a white ally has traditionally been difficult to find. She discloses that she used her own white friend Andrea, with whom she co-wrote an article on cross-race friendship, as a model of a white ally within one of her college courses. She argues that the white ally is a figure that needs modeling and publicity.[9]

When looking through the various models of whiteness available, the racist, the unconscious white, the guilty white, the abolitionist, and the white ally, the model of the white ally suffers from the fewest critiques. That is not to say that there are none. One criticism involves the tendency to use the noun "ally" as a label. Some argue that the term can be taken to mean that once someone achieves the status of an ally that the person has reached a sufficient level of consciousness across the board and can discontinue internal work. For this reason, I tend to speak of doing effective ally work as opposed to becoming *an* ally.

Another criticism concerns how the term "ally" generally refers to white people taking on activism work for the sake of people of color. Many raise concerns that actions done for the sake of another are less dependable. These critics remind us that continuing actions against racism are essential, but that white people must find a personal stake in the work. Thankfully, this is being done. One example specifically targeting teachers comes from Gary Howard's work, *We Can't Teach What We Don't Know.*[10]

I feel fortunate to be part of AWARE-LA, a grass-roots organization that is working to advance an approach to racial identity called *Radical White*

Identity.[11] This approach to white racial identity also aligns with the ideals inherent within the white ally model. AWARE-LA uses the term *radical* to highlight our interest in going deeply to the roots of the challenges we face.

The exploration the Radical White Identity requires and the way it locates white people as meaningful stakeholders in efforts toward social justice offer a sense of hope and inspiration. Within this approach, our antiracism efforts are not *in service of* people of color, they are part of our own effort to shed the socialization that has led to us behaving in ways that support and maintain the oppression of others. In this way, our sense of ourselves as being fully human is realized when we work toward educational, economic, social, and environmental justice.

Although space does not allow for a full and detailed description to be offered here, developing a Radical White Identity essentially asks individuals to devote concentrated time to exploring (1) our ethnic roots so that we can appropriately deal with the effects of our assimilation process, (2) our history of privilege and the systems that have oppressed people throughout our country's existence, (3) the way privilege works in concert with our other multiple social identities, and (4) our individual and collective potential to work against racism, oppression, and the enactment of skin privilege.

Doing this work with other white people, we are building what we call *Radical White Community.* Essentially, this is the community I lacked when I began to struggle with my new understanding of race. Within this community are people who can help me see privilege and racism more clearly, motivate me to continue constructing a healthy and effective antiracism practice, and support me to keeping moving forward in times when I fail. One important aspect of this group is that it welcomes people who are new to the ideas as well as those who have been working in antiracism efforts for many years. In this way, AWARE-LA hopes that a healthy antiracist white identity can begin to be formed even as we take our first steps toward ally work. (To learn more about AWARE-LA, please visit www.awarela.org.)

A FOUNDATION FOR ALLY ACTIVITY: WITNESSING

From the earlier discussion regarding the potentially adverse consequences of guilt on our relationships and work, we can see that there is good reason for the general discomfort among white people regarding consciously forming a white racial identity. Whiteness does not have a positive list of associated meanings, and when we turn to face race issues we often struggle. If we continue working on race issues, we come across two models that offer promise, the abolitionist and the ally. At least here there is support for our need to keep an eye trained on whiteness and a promise of a better, more complete sense of self as antiracist white people.

As I began to face what it means for me to be white and tried to find a healthy sense of myself as a person committed to antiracism, each of the previously discussed models somehow left me wondering. I like the ultimate goal of the abolitionists, but my psychological training just will not allow me to ignore how deep the problems lie. The white ally is a laudable model, one that I work toward as I build my Radical White Identity, but it is one that I still feel uncomfortable claiming sometimes.

Developing an effective white ally practice still feels like a goal on most days. I know what most folks of color expect of an ally, and I continue to struggle to become as consistent and skilled as that requires. Throughout all of this, what seems unacknowledged is what a massive leap it takes to move from being in an unconscious or guilty phase to becoming effective in ally work. There is so much to learn. Creating a clear vision takes time. Developing the skills to proficiently move into activism requires a sophisticated analysis.

White people need a positive, supportive foundation if we are going to collectively investigate our own whiteness. We need a model dedicated to inner psychological work leading to altered behavior. We need a model that starts with the development of a racial identity oriented toward equity and justice that helps us increase our perception.

The model of *witnessing* proposed and described in this book is just such a model. My hope is that developing the skills to witness helps people construct a foundational bridge on the path to becoming proficient at ally work. To my thinking, Sarah Sentilles began to witness while teaching in Compton. She said:

> I struggled while I was teaching in Compton. When I stopped teaching, I struggled harder still. I didn't know what to do with what I had experienced. I asked myself, again and again, "How must my life change in response to what I have witnessed?" My conversion, my awakening to the understanding that I am accountable and responsible for what is happening in Compton and in places like Compton across this country, devastated me. But it also liberated and empowered me. If I am accountable and responsible, then what I do matters.[12]

What we do matters. How we *witness* matters greatly. Becoming adept at witnessing our whiteness involves more than a simple decision to see race as meaningful. Witnessing asks us to create an inclusive vision of ourselves and our communities.

Witnessing involves creating sufficient insight to imagine and support becoming active in racial justice efforts both within and outside of our school, work, and social settings. Witnessing means knowing that we remain unhealthy as long as we are unconscious perpetrators and bystanders to racial injustice. Ultimately, witnessing requires us to know that our society remains unhealthy as long as we do not recognize our privilege and do not give voice to the ways that racial injustice continues to create dis-ease and distress in all of us.

This idea of witnessing our whiteness comes out of my reading of Kelly Oliver's philosophical book *Witnessing: Beyond Recognition,* which describes how witnessing holds two meanings simultaneously.[13] Extrapolating from the definition as given in the *Oxford English Dictionary,* Oliver notes that witnessing involves "*eyewitness* testimony based on first-hand knowledge, on the one hand, and *bearing witness* to something beyond recognition that can't be seen, on the other."[14]

In other words, we have to see with our own eyes *and* bear witness to the experiences of others that we cannot see on our own. In this double meaning, there is a "tension between eyewitness testimony and bearing witness, between historical facts and psychoanalytic truth."[15] Basically, this requires us to recognize that although seeing what is in front of our eyes is an essential aspect of witnessing, we have to also allow that the experience of trauma does not always correlate exactly with the degree of danger present in a situation.

For example, if you take a walk along a mountain path late one evening and trip over something long and thin in the road, you might run in terror from what you have every reason to believe is a snake. Your experience that evening, the trauma you felt in that moment, will not be lessened when you discover the following day that the snake was a rope. In other words, psychological truths hold meanings of lived experience that objective, historical facts cannot always verify. When our intent is to increase healing, arguing over fact can invalidate psychological experience and pour salt in wounds. So our witnessing is not simply about determining the facts of a situation. Bearing witness means being present to the experience of another person.

Facing our whiteness also means facing our past. Oliver argues that, "forgetting the past through the double oblivion of forgetting what has been forgotten almost guarantees that we will repeat rather than work through racism."[16] Seeing the links between past and present are essential for us to work through racism. In light of this, developing the ability to witness begins with knowing the legal, political, economic, philosophical, and social histories of whiteness.

NOTES

1. Tatum, B. D., "Teaching White Students about Racism: The Search for White Allies and the Restoration of Hope," *Teachers College Record* 95, no. 4 (1994).

2. Sentilles, S., *Taught by America: A Struggle of Struggle and Hope in Compton* (Boston: Beacon Press, 2005).

3. This pattern continues to emerge each semester as my students do their demographic studies on public schools within California. Although recent legislation has increased the number of credentialed teachers in classrooms, my students regularly find that suburban, affluent schools continue to report more stable, experienced teaching staffs, whereas inner-city schools serving minority populations continue to have more turnover and less-experienced teachers, exceptions notwithstanding.

4. Bigelow, B., B. Harvey, S. Karp, and L. Miller, eds., *Rethinking Our Classrooms,* vol. 2; *Teaching for Equity and Justice* (Milwaukee, WI: Rethinking Schools, 2001).

5. Association for Supervision and Curriculum Development. *Closing the Achievement Gap: A Vision for Changing Beliefs and Practices,* ed. B. Williams (Alexandria, VA: ASCD, 2003), 100.

6. Obidah, J. E., and K. M. Teel, *Because of the Kids: Facing Racial and Cultural Differences in Schools* (New York: Teachers College Press, 2001). This is a good text for examples of how a well-meaning white teacher can be party to the disengagement of students of color due to a lack of race consciousness

7. RaceTraitor.org, available at http://racetraitor.org/.

8. Tatum, "Teaching White Students about Racism."

9. Tatum, "Teaching White Students about Racism."

10. Howard, G., *We Can't Teach What We Don't Know* (New York: Teachers College Press, 2006), 104.

11. Goldberg, S. and C. Levin, AWARE-LA, *Toward a Radical White Identity,* http://awarela.wordpress.com/toolbox/.

12. Sentilles, *Taught by America,* 192.

13. Oliver, K., *Witnessing: Beyond Recognition* (Minneapolis: University of Minnesota Press, 2001).

14. Oliver, *Witnessing: Beyond Recognition,* 16.

15. Oliver, *Witnessing: Beyond Recognition,* 16.

16. Oliver, *Witnessing: Beyond Recognition,* 131.

Chapter 3

Uncovering a Hidden History

Mrs. Pearson, my fifth-grade teacher, stands out as the most impassioned of my early educators. She loved early U.S. history, the story of the Pilgrims' survival, Williamsburg, the Founding Fathers, and the colonists' fight for freedom and independence. In the spring of my fifth-grade year, in support of my teacher's work, my mother took me to visit Washington, D.C., Williamsburg, and Mount Vernon. That experience left me valuing the people who survived those early days with little technology and few medical advances. Both my parents and my educators oriented me toward that which inspired pride in our country, concentrating on historical figures with whom I could most easily identify, those who looked like me (even if most were men). My tenth-grade U.S. history class offered me more of the same, albeit without Mrs. Pearson's passion.

The limits of my education now stand out in several ways. First, the shameful aspects of our history played a minor, almost tangential role. A few pages here and a few pages there, the bulk of the text focused on heroic tales of overcoming by European colonists, immigrants, and settlers. Second, those few pages offered a sanitized view of the tragedy infused within our country's beginnings. Slavery was presented as a blip in the colonial experience, and the details of the extensive and inhumane treatment of African Americans throughout our country's history (not just during slavery) were largely left out. The takeover of Native American lands were offered as westward expansion, not the genocide of indigenous peoples.

Third, the small amount of information offered did not grab hold of my psyche and push me to investigate further, most probably because the negatively-affected groups were not part of my day-to-day experience. For that, I am responsible. As I got older, I could have known more. I chose to orient my attention elsewhere.

Thankfully, multicultural educators today are increasingly expanding curricula, locating and producing supplementary texts and media, and offering diverse points of view in order to move away from the type of Eurocentric education I received. They are responding to the needs of their diverse body of students, often offering both a critical analysis as well as ensuring that students see themselves represented within history along with their rich cultural traditions and important contributions to our country. Yet multicultural education is not without its detractors and, sadly, it remains sporadically implemented.

Most relevant for the focus of this book, however, is that although the information I was exposed to included various European immigrant groups' struggles to find success, not one page discussed the history of Europeans developing a white identity and how that history informs today's society. Yet, if we do not know the history of whiteness, how can we understand how this particularly shadowed aspect of our past plays out in our contemporary lives, shapes our use of language, and affects our relationships with others?

Let us not imagine that this investigation is in any way novel, however. Scholars of color have been looking into issues of whiteness, its historical roots, and psychological consequences for many decades. Some essential historic and contemporary researchers include W. E. B. Du Bois, Frederick Douglass, bell hooks, and Gloria Anzaldua, among a long list of others. Important to recognize is that the field of "whiteness studies" rests on the shoulders of these early voices. Without them, few of us would have known where to begin. Their work paved the way for this book as well as the various works that I draw upon to formulate a thread of thought that might help us move forward.

A first step involves exploring how the experiences of the earliest colonists and what occurred throughout the 1700s and 1800s, have contributed to the way we live our lives in the twenty-first century. If we form a deeper understanding of the invention of the white race and how whiteness has been created, maintained, challenged, and changed over time, then we are not destined to live out the influences of the past and we can find a more solid ground on which to stand and from which to move. Through this investigation, we can develop a perspective that clarifies our relationship to whiteness, offers insight into our cross-race experiences, and sheds light on some of the issues we currently find debated in the public sphere.

Before we delve into this history, though, I need to say up front that this chapter does not pretend to offer a comprehensive view of U.S. race history. Thorough studies of the history of racism and its manifestations in our country are easily obtained elsewhere.[1] This chapter also only begins to discuss the complex nature of white racial identity formation. Equally, volumes exploring this subject already exist.[2] This chapter offers just one perspective, one orientation that holds a particular truth.

From my background in depth psychology, I understand that any historical analysis is created as much out of the present and future as from the past. Each author brings an orienting view, a paradigm, an axe to grind, or a wish to the subject. Acknowledging that every historical tale is in some way a work of fiction, in my view, makes the offering more honest.[3] With this in mind, the value of this story will lie in its ability to resonate and make sense. Also, reminding ourselves how variable any individual's experience of whiteness can be might prove helpful here, as each of us will form our own conclusions regarding the degree to which the history of whiteness impacts our lives.

Lastly, each section within this chapter draws extensively from particular works that I have found invaluable in understanding the various aspects of this complicated history. Although generally frowned upon, in two areas I do quote these authors' secondary source materials in order to both admit when I am following the logic thread of the works cited and make use of the most essential voices referenced. That said, my efforts here are to present an overview of the disparate works to which I have been exposed that, when put together, offer a point of view I consider helpful.

There are several aspects of our hidden history that this chapter explores. First, when, how, and why was the white race invented? Second, when and why did European Americans take on a white racial identity? Third, in what ways is the development of a modernist perspective associated with whiteness? Fourth, how did science play a role in this history? Fifth, how did legal rulings help define the parameters of whiteness in the United States? We then use the answers to these questions to inquire into how this history lives on in our society today.

THE INVENTION OF THE WHITE RACE

The history of how the white race developed receives scant attention, and when the history is discussed, there is disagreement. True, as the first English explorers encountered West Africans, they began to use the word "black" in their descriptions of African people. Although an exaggeration of the actual appearance of the African people, the language used highlights the powerful impact that the difference in skin color made upon the English.[4]

Yet the use of the word "black" to describe Africans did not inspire the English to see themselves as part of a separate race called "white." Yes, they used the terms "white" and "black" to describe humans' complexions, but early theories regarding the differences in skin color involved explanations related to environmental factors, such as exposure to the sun.[5] Yes, the English most certainly compared themselves to Africans using color symbol terminology in such a way that the English saw themselves as godly, pure, and infused with light—in short, finding themselves superior.[6] Christianity's scripture and symbols certainly played a significant role in European people's justifications for denigrating, abusing, and enslaving African people.

But this was *not* the beginning of the word "white" as used to delineate a race of people. Early uses of the term "race" generally referred to differences between populations that are now considered ethnic, such as language and cultural characteristics. Examples include the "French race" or the "Russian race."[7] The idea of a white race would take quite some time to develop.

Some might consider this line of thought splitting hairs. We have one group of people oppressing another group for whatever reason, an age-old us versus them, power-and-control situation. What difference does it make whether or not that oppression included a race-based analysis? For those from traditionally oppressed populations, the only important difference worth discussing might be the level of extreme inhumanity characterizing the European slave trade as opposed to other forms of ancient slavery.

But for those of us who are part of the dominant group, those of us who have been convinced that white racial identity emerged as soon as Europeans encountered Africans, the idea that the white race was actually constructed later in colonial history makes a big difference. Finding out to what degree our own ancestors were duped into an exploitative system marked by white supremacy for the benefit of the powerful and wealthy can actually open the door for us to begin to see the impacts of this system more clearly and work toward its dismantling.

Theodore Allen's text, *The Invention of the White Race,* cites, agrees with, and refutes many classic history texts on race.[8] He weaves a particularly provocative and compelling thread, arguing that the invention of the white race involved an effort to manipulate European Americans into remaining divided from other groups.[9] The story goes something like this: First, the existence of slavery in the early British colonies was not necessarily an oppression based on race. When the African population was first enslaved in the colonies, the colonists had not yet begun to think of themselves as part of a white race.

To understand how slavery could exist without the race construct already in place, we have to recall the short-lived 1547 slave law in England that made slaves of unemployed Englishmen who would not work for simple board.[10] If the English were not above enslaving their own, it is not necessary to attribute the origins of slavery in the colonies to a racial factor. Interestingly, when the

1547 Act was repealed in England within only a few years of its enactment, it was largely due to the unseemliness of Christians owning other Christians.[11] In 1600s Virginia, the Africans were not Christians. No doubt, Africans were considered other and "less than"—but this did not mean that Europeans thought of themselves as a separate, white race. They thought of themselves as God's chosen people.

Second, in the colonies' earliest years, African Americans held a legal position somewhat similar to that of the European American indentured servants. Examples exist of African American families who possessed bond-laborers themselves in the early 1600s, at times owning, buying, and selling European American bond-laborers.[12] In Northampton County, Virginia, in 1666, almost 11 percent of rural Africans Americans owned land. In that same year, 17 percent of the European Americans owned land.[13]

While some African Americans were experiencing lifetime servitude, European American chattel bond-laborers were also subject to severe oppressions that included extensions of servitude, extreme punishments, and rules barring family development.[14] This is not to argue that the experiences of European Americans equaled those of African Americans. African Americans were regularly treated more harshly than their European American counterparts. Accounts from the early 1600s suggest that lighter sentences were given to European American servants than African American servants who tried to escape their bondage.[15] Also, whereas European American servants were legally guaranteed freedom upon finishing their terms, African Americans purchased to be slaves had no such guarantee.[16]

The point, though, is that European American bond-laborers were treated increasingly harshly by the mid-1600s. They were kept in servitude for longer periods of time than they had been previously, and this situation resulted in significant social tensions. Class antagonisms between proletariat and bourgeois classes heightened. This resulted in the disintegration of the buffers that normally allowed English societies their stability and social control.[17]

The increasing exploitation of the European American bond-laborers was part of an effort by landowners to retain as much of their unpaid workforce for as long as possible. In Maryland, this effort even involved a law in effect from 1664 to 1692 that held that any free woman "who married an African American lifetime bond-laborer was bound to serve" the man's master for the duration of the man's life. This law inspired owners to foster marriages between European American women and African American men so that their progeny would add extra unpaid labor.[18] Consistent with this effort was the push toward hereditary, lifetime bond-servitude for African Americans.[19]

Whereas some previous judgments affecting African Americans in the colonies remained consistent with English common law, the 1660s witnessed some important changes.[20] One such alteration enacted by the Virginia General Assembly in 1662 discarded the English common law practice *partus sequitar patrem,* descent through the father,[21] for a new practice holding that "the condition of the child follows the condition of the mother."[22] This change helped open the door for lifetime, hereditary bondage for African Americans in the colonies, wherein any child born to a bondswoman automatically would be considered enslaved for life.

Another change negated the English common-law custom outlawing holding Christians as slaves.[23] In 1667, the General Assembly decreed that baptism into Christianity would no longer alter the conditions of a person's bondage, eliminating a way that African Americans might otherwise gain freedom.[24] Further developments during that time period included a 1670 change wherein "the Virginia Assembly made it illegal for African American planters to buy 'Christian' bond-laborers, limiting them to the purchaser of persons 'of their owne nation.'" Additionally, "the purchase price for Africans was half again as much as that for Europeans."[25] The significance of this history lies in the fact that there was a shift in approach during the latter half of the 1600s toward people of African descent. Whereas laws once treated both Europeans and Africans somewhat similarly, new judgments increased the differential treatment markedly.

Laws allowing increased oppressions for bond-laborers led to increasing levels of discontent.[26] Adding to the tense situation was a large increase in numbers of African slaves stolen and purchased directly from Africa at that same time. The large numbers of discontented and enslaved workers raised questions of management within the colonies.[27] The time was ripe for a rebellion. Who would control the increasingly exploited European American bondsmen and African Americans experiencing lifetime hereditary servitude? Who would help manage and enforce this increasingly inequitable and strained social system?

A rebellion would come within a decade. By 1676, laboring-class workers, both free and bond, of both European and African descent, fought side by side during portions of Bacon's rebellion. These workers came together based on a common desire to see an end to the type of capitalism existing in the colonies that concentrated wealth in the hands of the plantation elite.[28] Those fighting the rebellion sought an end to unpaid labor and an increased "opportunity to become independent farmers." In essence, they fought for upward social mobility.[29]

The wealthy, landowning elite recognized the threat this posed, realizing that if the system of capitalist agriculture, which was dependent upon lifetime hereditary slavery, was to last the ruling elite would need to induce "a new birthright" for all European Americans, both free and bond. This would need to be an identity that could set them apart from people of African descent and enlist them as supporters of lifetime hereditary slavery.[30] This new identity was "white." Soon after Bacon's rebellion, enacted laws began utilizing this new terminology.

The creation of this new white identity involved the Virginia General Assembly, which deliberately fostered contempt between free whites and African Americans and Native Americans through a series of white-skin privilege laws.[31] One 1691 law forbade owners from setting African slaves free. Another 1691 law banished whites caught intermarrying with nonwhites, a marked alteration considering that previous decades saw the encouragement of these unions to increase unpaid, bond labor.

The 1705 Virginia Codes offered additional privileges to white servants. These included a ban against beating or whipping a Christian white servant and a definition of dues owed to white limited-term bond-laborers of corn, clothes, and a gun. As well, the new codes denied rights to free African Americans. This included the confiscation of livestock raised by African American bond-laborers who had previously been allowed to raise livestock on their own account.[32]

The Act of 1723 further imposed a system of racial oppression with new laws against free African Americans. These included, among others, disallowing any free African American the right to hold public office, banning free African Americans from testifying against a white person, instituting a policy of public lashing for any African American acting violently against any European American, "excluding free African Americans from the armed militia, and forbidding free African Americans from possessing any gun, powder, or shot, or any other weapon whatsoever, offensive or defensive."[33]

Additionally, to ensure that even if these divisive techniques did not prove sufficient for whites to stay apart, the act included a provision such that whites "found in company with any [illegally congregated] slaves" would be either fined or receive lashes.[34] This effectively created a system of *racial* oppression throughout the colony whereby rights were now based on race, rather than bond or free status.

After an exhaustive look at the circumstances leading up to Bacon's rebellion and the repressive and divisive legislation enacted following, Theodore Allen agrees with the conclusions of Edmund S. Morgan regarding the white-skin privilege laws, that:

> The answer to the problem [of preventing a replay of Bacon's rebellion] . . . was racism, to separate dangerous free whites from dangerous slave blacks by a screen of racial contempt. In this way, he emphasizes, the [Virginia]

Assembly deliberately did what it could to foster contempt of whites for blacks and Indians.[35]

Further, Allen agrees with Philip Bruce, who states that:

Toward the end of the seventeenth century there occurred a marked tendency to promote a pride of race among the members of every class of white people; to be white gave the distinction of color even to the agricultural [European-American bond-] servants, whose condition, in some respects, was not much removed from that of actual slavery; to be white and also to be free, combined the distinction of liberty.[36]

Finally, Wertenbaker is also quoted as coming to a similar conclusion that "Every white man, no matter how degraded, could now find pride in his race . . . Moreover, the immediate control of the negroes fell almost entirely into the hands of white men of humble means."[37] From this we find that being part of the "white race" involved a status of being free, Christian, nonslave, and of pure blood, one who might also be a voter, holder of public office, judge, juror, or witness in a trial.

Although European American bond-servants continued to experience little opportunity for social advancement, being given the distinction of being white, and therefore, free, allowed a pride among the newly-constructed white race to develop such that by the early 1700s, "the bourgeoisie had drawn the color line between freedom and slavery, and established white supremacy as article one of the Anglo-American constitution. Only European-Americans, as 'whites,' were thereafter to be entitled to the full rights of the free citizen."[38] Being white allowed even the poorest of whites to feel a sense of self-pride and hold power over anyone considered not white, enacting violence without fear of reprisal. Even with this, since a primary feature of capitalism is the "tendency toward concentration of capital ownership," many poor would-be planters moved to the frontier, a lateral mobility, claiming their readiness to "take lands from the Indians in the name of 'a white man's country.'"[39]

In sum, this perspective holds that racial whiteness was intentionally developed by the wealthy and political elite as a way to separate low-wage, or no-wage, laborers from each other in an effort to protect the interests of the still-growing capitalist system through the introduction of both (1) white-skin privilege laws and (2) more severe laws further limiting rights and freedoms for African Americans and Native Americans. In other words, in the late 1600s and early 1700s, laboring-class European Americans were offered a privileged status to keep them from uniting with African Americans and Native Americans in a fight against economic exploitation.

The result of this, over time, was the inculcation of white identity to such a degree that by the mid-1700s, European American workers were claiming white-skin privileges for themselves.[40] Laws offering job preference to whites, such as a 1750 law in South Carolina stipulating that handicrafts tradesmen could not teach African Americans their trade, further solidified the economic value of white skin.[41]

The economic gains that came with white racial membership help explain why other European immigrants, such as Irish workers, who were not yet seen as white, struggled to be accepted as white during the 1800s by siding with anti-abolitionist and white supremacist political movements.[42] Lastly, even with the abolition of slavery, demands to limit or deny nonwhites from competing for employment, essentially appealing to "white race solidarity" remained a strong feature in U.S. politics.[43]

Ultimately, this argument suggests that white racial identity did not emerge simply in response to Europeans trying to investigate their world and understand its diversity. Whiteness as a racial construct was deliberately invented for political and economic purposes. Yet there is certainly more to the story than the colonists being manipulated by the powerful and wealthy.

A NEW IDENTITY: BECOMING AMERICAN, BECOMING WHITE

The development of a white identity involved more than offering European Americans economic and social privileges. The development of a new racial identity also included creating defining characteristics and norms. To some degree, the development of this identity interpenetrates and infuses the economic pressures previously discussed. Yet additional assimilation pressures also contributed to the development of a white, American identity.[44] (See notes for a discussion regarding the use of the term "American.")

Philip Cushman's work *Constructing the Self, Constructing America* offers a psychological analysis that dovetails with the political discussion offered in the previous section.[45] Essentially, Cushman's work offers the psychological underpinnings that allowed the economic and political tactic of racial division, described by Allen, to take root during the 1700s and 1800s. The first hint of this is his argument that capitalism and racism were "aspects of a fledgling immigrant nation searching for its identity—part of an attempt to configure the self in a time of rapid and disorienting socio-historical change."[46] Put simply, the early colonists, by and large, sought new lives in a land with little familiarity and rapid change. These new lives, built around capitalism and racism, required a new identity.

Of primary importance is that the early colonists' disorientation involved an economic crisis that also brought about a moral crisis. Let us recall that many of the early colonists held a religious view valuing the humility of a "self" working as part of a communal whole. But this moral way of being did not support the growing capitalist system. In order to survive within the system, the colonists had to shift from believing in the ideal of a communal self to adopting a more individualistic, ambitious self.

The colonists needed to see God as expecting his followers to become personally ambitious, fending for themselves and their families, acquiring wealth, increasing in knowledge, and seeking material possessions.[47] Due to the pressure to fit into the capitalist system for survival, the communal self lost favor rather rapidly, but the creation of a coherent vision of what it meant to be an American took some time to develop.

Over time, the increase of urbanization, industrialism, secularism, and immigration within the colonies exacerbated the colonists' identity crisis. Since the colonists and new immigrants had either moved away from something unwanted, or landed in a sociocultural atmosphere that made their prior way of being impractical, they all needed a new and cohesive identity that would allow them to better survive.

The variety of groups from Europe settling simultaneously in the American colonies created a situation in which no communal identity existed within the United States in its early years. To deal with this absence of a common identity, American society developed a "negative identity," a way of seeing the self, a way of determining the correct way of being by determining what was "other than American." This other then became the justification of the white self, solidifying what it meant to be white by illustrating what being white was not.[48]

What it meant to be white was constantly reinforced through the images of what it meant *not* to be white. There is ample documentation of the negative images created to dehumanize and make fun of different racial groups in American history from the country's origins. Native Americans and slaves became two readily available images against which the European colonists and immigrants contrasted themselves. Images used to ridicule the Chinese in California and the Hispanic populations in the Southwest were also used at various times and in various places as contrasts while European immigrants became white.[49] The American self thus became a white self as negative portrayals of disparaged and oppressed groups defined what was un-American and, therefore, not white.

The minstrel stage was but one avenue used by European colonists to negatively characterize African Americans during the 1800s as a way to strengthen white self-identity. These images served as the contrasts against which Europeans learned to see themselves. Commonly, black African American men were portrayed as lazy, stupid, absurd, corny, clownish, jolly, flashy, and comic. Black African American women were portrayed as crude, unclean, and very sexual. Their marriages were shown as being controlled by the women, as the men were perceived as worthless. As audiences composed of European Americans watched these portrayals, they learned that being white meant the exact opposite of what it meant to be Black.[50]

We can also look at early American literature to locate the construction of the American, white self. Toni Morrison, in *Playing in the Dark: Whiteness and the Literary Imagination,* discusses how African and African American characters within white American literature helped whites to define what it meant to be white. She proposes that:

> Africanism is the vehicle by which the American self knows itself as not enslaved, but free; not repulsive, but desirable; not helpless, but licensed and powerful; not history-less, but historical; not damned, but innocent; not a blind accident of evolution, but a progressive fulfillment of destiny.[51]

Further, Toni Morrison offers two themes she sees as paramount to the psychology of white America that run throughout early American literature—specifically, the mythologies of innocence and autonomy. The concept of "newness" as related to characters within American literature is significant, and can be read as a sense of innocence, "without pollution, corruption, illness, or evil."[52] Our early literature demonstrates our construction of the "new man" of the world within the writings, a construction dependent upon establishing what was different. The maintenance of white innocence within this context depended upon the maintenance of Black people as disgraced, dirty, soiled, sinister, and wicked in some respect.

We can also read the themes of autonomy and freedom as efforts to support "individualism." Those with freedom and autonomy are white within early American literature. The characterization of the new man being innocent, free, and individualistic supported the development of the newly-constructed white identity, and in countless pieces can be contrasted with the un-free, un-autonomous characters that rarely displayed a white face.

A similar dynamic allowed white Americans to characterize Native Americans in negative terms in order to support an idealized way of being. Thus, Native Americans were found to be heathens, savage, ignorant, lazy, dishonest, and worst of all, communal, as they lived in a way that worked against capitalism and were seen as lacking bourgeois values.[53] To remedy this, during the 1870s Congress created a plan to "save" Native Americans by "civilizing" them, which essentially meant creating separate individuals through the breakup of tribal units and reconstructing its members.[54]

While much else could be said about the interactions between the Native American populations and white colonists and settlers, the important point for the sake of this discussion is that the Native American way of being was not only other, but it was wrong, according to white Americans. The correct way of being an American meant to take on the values of the white American self, a self that was independent and personally ambitious, and who accumulated wealth.

By disparaging other racial groups, whites could more clearly identify their own attributes. Some of the primary characteristics attributed to being white can be seen by looking at the significant white bourgeois class that had developed after more than a century of colonial experience. The small communities of Puritan, or other, settlers had given way to large cities with varied and diverse sections. The turn away from communalism was all but complete, and capitalism was the dominant economic paradigm.

The bourgeois white American self that developed by the 1800s was characterized as individualistic, hardworking, moralistic, frugal, able to postpone gratification, able to tame nature through hard work, and used others' labor for personal advancement. What was considered acceptable was rigidly defined.[55] White Americans valued emotional reserve. To have a lack of entrepreneurial ambition, initiative, inhibition, or individual competitiveness was to be ill. High levels of sexuality, communalism, fear, hopelessness, confusion, and mysticism were looked down upon.[56]

And yet, this identity needed continued strengthening, and new immigrants required indoctrination. Ultimately, in the midst of rapid socioeconomic change, the pressures faced by European colonists and immigrants prompted the creation of a rather rigid and isolated white American self. This self was contrasted with the other groups found in America for the sake of a cohesive community of white people with a similar set of values.

The common value system born from negative views of others held great value for white Americans. Ultimately, the contrast allowed the white American self to hold a positive sense of self-worth. But additionally, and extremely important for this discussion, the disparagement and stereotyping of other racial groups as wrong, ill, and worthless also masked the shadows that came with a rigid and restrictive way of being. Finding all devalued characteristics within the community of the other allowed our European ancestors to protect themselves from acknowledging their own wishes to push back against the productive, individualized, rigid white self. Most likely without consciousness, newly-created whites projected their own unacceptable thoughts and desires onto nonwhite groups.[57]

For example, with productivity at a premium, any thoughts deemed lazy were pushed off onto another group: "We are not that way, only those 'others' are lazy." In this way, the negative images of others, produced and consumed through such vehicles as the minstrel stage, can be seen as European Americans' attempts to deal with the "illnesses" faced by many whites, the shadows of the newly-formed culture, illnesses such as "personal rigidity, loneliness, isolation, and lack of imagination, humor, and creativity."[58] In other words, white Americans soothed their own distress by relishing in negative portrayals of others, in effect focusing blaming attention elsewhere instead of acknowledging the negative effects of their constricted way of being.

Important to consider is how the qualities attributed to whites developed during the colonial period mirror the generally accepted values of contemporary white society. The description of the white American self fits me fairly well. My family prizes independence and individual freedoms to a great degree. Conversations with my cultural elders taught me that logic trumps empathy, and I admit that I am often emotionally distanced from what occurs around me. All the while, I learned to work hard, follow a strict moral code, and postpone gratification so that larger goals could be achieved.

I also value frugality and absorbed the cultural idea that what some call "exploitation" is what my ancestors saw as "paying one's dues" to offer me a better future. Productive is the word most often used to discuss how I walk in the world. To be competitive and ambitious has always felt required. I cannot even fathom how much the stories of heroes and heroines—individuals fighting against the odds for the sake of their dreams—have influenced me.

Yet this approach left me somewhat isolated for quite some time. For years I followed the prescribed plan more often than I created my own, and it took a long time for me to start nurturing my own creativity. My cultural matrix bred a particular type of perfectionism in me that I constantly struggle against. Why do I have such a hard time taking a break, letting go of my work ethic for even a short time? Why do I have trouble acting silly or letting myself dance with abandon? Why must I always see myself as a model of propriety? As with other issues raised within this book, years of conversations with other white people have convinced me that I am not the only one who struggles with these concerns.

Let me be clear. The point here is not to devalue all of what people call American values. As someone thoroughly entrenched within them, there is much about my way of being that I prize. But there are two serious issues worth considering. First, many of our current American values are the same as those used to construct the white identity in early American history. Some of our American values are the same ones historically used to disparage others. In essence, our American values are also the same values we constructed as identifiers to mark what it means to be white. Second, taking on the traditional white American identity involved splitting off aspects of our psyche and projecting unacceptable feelings and thoughts onto others. In other words, some of our American values are the same values that led to rigid norms from which we still require healing.

Additionally, this discussion of what it means to be white in America today would be incomplete without recognizing the cultural loss that many whites feel. True, each European ethnic group has its own particular history in this regard, and some groups gave up more of their cultural identity than others in their assimilation process. However, descendants of European immigrants often no longer retain a deep sense of ethnic identity and culture apart from being American. Even though this shift from ethnic European to American might have played out differently for each family and for each generation, we can recognize that something was given up when we became white. As we gave up one cultural way of being, we took on another.

For some of us, in taking on a white self that could not value many aspects of being in the world, we became exiled from ourselves. Many of us suffer from a lack of experience. We no longer fully understand what it means to have a communal, interdependent attitude. (This is not to romanticize. There are shadows to every way of being.) For all of its benefits and privileges, there is something that has been sacrificed in our assimilation into the group called white. Many in today's culture feel it as an ancestral loss. To some it suggests that something more soulful has been replaced with materialism and consumerism. To others, it is the loss of community traditions that do more than preserve familial and personal rituals.

Fundamentally, this perspective can help us understand that our historical construction of a white identity continues to complicate what it means to be part of American society and remains a salient issue for many people who may have very different relationships to the term "American values." To quote William Faulkner, "The past is not dead; it is not even past."[59]

A DISCONNECTED WORLDVIEW

Admittedly, the development of racial whiteness, although invented in the United States, did not occur in a vacuum. Even though I find the political, economic, and psychological perspectives previously discussed essential, we can gain additional insight when we include the way larger philosophical shifts impacted the development of white identity. Briefly, the idea is that the modernist worldview and its associated meanings are often considered white. Richard Tarnas offers a compelling and thorough description of the development of the modern, Western psyche in *The Passion of the Western Mind.*[60] Where our discussion of white identity crosses paths with Tarnas' work is in the movement from the classical and medieval Christian world-views to the modern perspective that took place throughout the time period of European exploration, colonization, and exploitation, from the 1500s through the 1800s.

Several distinguishing changes occurred during the shift to the modern perspective worth noting. First, instead of the world being alive with spirits and divine forces with which humans can relate, the modern universe is a naturally regulated, impersonal phenomenon whose secrets can be learned only through scientific, rational inquiry. *Science* and *rational thought* begin to rule. Second, in the modern world the objective world is separate from the subjective mind, and both are seen as operating on different principles. The modernist view holds that the objective world can be studied and offers factual knowledge, while the subjective mind is associated with emotion and holds far less value. Enter the increased value of *objectivity.*

Third, this shift in world perspective altered humanity's view of the self. Fundamentally, by the 1800s, the direction and quality of the modern character:

> reflected a gradual but finally radical shift of psychological allegiance from God to man, from dependence to independence, from otherworldliness to this world, from the transcendent to the empirical, from myth and belief to reason and fact, from universals to particulars, from a supernaturally determined static cosmos to a naturally determined evolving cosmos, and from a fallen humanity to an advancing one.[61]

With the advent of the modern view, the human subjective experience lost its value. The rational, objective, scientific mind became the hallowed vehicle for understanding the world and one's place within it.

The modern view encouraged the autonomous, separate self. The modern awareness became complex and productive as it increasingly found power and authority in independent judgment and human achievements as opposed to religious structures. The modern view also made it possible to use power to exploit during imperialistic voyages, industrializing efforts, and the secularization of society.

The modern perspective, encouraged by the scientific, democratic, and industrial revolutions, developed simultaneously throughout Europe and in the American colonies. Take a moment to note that many of the characteristics described earlier, as part of the American colonists' definition of the white self, found their base in the modern character: the reliance on the individual, autonomous self; the move toward the capitalistic acquisition of material wealth; and the value of rationality and logic. Recall that Cushman's analysis of the moral crisis affecting the colonists required a new way of seeing what God wanted in a congregation. This crisis reflects the larger-worldview shift with its focus on science, rationality, independence, and the exploitation of nature and its peoples as machines.

If we can see this admittedly complex, but interwoven, relationship between the modernist perspective, the creation of a white racial identity, and the political decisions that put a system of white supremacy in place within the American colonies, we might be able to see how for many people, the modernist perspective is practically synonymous with being white. If we keep in mind that "the entire western intellectual canon [developed during the modern era] is defined and privileged by a more or less exclusively male, white, European elite,"[62] then we can see how Western became associated with white.

For many, as Western nations and peoples gained power over others, pushing the modernist perspective across the globe and dehumanizing indigenous peoples for their supernatural belief systems, modern became synonymous with Western. In this way, for many people, since Western equals modern and modern equals white, then white equals Western. Clearly, this perspective raises immediate concerns as its breadth sweeps any person of color who holds a modern worldview into the large unfixed zone of whiteness. Yet this is precisely what some believe to be true, and therefore it is worth looking at these associations and meanings in order to better understand this viewpoint.

As the modern philosophical paradigm still holds a dominant position in much of our twenty-first-century society, the connection of modernism and whiteness as intrinsically related has serious implications for how white people experience the world and how people of color either do or do not relate to the white, modern worldview.

UNDER THE COVER OF SCIENCE

The earlier-discussed political, economic, social, and philosophical developments intertwined to prompt the invention and development of the white race. Capitalist desires to amass wealth combined with the moral crisis, asking new colonists to find a new way to relate to the social, religious world. Religion, political policies, and propaganda combined to help whites see themselves as superior to other groups, fostering a new, white American identity. These are our hidden histories, absent from most textbooks. These various factors are the roots—the foundations, if you will—for those who would put forth theories of racial difference beginning in the mid-1700s.

To make the point more clearly, the theories of race that became popular in the mid to late 1700s did not begin race thinking in the United States. Instead, they operated under the banner of science to build on what had already become widely accepted views among Europeans in the United States.[63] Racial-difference theories are hardly hidden. Many of us continue to learn about these now-discredited theories as part of our history of science. Even though these theories cannot be considered hidden, we turn to these fictive, pseudoscientific justifications for racial oppression very briefly in order to highlight how these theories maintained a white racial identity characterized by white supremacist ideology.

Dr. Joy DeGruy Leary discusses the false nature of racial classification theories and how they helped whites reduce their own psychological anxiety regarding treating groups of people as less than human in her text *Post Traumatic Slave Syndrome*.[64] In short, she discusses how the racial classification of humans began with Carl Von Linnaeus in the mid-1700s, well after racial oppression developed within the United States, with the extension of his taxonomic system of plants and animals.[65] His text, *Systema Naturae*, offered a system based on a color criterion with humans described as white (Homo Europeaus), black (Homo Afer), red (Homo Americanus), or sallow (Homo Asiaticus). This text also offered opinions on the moral and intellectual capacities of each group. Dr. DeGruy Leary refers to Haller's *Outcasts from Evolution* to detail the differential descriptions.

> Linnaeus describes Homo Americanus as reddish, choleric, obstinate, contented, and regulated by custom; Homo Europeaus as white, fickle, sanguine, blue-eyed, gentle and governed by laws; Homo Asiaticus as sallow, grave, dignified, avaricious, and ruled by opinion; and Homo Afer as black, phlegmatic, cunning, lazy, lustful, careless, and governed by caprice.[66]

Linnaeus' classification system opened the door for later researchers to offer their own systems. One such researcher was Johann Friedrich Blumenbach, whose *On the Natural Variety of Mankind* grouped humans into five categories: Caucasian, Mongolian, American, Ethiopian, and Malayan. In this classification system, group membership derived from a combination of color, hair, skull, and facial characteristics. Dr. DeGruy Leary uses a quote from Haller's *Outcasts from Evolution* to illustrate the ridiculously subjective and fictive nature of this theory. Regarding Blumenbach's research on Caucasians, Haller writes, "He took the name from Mount Caucus because its southern slope cradled what he felt to be the most beautiful race of men."[67]

In 1908, after a century and a half of research on racial typology, A. H. Keane's *The World's People: A Popular Account of Their Bodily and Mental Characters, Beliefs, Traditions, Political and Social Institutions* located all humans into four tight categories.[68] This framework retained the same color-coded system as Linnaeus' original work, white, black, red, and yellow, and used the terms Caucasic, Negro, American (Amerind), and Mongolic. In addition to this furthering of previous authors' work, this text continued with more detailed descriptions of the mental characteristics of each group. Overall, the descriptions offered of each group mirror the already prejudicial views held by whites, views developed as part of a European's indoctrination into white identity.

The fact that these theories today appear absurd to those of us who recognize that they simply reflect the previously existing pervasive racism can make highlighting them appear unimportant. However, race theories played a key role in many legal decisions that helped shape the racial makeup of the United States today. The courts used these theories as they determined who was or was not white, shaping our sense of what it means to be white in America.

PRIVILEGE AND CITIZENSHIP: WHITE BY LAW

As detailed in the earlier section on the invention of the white race, laws discriminating between Blacks and whites helped set the foundation for racial oppression and the development of white racial identity in the colonies. But later legal history can help us understand exactly who fit into the white category. Ian F. Haney Lopez, in *White by Law,* documents how the courts decided who would be defined as white—and therefore who could become a naturalized citizen—in the United States.

Reviewing this history astounded me. My education left me woefully ignorant as to how the legal system helped shape our understanding of whom we consider white, who could be naturalized as an American citizen, and how those decisions were made. This brief look also adds support for those who argue that our country purposely connected being American with being white.

Recall that the Virginia Codes, enacted in 1705, outlined a privileged system for Europeans in an effort to create a separate group of people who would claim whiteness as an identity. By 1790, the conception of the "white race" was strong enough for the passage of the Naturalization Act, which made being white a prerequisite for naturalized U.S. citizenship.[69] For the next 162 years, an immigrant's ability to naturalize depended upon the applicant's race. Let me say this more clearly: From 1790 until 1952, U.S. naturalized citizenship was restricted to whites.

The only exceptions to this rule were, first, the post-Civil War 1870 alteration that allowed persons of African origin to naturalize in order to accommodate the newly freed slaves. In other words, following 1870, the right to naturalize as a U.S. citizen required the applicant to be classified as either white or Black.[70] The second exception involved Native Americans whose citizenship was enacted in "piecemeal fashion, often tribe by tribe" until 1924.[71] Third, "the basic law of citizenship, that a person born here is a citizen here, did not include all racial minorities until 1940."[72]

Throughout the 162 years that naturalization depended upon racial classification, the courts heard fifty-four cases and struggled to decide who would be white. Of those fifty-four cases, only one did not involve the applicant claiming to be part of the white race, highlighting how immigrants easily perceived the social value of whiteness. Throughout those cases, applicants from Hawaii, China, Japan, Burma, and the Philippines, as well as all mixed-race applicants, failed in their arguments. On the other hand, courts ruled that applicants from Mexico and Armenia were "white," and on alternate occasions deemed petitioners from Syria, India, and Arabia to be either "white" or not "white."[73]

The court records reveal that what made someone white could never be nailed down and fixed.

Overall, decisions drew from four distinct rationales: (1) common knowledge (popular speech or use in literature), (2) scientific evidence (theories of racial difference), (3) congressional intent (searching within the statutes for clues as to earlier intention), and (4) legal precedent.[74] Similar to the previous discussion on creating a new white identity, the key to knowing who was white depended on defining who was not white. Added to this was the legal statutes' wording that membership to the white race was the key to citizenship, not the applicant's European descent.[75] Decisions were made on a case-by-case basis, often utilizing racially-prejudiced personal characteristics to denigrate those denied citizenship and label those considered not white as inferior.[76]

For the most part, within the early years of these prerequisite decisions, the common-knowledge and scientific-evidence rationales tended to support each other.[77] The pattern of immigration also reveals that during that time, citizenship questions largely revolved around those who were more easily distinguished white or Black.[78] The "one drop of blood"[79] rule, which renders anyone with known African ancestry as Black, was in effect. Since only whites were allowed to become citizens, anyone of mixed-race was denied citizenship. This led to some odd decisions, however. For example, one court case in 1854 categorized a Chinese man as Black in order to justify disallowing his testimony against a white man accused of murder.[80] Decisions such as these allowed the courts to protect the value of whiteness, further defining and protecting white identity.

Yet cases heard between 1909 and 1923 demonstrate a divergence between the science of the time and popular understanding, which led to contradictory results and rationales.[81] During this period, six decisions relying on scientific evidence allowed naturalization, while seven decisions relying on common knowledge did not. The explanation for this involves some courts' reliance on theories of race, which at that time conceptualized Caucasian as a broader category than what was commonly considered white.[82] For those courts, racial categorization did not hinge on skin color. This is in contrast to the courts that rejected the equaling of Caucasian and white and discredited the science of race.[83]

The contradictory decisions came to a halt in 1923, however, when the Supreme Court heard two cases within that same year, *Ozawa v. United States* and *United States v. Thind*.[84] Briefly, Ozawa was a Japanese immigrant who argued that his skin was white. He offered a letter outlining his dedication and service to the United States and by any standard he would have appeared the epitome of assimilation. But the Supreme Court rejected skin color as the sole test to determine race. In this case, the court ruled that Caucasian and white were synonyms and that the Japanese, not being Caucasian, could not be white. Ozawa's application for citizenship was denied.[85]

However, Thind, an Asian Indian, argued that he was Caucasian, and therefore was white. Here, the Supreme Court denied the link between Caucasian and white and used common knowledge to deny him citizenship.[86] This set in motion a program to strip other Asian Indians of their previously-granted citizenship.[87] According to Lopez, "Comparing the rationales put forth in Ozawa and Thind suggest that the Supreme Court abandoned scientific evidence explanations of race in favor of those rooted in common knowledge when science failed to reinforce popular beliefs about racial difference."[88] The reliance on common knowledge over science would continue thereafter. Important to highlight is how science can be held up as objective evidence when supporting racist ideology but struck down when challenging popular conceptions.

With such a fundamentally racist approach, one might wonder what might have prompted this program of racial discrimination to change. Issues surrounding World War II can be seen as those that pushed the United States to change its white prerequisite policy.[89] Consider this: With Hitler's policies enacted in Germany in 1935, Germany became the only other nation besides the United States to use race to restrict naturalization. The hypocrisy of the United States embracing the very racism that it purported to be fighting overseas was visible to international allies. To avoid charges of racism, Congress enacted reforms in 1940, with complete reform by 1952.[90] Naturalization would no longer be tied to an applicant's race. This does not mean, however, that the country of origin became meaningless.

A significant point to gain from knowing this history is that the predominance of white citizens in the United States is no accident. Not only did the naturalization laws favor whites in becoming U.S. citizens, but the enactment of racial quotas for immigration were also conscious attempts to retain the racial status quo in the country.[91] For example, the National Origin Act of 1924 included a temporary quota system limiting the number of Eastern and Southern Europeans allowed into the country.[92] This law set aside 50 percent of available slots for British citizens, excluded Asian immigrants, and heavily restricted Jewish immigrants. Even refugee status did not make a difference, with the United States turning away thousands of European Jews fleeing Nazi persecution during World War II.[93] Until 1965, these types of national-origin quotas remained in place.

The vestiges of this privileged legal status of whiteness are in evidence today. Many still recognize the unhyphenated term "American" as referring to whites, unless otherwise noted. Also, large numbers of immigrants choose to racially classify themselves as white, especially as they feel increasingly economically prosperous.[94] This legal history helps us understand the problematic nature of white racial identity; in some instances, the legal definitions do not directly correspond to the image accepted by society at large.

We are now at a point of summary. Multiple threads woven together form a provocative hypothesis concerning how and why the white race was created. Admittedly, the evidence is but a brief outline of one slice of our history, but its importance is that it points toward what for many is a blind spot. The totality of the perspectives presented reveals an argument favoring the view of the white race as a:

1. social construction,
2. initiated for the sake of economic and political privileging of one group of people over another
3. in the service of social control and economic/political stability
4. that depended upon increased individualism and the devaluation of communalism,
5. which was made possible by the modern philosophical worldview
6. and the creation of a new American identity based on negative views of others
7. that was supported by prejudicial pseudoscience
8. and was reinforced by the U.S. court system that linked naturalized citizenship with membership in the white race until 1952.

The evidence presented here can be taken or left behind with little consequence if there is no acceptance that these factors have something to do with our current cultural matrix. Clearly, my argument is that the historical creation of the white race has *much* to do with our current lives and raises complicated questions concerning the associated meanings of whiteness and how they enter our social and work lives, relationships, and institutions.

There are also many questions the analysis raises. First and foremost, why do we not learn about this history? To this I can only respond that much of the information outlined here clearly is critical of the United States. From my experience, there has been a general effort among many to focus on the positive elements of our shared history as a way to promote pride and patriotism. There is also a strong push to stay focused on our similarities and successes, while putting aside our differences and past bad acts.

This fits squarely with our tendency to believe that race is in the past and that to focus on this history only exacerbates negative feelings that no longer have a valid place in our national dialogue. Recent decades have brought much of this to light, however, and many high school and college students today do learn some elements of this history. However, there remains an active resistance and a concentration on this material remains relatively rare.

I did not learn about any of this information during my high school or college years. Ultimately, the people of color I met during my elementary teaching years alerted me to certain texts that I then chose to read. A particularly important one in my own development was *A People's History of the United States* by Howard Zinn.[95] This book offers a look at history from the point of view of those who were decidedly not the winners of the battles. Ingesting a different historical view did prompt me to feel pangs of guilt; I will not lie about that. But the increased knowledge also prompted further interest. I became dedicated to delving more deeply into what felt hidden, and that is when I found the information offered within this chapter.

My doctoral studies also offered me an opportunity to look at the psychological and philosophical developments. But my own outrage led me to look at the legal history, which for me was the most shocking. As I am sure is also true for many people, this history had previously felt far removed from my life. Learning how recent this history is, as well as how clearly it seems to relate to contemporary issues, made a profound difference in the way I see myself in the world. Our present unbroken ties with our past then became easier to witness.

A LIVING HISTORY

If we believe that we have moved beyond our racial history, we remain ignorant of the ways this history of whiteness continues to affect our lives. Many of our twenty-first-century issues have racial implications related to the themes just discussed. If a small group of people were to sit and do a simple brainstorm, a myriad of ideas might flow forth. But for the sake of offering at least a few examples, what follows are some perhaps subtle and not-so-subtle connections between the past and the present.

The history of whiteness exists just under the surface of every debate concerning American values, multiculturalism, and diversity. Very often, resistance against the language of "American values" is quickly deemed unpatriotic. But knowing the history as just presented helps us to understand why the same person can value democracy and freedom and yet resist calling them "American values" at the same time.

Knowing this history helps us understand why, to many people, "American values" suggests support for individualistic, competitive consumers who privilege objectivity and science to the detriment of people who value a cooperative, communal lifestyle, a resistance to environmental degradation, and indigenous spiritual belief systems. In short, knowing this history complicates our use of the term "American values" as we recognize that many associate those very values with oppressive and degrading treatment of people considered not white, not Western, or not modern enough to fit within our capitalistic, consumer-driven society.

In light of this, we can see why this issue of what counts as essential "American" history underlies debates over history curricula in schools. Essential to admit is that the teaching of history is not politically neutral. All approaches fundamentally take a stand, even if that stand is to allow the status quo to rest as is. In the dialogue surrounding the teaching of the traditional, Eurocentric form of U.S. history versus adopting a multicultural approach, not infrequently the debate becomes characterized as a fight between racists on the right and guilty liberals and special interests on the left.

I am not naïve enough to believe that reading this short history is going to radically alter anyone's fundamental political orientation. I do hope, however, that this information allows us to see that our beliefs and values are shaped by our relationship to this history and that there are very good reasons for people to (1) push against a sanitized, feel-good version of our past and (2) find themselves uncomfortable relating to systems and ideals historically aligned with the development of white identity. Regardless of whether or not we agree with the full text of Reverend Wright's statements about the U.S. that were publicized and debated during the 2008 presidential election cycle, knowing the history of whiteness might at least provide sufficient context to help us understand why he and many of his parishioners might feel the need to criticize the U.S. in extremely harsh terms.

Moving forward and looking more broadly, many of us interact with young people who have inculcated the belief that doing well in school is a *white* thing, that achieving middle-class status, delaying gratification, and being productive within the academic and business communities involve assimilating into whiteness. Although this resistance does not characterize most students of color, there is a decently large and disaffected group of youth of color who reject traditional curricula. Of primary importance to me is what we do about this situation. If we cannot see the linkages between our past and present, we will do nothing.

But if we recognize that those resistances are very understandable reactions to our country's racist foundations, we might approach our conversations differently. Can we help ensure that our young men and women of color access the information highlighting their forebears' important scholarly and scientific contributions? Do we understand the complexities of their resistance sufficiently to host an open and honest dialogue that can convince them that success, productivity, and academic intelligence are *not* only for whites, admitting that we see the historically racist precursors for that way of thinking? Essential to understand is that we cannot effectively do this unless we, ourselves, know this history well and have fully-developed understandings of the ways our own racial placement affects our view of the world.

It was not long ago that I witnessed a teacher speaking to a group of parents on back-to-school night, many of them immigrants, letting them know in no uncertain terms that they were now in a competitive country and their students would need to stop relying on each other for their success. How do you think this attitude informed this teacher's delivery of instruction, her relationship with her diverse student body, and the parents' view of the school?

The fact that we have a competitive system is not the core of the problem upon which I hope to shine light. The essential problem is that when we are blind to how this system developed alongside a white identity, we cannot step outside of ourselves in order to evaluate when it is beneficial and when it causes problems. The unconscious nature of our acceptance of values termed "American" and our inability to witness how their adherence affects us as well as others is ultimately what requires focused attention.

UNCOVERING A HEALING HISTORY

If we stop our inquiry after uncovering the hidden history regarding the development of the white race and its cultural associations, we risk leaving ourselves with a frustrated sense of paralyzing guilt. For me, concentrating only on the history related to whites' enactments of injustice brought a tremendous sense of heaviness. I began to ask, what are we supposed to do with this information? We certainly were not born during the early formations of white racial identity. Yes, we might take seriously the various ways that we now see the associations with whiteness pervasive in our country's current debates. But each of them is also related to other issues and figuring it all out can be quite confusing. What is the next step?

Fortunately, there is another aspect of our history that has been covered over, one that can offer us a way forward. We need to not only challenge ourselves to go more deeply into the guilt and shame-inducing history, but we must also seek out the examples of those who found ways to respond to the injustice. There is a long history of white antiracism that needs to be brought out from the shadows. Since the beginnings of our country, there have been white people fighting against racism and the systems that bestow advantage upon people with white skin.

Whether or not we are ready to follow in activist footsteps, we can learn from the past antiracist history and investigate how that history informs current antiracist efforts, many of which also incorporate anti-imperialist, anti-oppressive movements. Becky Thompson's *A Promise and a Way of Life* is but one general reference.[96] Her book charts the history of antiracism and offers a good look at the lives of those who reject associating with oppressive actions in the world.

Witnessing this history is one of the first steps on the way toward doing *ally* work. The various avenues offered by antiracist activists can offer us models of what it can look like to become responsive to oppressive actions associated with whiteness. These guides can help us know how to act on new principles, principles that go beyond being "American," loving freedom and democracy, toward those that allow us to link those ideals with witnessing actions that truly build justice for all within our society.

Enacting a search for guides can be a liberating undertaking. We do not have to remain mired in the dis-ease that comes from either turning away from our whiteness, or facing it and then becoming guilt-ridden. Finding people that show us a better way to deal with racism existing today, racism that has its origins in our history, can offer us a sense of direction.

NOTES

1. A quick online search for racism in regards to any aspect of history is likely to be fruitful. A first step, however, would include reading Howard Zinn's *A People's History of the United States: 1492–Present* (New York: Harper, 1980).

2. A couple of good resources related to white racial identity, one contemporary and practical, the other historical, include Janet E. Helms' *A Race Is a Nice Thing to Have: A Guide to Being a White Person or Understanding the White Persons in Your*

Life (Topeka, KS: Content Communications, 1992) and Noel Ignatiev's *How the Irish Became White* (New York: Routledge, 1995).

3. Hillman, J., *Healing Fiction* (Woodstock, CT: Spring, 1983).

4. Jordan, W. D., in J. Hillman, "Notes on White Supremacy: Essaying an Archetypal Account of Historical Events," *Spring* 46 (1986): 29–58.

5. Jordan, W. D., *White over Black* (Baltimore, MD: Penguin, 1969), 11.

6. Hillman, "Notes on White Supremacy."

7. Jay, G., "Who Invented White People? A Talk on the Occasion of Martin Luther King, Jr. Day, 1998," http://www.uwm.edu/~gjay/.

8. Allen, T. W., *The Invention of the White Race,* vol. 2 (New York: Verso, 1997). No doubt many can cite different authors in an attempt to discredit the line of thinking offered here. But before dismissing the ideas presented by Allen, I suggest looking at Allen's text in order to get a sense of its comprehensive detail and thorough analysis. Or you might consider reading a summary of the book's argument created by the author, available at http://clogic.eserver.org/1–2/allen2 .html.

9. Allen, *The Invention of the White Race,* 249.

10. Allen, *The Invention of the White Race,* 20.

11. Allen, *The Invention of the White Race,* 21.

12. Allen, *The Invention of the White Race,* 186.

13. Allen, *The Invention of the White Race,* 185.

14. Allen, *The Invention of the White Race,* 147.

15. Zinn, Howard, "History Is a Weapon: Drawing the Color Line," http://www .historyisaweapon.com/defcon1/zinncolorline.html.

16. Allen, T. W., "Summary of the Argument of *The Invention of the White Race,"* (Part Two) http://clogic.eserver.org/1-2/allen2.html.

17. Allen, *The Invention of the White Race,* 147.

18. Allen, *The Invention of the White Race,* 134.

19. Allen, *The Invention of the White Race,* 125.

20. Allen, *The Invention of the White Race,* 195.

21. Allen, *The Invention of the White Race,* 197.

22. Allen, *The Invention of the White Race,* 195.

23. Allen, *The Invention of the White Race,* 197.

24. Allen, *The Invention of the White Race,* 197.

25. Allen, *The Invention of the White Race,* 198.

26. Allen, *The Invention of the White Race,* 198–99.

27. Allen, *The Invention of the White Race,* 198.

28. Allen, *The Invention of the White Race,* 239.

29. Allen, *The Invention of the White Race,* 239.

30. Allen, *The Invention of the White Race,* 248.

31. Allen, *The Invention of the White Race,* 249.

32. Allen, *The Invention of the White Race,* 250.

33. Allen, *The Invention of the White Race,* 250.

34. Allen, *The Invention of the White Race,* 251.

35. Allen, *The Invention of the White Race,* 249, quote from Edmund S. Morgan, *American Slavery, American Freedom: The Ordeal of Colonial Virginia* (New York: Norton, 1975), 328.

36. Allen, *The Invention of the White Race,* 249, quote from Philip Alexander Bruce, *Social Life in Virginia in the Seventeenth Century: An Inquiry into the Origins of the Higher Planting Class, Together with an Account of the Habits, Customs, and Diversions of the People* (Richmond, VA: Printed for the author by Whittet & Shepperson, 1902), 137–38.

37. Allen, *The Invention of the White Race,* 252, quote from T. J. Wertenbaker, *Patrician and Plebeian in Virginia* (New York: Russell & Russell, 1959), 212.

38. Allen, *The Invention of the White Race,* 45.

39. Allen, *The Invention of the White Race,* 257.

40. Allen, *The Invention of the White Race,* 253.

41. Allen, *The Invention of the White Race,* 252.

42. For a thorough history of the Irish workers' struggles, please see D. R. Roediger's, *Wages of Whiteness: Race and the Making of the American Working Class* (New York: Verso, 1991). Some important issues considered include: Why were the Irish not seen as white? The text suggests that

There were good reasons—environmental and historical, not biological—for comparing African-Americans and the Irish. The two groups often lived side by side in the teeming slums of American cities of the 1830's. They both did America's hard work, especially in domestic service and the transportation industry. Both groups were poor and often vilified. Many Northern free Blacks who lived alongside Irish-Americans not only knew that their families had been torn from Africa by the slave trade but had also themselves experienced the profound loneliness, mixed with joy that Frederick Douglass described as the result of escaping North from slavery, leaving loved ones behind (134).

Another questions is, How did the Irish struggle to achieve white status? To which the text answers, in part, Irish Americans "solidly voted for proslavery Democrats and opposed abolition as 'nigerology.' . . . They also "became leaders of anti-Chinese forces in California" (136). Additionally,

the making of the Irish worker into a white worker was thus a two-sided process. On the one hand . . . Irish immigrants won acceptance as whites among the larger American population. On the other hand . . . the Irish themselves came to insist on their own whiteness and on white supremacy. The success of the Irish in being recognized as white resulted largely from the political power of Irish and other immigrant voters. The imperative to define themselves as white came but from the particular "public and psychological wages" whiteness offered to a desperate rural and often preindustrial Irish population coming to labor in industrializing American cities (137).

"Politicians began to speak of Irish as part of the Caucasian race during 1830's and it continued" (141–44). "Irish sought to rid their places of employment of blacks (after having taken over their jobs) to escape the connection with blacks" (150). Another essential source is Ignatiev's *How the Irish Became White.*

43. Allen, *The Invention of the White Race,* 253.

44. I have to admit my own struggle as I discuss this topic. The use of the term "American" offends many people. I understand why people take offense. I am a citizen of the United States, living on the North American continent. Quite logi-cally, I am North American. Using the more general term "American" to describe those living within the United States excludes all those living in Central and South American countries, as though they are not Americans. To many, speaking as though we, in the United States, own the term "American" smacks of privilege, arrogance, and a dismissal of those south or north of our borders. My choice to use the general term American to describe the development of a white racial identity particular to the United States is not made lightly. I struggle with this language and would hope that we might find another way to relate to ourselves in the future. However, at this time, this is my most likely path to connect with the majority of white U.S. citizens, who consider themselves, simply, American.

45. Cushman, P., *Constructing the Self, Constructing America: A Cultural History of Psychotherapy* (New York: Addison-Wesley, 1995).

46. Cushman, *Constructing the Self,* 36.

47. Cushman, *Constructing the Self,* 39.

48. Cushman, *Constructing the Self,* 61, 346.

49. Morales, A. L., *Medicine Stories: History, Culture and the Politics of Integrity* (Cambridge, MA: South End Press, 1998).

50. Cushman, *Constructing the Self,* 43.

51. Morrison, T., *Playing in the Dark: Whiteness and the Literary Imagination* (New York: Vintage Books, 1992), 52.

52. Morrison, *Playing in the Dark,* 34.

53. Cushman, *Constructing the Self,* 41.

54. Cushman, *Constructing the Self,* 57.

55. Cushman, *Constructing the Self,* 61.

56. Cushman, *Constructing the Self,* 59.

57. Cushman, *Constructing the Self,* 51.

58. Cushman, *Constructing the Self,* 52.

59. O'Connor, Anne-Marie, "Diverse Realities of Mysteries," *Los Angeles Times,* July 5, 2006.

60. Tarnas, R., *The Passion of the Western Mind: Understanding the Ideas That Have Shaped Our World View* (New York: Ballantine Books, 1991).

61. Tarnas, *The Passion of the Western Mind,* 319.

62. Tarnas, *The Passion of the Western Mind,* 400.

63. Haney Lopez, I. F., *White by Law: The Legal Construction of Race* (New York: New York University Press, 1996), 96.

64. DeGruy Leary, *Post-traumatic Slave Syndrome.*

65. DeGruy Leary, *Post-traumatic Slave Syndrome,* 59.

66. DeGruy Leary, *Post-traumatic Slave Syndrome,* 60.

67. DeGruy Leary, *Post-traumatic Slave Syndrome,* 61.

68. Haney Lopez, *White by Law,* 97.

69. Haney Lopez, *White by Law,* 43.

70. Haney Lopez, *White by Law,* 44.

71. Haney Lopez, *White by Law,* 41.

72. Haney Lopez, *White by Law,* 41.

73. Haney Lopez, I. F., "White by Law," in *Critical Race Theory: The Cutting Edge,* ed. R. Delgado (Philadelphia, PA: Temple University Press, 1995), 542.

74. Haney Lopez, *White by Law,* 63.

75. Haney Lopez, *White by Law,* 52.

76. Haney Lopez, *White by Law,* 28, 56.

77. Haney Lopez, *White by Law,* 544.

78. Haney Lopez, *White by Law,* 50.

79. Haney Lopez, *White by Law,* 27.

80. Haney Lopez, *White by Law,* 51.

81. Haney Lopez, *White by Law,* 67.

82. Haney Lopez, *White by Law,* 71.

83. Haney Lopez, *White by Law,* 72.

84. Haney Lopez, *White by Law,* 69.

85. Haney Lopez, *White by Law,* 80–86.

86. Haney Lopez, *White by Law,* 86–91.

87. Haney Lopez, *White by Law,* 91.

88. Haney Lopez, *White by Law,* 79.

89. Haney Lopez, *White by Law,* 44.

90. Haney Lopez, *White by Law,* 46.

91. Haney Lopez, *White by Law,* 37.

92. Haney Lopez, *White by Law,* 38.

93. HistoricalDocuments.com, "The Immigration Act of 1924," http://www.historicaldocuments.com/ImmigrationActof1924.htm.

94. Moore and Fields, "The Great 'White' Influx."

95. Zinn, *A People's History of the United States.*

96. Thompson, B., *A Promise and a Way of Life: White Antiracist Activism* (Minneapolis: University of Minnesota Press, 2001).

Part II

The Journey into Witnessing

Chapter 4

Fellow Travelers
Engaging the Journey

Being one of only a few white people in a crowd of people of color felt natural after years competing as one of only a few white sprinters during college. This sense of normalcy served me well few years later during graduate school when I responded to an advertisement for a research assistantship at a local elementary school. Heading east from my private college in an affluent neighborhood for an interview at the elementary school, the landscape changed markedly. In a few short miles I arrived in an inner-city neighborhood populated primarily by people of color, a community called "the bottoms" that was known for gang violence and economic struggle.

I spent the first several months at the school volunteering. Observing the students, teachers, counselors, and mentors allowed me to notice those who appeared most able to form transformative relationships with the students in the school's violence-prevention program. Two of the Black mentors seemed to get it right. Their knowledge and insight astounded me, particularly when placed against what I perceived as less-than-helpful approaches from the white psychiatrist and psychologist.

Recognizing the stark difference in worldview between those two mentors and the other program supervisors, my curiosity grew. I sought these men out for conversation, hoping to learn more about their vision and understanding. Over the next few years I became a regular part of their multiethnic, multigenerational community-based organization. This group is dedicated to personal and social transformation and it has allowed me to experience relationships that go far deeper than our racial backgrounds. This group includes many who recognize and study the philosophy and spirit underlying indigenous practices, healing arts, and hip-hop culture, their radical potential for increasing consciousness and bringing people together across race. My decision to pursue study in depth psychology is largely attributable to the influence of this group.

After a couple of years working with the violence prevention program, I began to teach at the school. Those years teaching also forced me to develop a more in-depth and complex understanding of race, class, and community. So, by the time I left my fifth-grade classroom to pursue another degree, the experiences I had within the community group and my teaching practice had intertwined. They left me with a desire to learn how to inform my home (white) community of the brilliance and potential residing within people of color living in violence-ridden cities throughout the United States. Projects I designed for my new academic program focused on the struggles of inner-city youth of color and the need for people to stay open and observant in order to see and support the gifts lying within these strong, vibrant individuals.

What became clear to me, however, was that the ability to truly *see* people and the search for life inherent in their pursuits has a lot to do with our ability to witness how our thoughts, attitudes, and behaviors are informed by our racial experiences. After years of receiving important mentorship from people of color, I felt the need to find other white people who had looked deeply within to identify how being white affected them, white people who could be my guides as well.

I looked for really particular people. They needed to be competent in maintaining close cross-race relationships *and* had to see race as playing a significant role in our society. This was really important. There are plenty of people, both whites and people of color, who move through the world believing that race does not affect their cross-race relationships. For some, that belief arises out of community-based practices, which in some ways mirror my experiences described above. Yet, for others, and my sense is that this is the majority, we skirt the shadows and fight to keep the peace at all costs. To keep learning myself, I really needed to talk with people dedicated to confronting race issues in a deep and penetrating way.

In other words, I needed to speak with people who understand the magic of Hecate's transformative brew, who see the need to focus on the hidden, battered side of our psyche in order to find healing for our deepest wounds. Within this general search, I especially wanted to find white people who have sat in the fire, white people who have withstood the heat of anger, resentment, and rejection from people of color, white people who know the importance of bearing witness to the dis-eases bred from racial injustice.

People with various backgrounds across the nation received calls from me. I requested to speak with them about race, friendship, and whiteness. More times than not, I first contacted people of color whom I either knew or had heard of who then suggested that they had a white friend who fit my interest.

Occasionally, connections occurred in the opposite direction. Important to point out as well is that those interviewed are all elder to me. Although their life experiences may be extremely different than those who have come of age more recently, they have learned a lot traveling the path before us and there is much to be gained from their stories.

In the end, I interviewed sixteen people, eight white people and eight people of color. Sitting with them required me to travel north, east, and south. Starting in Los Angeles, I visited Berkeley, Seattle, Chicago, Washington, D.C., and New Orleans. Of the eight pairs, seven are highlighted in this book. To be clear, in no way are these people superhero personages. Each of them recognizes needed areas of growth. In this way, they are perfect models because they are relatable human individuals who are out there struggling, perhaps a bit farther down the path, but not yet fully arrived.

My learning process involved interviewing the white people and their friends of color for equal periods of time, both individually and as a pair. The project that originally came from these dialogues offers a balance of their voices. However, based on the intention to inspire white people to witness their whiteness, the white voices here receive increased space in this chapter. This chapter concentrates on how the white people became conscious of their racial identity and what facilitated developing that perspective. In some instances, their friends of color enter the dialogue, offering us insight into how we might maneuver through this challenging territory ourselves.

Chapter 5 then explores the various meanings these people associate with whiteness, Chapter 6 considers the role that conflict plays within the relationships, and Chapter 7 delves into the lingering racism they continue to face and how they deal with it. Collectively, the voices offered in these four chapters illustrate many of the essential issues we need to face when deciding to confront dis-ease regarding race and to construct a viable, healthy antiracist identity and practice that subverts white dominance.

Structurally, the men are introduced first, followed by the women. The order of appearance reflects no privileging of male voices, but actually serves a more specific purpose. Each of the women not only describes her early experiences regarding developing her sense of what it means to be white, but she also identifies her friend of color as an essential facilitator in the developmental process. For that reason, their stories are a set of extended voices following the shorter men's introductions.

Questions to consider at the start:

- When did you first realize you were part of your race?
- When was the first time you learned about racism?

- Has anyone been important in your learning regarding race issues?
- What does it mean for your life to be a member of your race?

THE MEN

Michael Meade is a storyteller and mythologist who lives on Vashon Island in Washington. He is the author of *Men and the Water of Life.*[1] Michael produces and leads multicultural conferences through his nonprofit organization, Mosaic Multicultural Foundation. Luis Rodriguez, a Los Angeles-based community activist who is best known as a Chicano poet and the author of *Always Running: Gang Days in L.A.,* identified Michael as one of his closest white friends and partners.[2] I have known both of these men for many years, have regularly attended their workshops, and consider them mentors. I find their contributions essential, as their wise counsel has taught me to keep one eye on our essential connectedness and humanity while keeping the other on social justice.

Currently, Michael moves people through social strata issues such as race and class in order to connect people through mythology and poetry. But he could not do this work without a real psychological shift that prompted him out of his youthful environment. Michael talked to me about his upbringing. He said, "I grew up in a blue-collar, Irish, bigoted, and racist community [in New York]. I mean, ridiculous, so racist that Italians were considered a different racial group. And anybody who wasn't fair-skinned, freckled, eating potatoes, or something was like an enemy group." And yet, Michael remembers, "in the midst of it feeling there's something wrong with this . . . It feels stupid and forced."

Michael's story reflects the history of the creation of whiteness offered in Chapter 3 wherein certain groups, specifically the Irish and Italians, were not originally considered white during early immigration phases. Over a century later, we still see how our early history continues to shape people's perspective regarding who fits into the white group.

Michael then talked about a moment when his perspective radically altered when his crew left their neighborhood to go to the beach.

Once, we went to the beach with our little crew of fourteen- and fifteen-year-olds and with the older crew from the neighborhood. They seemed much older, yet they were probably seventeen, eighteen, and nineteen. They'd been through this for years and were pretty hardened. We were at Jones Beach. It was unusual to leave the neighborhood and no one would admit it at the time, but there was a certain amount of fear present already because we were way outside our boundaries. And the way people from the neighborhood act when we're outside our boundaries is get defensive and ready to fight. Fear turns into defense on one hand, but with very little provocation, violence on the other . . . Drinking beer, hanging out on the beach, . . . playing the role. There were a couple of guys, clearly friends, sitting near us on the beach. One was Black and the other white. I saw it right away and thought, "Oh, I hope those guys move or else somebody's going to get hurt."

The older guys from our neighborhood tended to do harm before considering what the meaning of something unfamiliar might be. So, I size up the situation and figure unless the wind blows the right way, those two guys are going to get their asses kicked in a way that they've never seen before. I have my eye on it, I'm not in favor of it, but I don't know what to do about it. Finally someone said something and I know that words will lead to action real fast. So I said something to try and deflect it, which was dangerous because it could turn on you fast, especially with the older guys. That led them to say, "OK, you go over there and tell that Black asshole and his fucking fairy friend [it gets to racial phobia and to homophobia real fast] to get off the beach. And if they don't do it, you kick their ass right there." That's how the game goes. So I can't really say no, in terms of my understanding at the time. So I go over and say "Listen, don't even think about this situation. Get your stuff, get up, and just walk away. If anybody says anything, just keep walking."

They said, "What are you talking about?"

I said, "The people I'm with are gonna kick your ass real soon."

"Why?"

"I don't have to explain why. Just take me at my word. You will get hurt. Get up and get going."

So, the Black guy understands. He looks around and says, "Let's go."

The white guy says, "Well, that's not right."

And I said, "Aw, man. What a dummy." Where does this guy come from? Probably a nice neighborhood or something. "It's not about what's right. It's about saving your ass. Get out of here now."

Maybe ten minutes later, the white guy comes back. He walks up to the group . . . I thought, oh no, this guy doesn't know how bad he could get hurt . . .

He stood there with his voice cracking and said, "This is not right; not fair. This is inhuman." He didn't even curse. And no one did anything because he was telling the truth. But that didn't mean he was going to survive the experience.

Now, they all looked at me, 'cause it's now my job. So I got up and went over to him and said, "That was brilliant. Now get the fuck out of here." I think that was the right combination. He needed to somehow know that he was right, but that he wasn't so stupid as to want to lose all his teeth at this moment. So, he left and it was over. But, for me, I was like, wow . . .

I realized that what he said was the absolute truth. I knew that how we acted was distorted . . . That was a pivotal experience for me. And one thing that came out of it was feeling real scared afterwards . . . scared of the realization of how dangerous it is to be genuine, to have knowledge and act on it.

Hearing Michael's story I was struck by how this experience, and others like it, prompted him to reject racist ideology and create his own sense of self. As he continued to share, the approach he used to create his own identity reminded me of aspects described in Chapter 1 regarding a focus on ethnicity. Since Michael does not feel part of what he sees as the white group, he identifies with his Irish heritage, an identification that is both literally and imaginatively true.

When I identify as Irish—I mean I'm not Irish, I've been to Ireland as a visitor and my mother was born here and my grandmother was born here. But when I was really looking around for a way to explain what was happening to me, I didn't feel part of the mainstream. Once I got into serious issues in my life, I didn't feel like a part of the white culture in the sense of the forced homogenization that white people go for. And I instinctively knew that it meant losing my sense of self. And I also noticed how quickly, if you go against it, you are out. You are not even second-rate. You are gone. And I realized that I don't want to be a part of something that just casts you out like that. That's why I think I've had some sympathy for people of color because I realized how a white person can be cast out of the white group for not having the white idea, even if you look like you should have that idea. So those things made me alert to it. I said, OK, what's legitimate here? I can't say I'm not white in the sense of not being of European ancestry. I mean I look like I am.

So what is there in the range of things, and I think I'm lucky because both sides of my family are from Irish roots. So I adopted Ireland on an imaginal level. I began to check my ideas and ways of looking at the world against James Joyce and Yeats. That's who I felt aligned with. Not just because I love the beauty of what they're doing, but because I think there's some internal resonance that I've inherited. I memorized Yeats' poems when I was driving in my car. I did it to find myself, to locate myself on the highways, you know, in the confusing chaos of the highways of life. And I would find things in the rhythms of the poems. I would feel like I come from this mostly unseen place.

At first I wondered if Michael was avoiding dealing with race by identifying with Ireland on an imaginal level, finding a sense of grounding in something beyond being white.

Yet as Michael continued it became clear that he does not turn a blind eye to his whiteness. His attention toward his cultural heritage and personal rejection of mainstream whiteness is not an escape from the difficult history of oppression in this country. He was quite able to talk about his own family's past and the part they played within the larger history of whiteness:

> There's a point in American history where had the Irish and Scottish been more courageous and genuine they would have aligned with the Black and enslaved and indentured folks because the Irish and the Scots were also indentured. But they saw a way to slip out and I have to own that, too. It's part of my own heritage and one of the greatest mistakes in the history of this country. There they were, a white-appearing group who were escaping colonization in their own land and could have deepened that sense in this land as well. Being "white" became a way up and out and I know my own family went for that.

Michael's example demonstrates how we can hold the tension of multiple realities. On one hand, he recognizes the value of reclaiming an ethnic identity that holds beauty and the promise of connection and a sense of place, albeit imaginal. On the other, Michael sees the meanings of whiteness and rejects adopting the values traditionally associated with being white. Yet, what makes his story really instructive is that he finds a way to reject the values of whiteness without denying his connection to its history and current manifestations.

The second man spoken with was Bob Roberts, a white man I interviewed in pre-Katrina New Orleans, Louisiana. I learned of Bob through the documentary film *The Road to Return,* which featured the work of Project Return. Bob was the executive director of Project Return, a nonprofit dedicated to reducing recidivism in parolees when we met.[3] He is also the author of *My Soul Said to Me,* a memoir about his community-building work in a Louisiana prison.[4]

Meeting Bob, I was struck by his openness and complete engagement. Talking to him in some ways was like sitting next to a starving man receiving a plate of food after a long period of fasting. He dove into the interviews, expressing his deepest concerns, pains, and hopes. His interview was one of the most emotional. It seemed that he longed to have more conversations like the one we shared in his small office with the air conditioning blasting and the buzz of a busy community center just beyond the door.

Bob talked about his early experiences. "I grew up in a tremendously conservative society, Shreveport, Louisiana. My neighbor, who was Jewish, used to say it was so conservative that we even called our rabbi Bubba." He also spoke of growing up poor: "Even though we were poor and my mother had to work to support us, my mother and father both, . . . we had a maid. As a white woman [my mother] could make more than a Black woman . . . so she could take part of her pay and pay [the maid]."

Segregation marked his upbringing. He said, "I never went to school with a Black person, all the way through high school, college, and even dental school, until I went back to school for social work. It was the first time." Bob also spoke of his first recognition that segregation was wrong:

> I grew up in the era of segregation. I never knew anything was wrong with segregation until I got on the trolley one time and my caretaker, my second mother, the woman who was our maid, sat in the back of the bus. She didn't belong back there. She was my mother. She took care of me. She scolded me. She spanked me. She held me.

Bob said that although "there was a time when I bought into the racial stuff in my high school years," that he extended respect to adult African Americans as a youth in a way that went against the norms of the time. This respect emerged when interacting with his elders: "I carry this thing of respect for elders. 'Yes sir, no sir.' I was a little Southern boy. I carried that right over racial lines. I can remember going through the cafeteria lines in junior high school and high school and the servers were all Black women and saying, 'Yes, ma'am, yes, ma'am.'"

His first close relationships with African Americans outside of his home formed the summer after his father's death when he worked in a warehouse. He writes that "the Black laborers in the warehouse" showed him kindness. He describes them as "men who had known and deeply respected my father . . . Those men took me under their wings and taught me how to endure hard labor, how to shoulder the hundred-pound flour sacks with my small frame, and how to put up with the incessant insults that the boss threw at all of us."[5]

Bob currently questions much about our culture and said that "there's nothing like getting outside your own culture to learn about your own culture, to go learn about another. I lived in Germany for four years and that's what really started opening my eyes." He spoke about a time during that period when he began to study WWII. He had some books and conversations that made him question issues of sanitization and culpability within warfare. He said:

> I was reading [a] book one night and [the author] talked about where after the beach had been secured and they moved inland from the beach, he said a crew would come on shore and this crew would pick up all the body pieces. He talked about finding a face in the sand. And he talked about leaving whole bodies lying there in the waves and then after they'd cleaned up all the pieces they would invite the journalists onshore to take pictures of whole bodies like you saw in the movies . . . sanitizing the true violence of war.
>
> And by then I had a collection of WWII books and some with pictures. And I even had this Time Life book with a series of pictures and it was two in the morning and I furiously got up and threw down all the books on the South Pacific and went through all the pictures—these were Time Life and were full of pictures—to see if I could see anything but a whole body. And the lie about

it all! And if there was ever a turning moment, a turning against our military and what it had done, and was doing in Vietnam, and is still doing it now. Boy, that was a moment. Realizing I had been lied to. All those movies with John Wayne and all the glorification and sanitization of violence and warfare . . . God, by the time Steven Spielberg came out with *Saving Private Ryan* . . . There was an opening scene where the first thirty minutes are the D-Day invasion . . . that opening scene was full of body parts and not whole bodies . . . and people complained about all of the violence . . . But it was the first movie that depicted the truth. And I wept. I was so angry that it took so long. I was fifty-five years old before anybody told the truth.

Emotion emerged as we talked and I asked Bob what that experience opened up for him. He answered that he found himself "looking at myself in the mirror thinking . . . how else have we been lied to? What else is being held back?" Bob shared with me that he finds this learning essential in terms of his ability to relate to people who come from different backgrounds in the United States. Realizing that he needed to question cultural assumptions and the media's portrayals prompted him to delve deeper, under the surface, in order to understand other ways of seeing, locating hidden truths by listening to different versions of history and people's experiences.

This last realization is what characterized my whole experience with Bob. He is a man dedicated to facing shadows. Sitting with him over the course of a weekend, he taught me a lot about owning up to lingering forms of racism as part of a dedication to truthfulness.

The third man interviewed was Spencer Brewer. Spencer is a white man who lives in the predominantly white city of Yucaipa, California. He is a composer, musician, and founder of a high-tech business. Spencer played a significant role in aiding the production of one of the most widely used anti-racist teaching tools in the country, *The Color of Fear.*[6] Lee Mun Wah, the producer and director of this and other educational films, spoke of Spencer as his longest-term white friend and colleague.

I knew neither of these men prior to the interview process. Since the connection came through Lee Mun Wah, my first contact with Spencer occurred when he breezed through Lee Mun Wah's home in Berkeley and into the backyard where I sat. He entered with a confident stride and a slightly off-kilter demeanor, presumably due to his hurried trip on the road. He had driven several hours to be a part of the process, and we began the formal interview almost as soon as he arrived.

We had little opportunity to share in the niceties that might normally precede such a personal conversation. However, Spencer seemed to take a deep breath and, for the sake of his friend, opened himself up to the process, trusting me with his personal tales without resistance. I find this significant because Spencer shared some really tormenting and personal stories, both about his own upbringing and his relationship with Lee Mun Wah. To be honest, I was stunned at the depth of his sharing, the way he sat at times at the edge of his seat, while at other moments he would think long before responding, giving me a chance to notice the breeze, the wind chimes, and the birds in the trees surrounding us. It was almost surreal, sitting in such a peaceful environment, speaking of such difficult experiences.

Spencer talked of being raised in Texas "in a family that believed . . . that Black people would never excel, and not to expect much from them because they are not intelligent . . . My grandmother was a blatant racist. My father . . . is a racist. And I didn't agree." Spencer said that as he got older he rejected his family's way of thinking. He spoke of an early confrontation with his grandmother:

> There was a woman who helped raise me. She also raised my father. She was a Black woman and she went to work for my grandmother when my dad was two. She lived in the back house with her husband and she raised my father. She was also my grandmother's maid and did everything. That was the time when that was status quo back in the 20s and 30s and Leena went on to take care of and raise us boys. She rode the bus six different connections through Dallas to get out there and did her thing and put up with all that stuff and wore her white shift, whatever you called those things, and rode the bus again after work, all six places to get back home. When I became a teenager I began to question my parents on all of this. Why doesn't Leena eat with us? Why is it Thanksgiving and she's sitting in the kitchen? Why is it Christmas and she's wearing this white shift and sitting in the kitchen? It got kind of rough with us until one time my grandmother just told me what's so. And I said, "I don't agree. This is not the way it is. This is not the way it is supposed to be."

Spencer continued to reject his family's messages about race but knew that racist messages were ingrained in him to a significant degree. He also mentioned the way that the socialization process in his home community demanded certain behaviors: "You know in Texas, I'd actually have to act a certain way even as a white male to walk past [some] guys . . . you have to go even further than being white in Texas. You've got to be the good ole boy."

The big shift for Spencer occurred while watching the film *The Color of Fear,* produced by his friend Lee Mun Wah.

> Now, understand, I still had this underlying face that I was brought up to believe that Black people are scary and don't expect too much out of them. When I began to walk, this is what I was told. You have blue shoes on and you are going to wear blue shoes. I never questioned it, until I started questioning it. I still couldn't get rid of the voices, the conversations that just came out immediately.

Oh, there's clouds outside, is it going to rain? There's a Black person, should I cross the street? It was just a gut instant reaction.

But, as I got older and did a whole lot more work on myself I started questioning all this stuff. Oh, . . . I'm having this reaction; I'm going to stay where I am on the sidewalk. I was challenging all these things that were coming up inside me constantly. This is bullshit. I don't believe this. Where is this coming from?

But when I saw the film, what changed for me is I started listening to each one of these gentlemen's truths that were in the film and they were saying it from the most vulnerable place they could. I had never been witness to that conversation before. I think that is what has been most powerful to so many people. They have never witnessed that conversation before, not said like that. I hadn't. So when I heard what they had to say, especially Victor—what an eloquent speaker Victor was, how incredibly scary looking he was just as a Black man—and so here's a guy who looks scary, and is incredibly intelligent and articulate and speaks very directly to the point and has an enormous amount of pain and anger inside him about his life going this way. I really, really got that. I mean I really heard it. Each of them, I heard each one in their own ways. When I walked away from that I was left with, I'm gonna change, I'm gonna do it differently.

Spencer talked about how this new perspective completely altered his sense of self and what he needed to do in the world. For me, Spencer is a prime example of someone who did not begin to see the importance of racial identity until well into his adulthood. He has struggled to understand its effects and he now pays a lot of attention to how issues of race arise on a regular basis.

The youngest man I interviewed was Dave Adelson. Dave is a white man living in Venice, California. A neuroscientist at the Veteran's Administration in Los Angeles, he also served on the Board of Directors for Pacifica Foundation. Meeting Dave was like entering a whirlwind of intellectual activity. His apartment where we met was filled with books and tapes and he could barely stay seated during the interview. One question posed would elicit minutes of story, answer, and analysis. He offered me CDs to fill in my gaps of knowledge and pulled multiple items from shelves to support points he made within our conversation. As with the others I interviewed, Dave spoke readily from the start.

An interview originally scheduled to last approximately two hours turned easily into three as we sat on his large couch with our hot tea resting on the cluttered coffee table before us. Differently than the other interviews, however, Dave's stories involved a higher degree of intellectual analysis and less emotion. What Dave offered was a thorough and complex analysis of how his life and racial make-up intersects with issues of class, group politics, media, systemic racism, and history. At the time, it was overwhelming. But, hearing his perspective also helped me grasp the complexity of the issues and how long it takes to develop a sophisticated understanding.

Dave's intellectuality made a lot of sense when he told the story of his upbringing. He grew up in a well-to-do area of Los Angeles, attending a predominantly white, elite, private school for gifted children. He recalled that he was unconscious of race as an important issue throughout his childhood. But, Dave did remember one experience where race felt significant:

> When I was nine I took a half a year off from this school and went to this experimental school called the Peripatetic Community School, which was a school that was in a van, basically. We drove around town in this van . . . and did stuff. We'd go to parks. I think there were nine of us, seven maybe. And being in school meant being in the van . . . We would go down intermittently to a school down in Watts. And there I remember going to school and everybody on the playground was Black . . . I could tell that I stuck out like a sore thumb and I didn't know how to act, and I didn't know how to be, and it was like "whoa," and that was kind of heavy.

During Dave's junior-high-school years he remembers once talking with his friend William about an issue that involved race.

> When we were kids race . . . didn't seem to me to be an issue. In other words, I was never conscious of think[ing] they're Black and we're white. It didn't strike me that way. But, I remember particularly in our last year in junior high we had a teacher who was somebody who would tease us all the time. And he would tease William particularly hard and transgress William's sense of boundaries and I remember us talking about [the teacher] being racist and I didn't get it. I was like "What do you mean? He teases us all? What are you talking about?" So, that was an interesting thing that happened where my unconsciousness about that might have been something that made me not understand where [William] was coming from.

Dave's interpretation of his teacher's behavior is perhaps in some ways similar to the way I saw my own teacher as simply being mean when he would yell at the English learners in our class.

After the private school experience, Dave attended Pacific Palisades High School, a public school in an affluent neighborhood. Yet, contradiction marked his last year of high school. "I got into some fights with my father, moved out, moved in with my mother. She got divorced and moved out. So I lived by myself at the top of Coldwater Canyon." He spoke extensively of this experience:

> I lived in a house on the top of a canyon in Beverly Hills, by myself, with three bedrooms and a pool. But, at the same time I didn't have enough money to eat. So at the end of the month I would eat rye bread with mustard on it.

He sums up this contradiction by saying that he was "a kid from privilege who didn't have a good time with it."

Yet, Dave also has an African American stepmother and two stepbrothers that offered him moments to experience firsthand how whiteness offers societal benefits. He recalled that one of his stepbrothers "used to talk about it . . . the way that being Black meant that he got treated." Dave recalls that, "I listened to it, but didn't absorb it." Dave, and his African American friend William, talked about how Dave can now look back and see the privileges he received due to being white, but how he simply did not perceive them that way at the time. Dave said.

> There were other experiences where, oh when we went to Bullocks to return Members Only jackets . . . And the security jammed [my stepbrother] for shoplifting and I'm right with him the whole time. And we're together and they come and jam him. We had the same stuff . . . and I'm sitting there doing the exact same thing with the exact same merchandise as Tim. But Tim gets arrested and hauled off and patted down and messed with and I didn't. And we still never had the discussion about it. I recognized it, but it still didn't penetrate.

The way being white played a role in Dave's life finally penetrated during his graduate-school years. Dave found KPFK radio station and became active in the politics within the organization:

> I started going to all of these left groups and [working with] community activists and I started bumping up into my own class, my own political background. One of the things that happens, you grow up in this culture, and the myth of America is this great, virtuous, generous culture that is bringing light and democracy to the rest of the world. And even if you don't buy into that in any direct way, it's still in the ether around you. So, I come in with the attitude that I'm trying to do good. I didn't really understand the reactions I would get where people didn't want to work [with me], and I came over time, some of it painfully, to realize that part of it was my own privilege, my own lack of understanding about who I was.

Understanding his own privilege and what that means for him on a day-to-day basis is still something Dave is working on. Practically, he spoke of trying to bridge the gap between people of color involved in the radio station who hold nationalist politics and those whites holding progressive ideals. Through these experiences he recognizes intimately how white people continue to seek to exercise power over people of color who hold differing views. Dave's response to this involves efforts to create a community-oriented media in which information is freely shared. Yet, there were many years of young adulthood when Dave did not hold this perspective and Chapter 6 will discuss how that affected his friendship with William.

THE WOMEN

Through close cross-race relationships, white people come to understand race experientially (not just abstractly) and to realize they cannot afford to distance themselves from the realities of racism.

—Becky Thompson

This section begins with this quote from Becky Thompson because each of the three white women interviewed mentioned the important role their friend of color played in their racial identity development. The first woman interviewed was Karen Teel, an affluent white woman. She is an assistant professor of education at Holy Names University in Oakland and currently lives in the predominantly white, Northern California city of Lafayette. I learned about Karen through Jennifer Obidah, her African American colleague, who was then a researcher and full professor at UCLA. Jennifer and Karen coauthored the book *Because of the Kids*[7], a text that documents Karen's efforts to become a better teacher for African American students with Jennifer's help.

Karen was the first person interviewed for the project. We met on a cool February day in a hotel room on a weekend when Karen and her husband had come to Southern California to attend a family function. I was nervous. Karen was gracious and warm. I began formally. Karen told stories. She moved back and forth through time, reaching for the moments where emotions ran deepest. Like Bob, she showed me her deepest pains and offered up her most heart-wrenching challenges for full view.

Karen grew up in Fresno, California, in the 1950s, an all-white, middle-class community. She described her upbringing as "idyllic."[8] About her family life, Karen said that she "wasn't raised in a family that [was] activist. My mother was very concerned about the so-called downtrodden . . . she was always ranting and raving about injustice. But she never did anything about it. Neither did my father." Yet Karen spoke of a time in college when she studied abroad and fell in love with a dark-skinned man from Tunisia. She said, "My mother immediately flew over and led me away to England."

Karen never had any cross-race friends growing up. In fact, she "felt like it would probably be impossible to get to know somebody really well from that culture, from that background, because I felt very guilty about my history and legacy as a white person." This may sound foreign to people today who grew up in diverse communities and who move easily within multiracial circles. But, there are still large areas of our country where segregated social circles are the norm and our undigested history of oppression remains a significant barrier to cross-race relationship building.

Karen said that her guilt erupted in graduate school as she recognized the oppression that African Americans face:

I started reading a lot of literature about that experience and a lot of new theories . . . about why African American students were not succeeding in our schools and a lot of it was associated with racism . . . I started to become more and more outraged by what I was reading . . . I became more reflective and angry and confused about everything I was reading and hearing. I was also visiting classrooms in the inner city and seeing the elementary schools and seeing these incredibly bright and enthusiastic African American children. And then I'm reading this literature about how they are falling through the cracks in middle school and high school and about the achievement gap and all the issues that African American educators were writing about.

And I was becoming very anxious. I felt like I wanted to do something to make a difference, to work on myself as a teacher and to prove through different teaching strategies and a different grading system that would be more supportive academically and culturally of African American students. I wanted to prove that they were indeed just as capable as any of the other kids. But at one point I questioned, why did I care? Why do I even care? Socioeconomically, I don't even need to work. My husband was a banker and there was no need for me to do anything. But I loved teaching. I had mostly taught all white students until I went to graduate school. So why was I drawn to this whole African American scene and allowing myself to go through all of this pain and concern?

Karen felt a sense of historic sadness and regret and says that she "was worried about this guilt driving my interest in working with African American students because I didn't want that to be the reason."

Ultimately, Karen did stop teaching her predominantly white classes and dedicated herself to teaching African American students—not out of guilt but out of determination to improve their educational experience and success. Karen even sought out help to improve her teaching practice, inviting Jennifer in to her classroom as a part of Jennifer's dissertation project. Karen revealed, however, that she had secretly hoped that Jennifer would find no criticisms. Instead, Jennifer challenged Karen far more than she had anticipated. Karen talked about why she valued the often tumultuous and painful process.

I just saw the power of it, the strength, and how enriching it was . . . I just saw when people got together and problem-solved, got together and made decisions, that it was just so amazing when you had more than one mind trying to work it out . . . And I've seen things that I didn't like about myself, and I wanted to change it, and I didn't know what to do about that. That, I think, is a gift . . . that

I blame myself and see myself as partly responsible. I don't know if you would call it a gift, but it's something you have to have in order to change, in order to believe that you need to change, how you are relating to people or doing this or doing that. You have to believe somehow that you are not perfect, that you are at fault, you have some weaknesses, or you don't quite have it all figured out, and you need help.

Karen's belief about our need to somehow see ourselves as not perfect is really essential. More than any other person interviewed, Karen is a model of continued openness to hearing about how she still acts out racism without conscious intent and she is dedicated to doing something about it. As hard as the path may be, she easily names the benefits she derives from this deep, internal work.

Karen spoke freely about the profound transformation her relationship with Jennifer has inspired, far beyond her work in the classroom. She described how Jennifer has helped her completely alter her worldview:

It has been an incredible journey, an incredible awakening for me as to what it is like to be African American in this country today and how much privilege I have as a white person.

[Jennifer] has been an incredible gift as much as my mother, which is a weird thing to say. But, you know, when you think about who has really seen through you. I mean she sees through me. And she brings out what's good and brings out the truth in my soul, in who I am, and I know it's right and I know it's beautiful.

It must be said, though, the learning Karen gains through this relationship did not come easily for either of them.

I asked Karen how often racial challenges come up between them. She told of both the frequency and quality of these moments:

When we are together? It comes up every time we are together because I will have a thought. I will say something. I will do something. And either I'll catch myself or she will point it out to me, that it is an example of being racist that is not conscious. And then we will get into this long conversation about it, analyzing it, and I will end up in tears because, again, I don't like it. It is ugly.

It just gets deeper. It is like I am an onion and I'm being unpeeled and all the layers of conditioning and socialization and living in a racist society are there and she is trying to unravel all of that, help me unravel all of that, so that I see the truth, I see myself and who I am and what's molded me and what's really happening in the society.

When I asked Karen what makes her stay and sit through those tears she said that it is "because it is wrong and I want it to change." After many years of collaboration and learning, Karen feels more confident speaking about her own increasing awareness. She said,

> I am more aware of what African Americans experience. And what I have done because of what Jennifer has shown me, explained to me, shared with me. I have been much more aware of things that happen around me when I am in a mixed group, or when my friends talk about African Americans and education, for example, and what they think is going on. So I am seeing, hearing, denial whether white institutions could be racist and denial. I mean I had an experience with a group of white friends I meet with once a month. They are all teachers in education. [They] read our book and said, "We don't believe you are racist. We know you. You're not racist." And I just looked at them and said, "You don't know me. And I don't think you know yourselves."

Even after countless conversations and realizations, Karen still feels a great deal of tenuousness when it comes to relating to people of different backgrounds.

> I worry that they won't . . . this is where I get emotional, they will think I have some motive for wanting to be their friend, that there is something I am after. Why would I want to be their friend? And that's totally . . . Jennifer would say, you are trying to think for them. You're trying to lay stuff on them and that is so racist.

Karen admits that there is still a lot that she does not see. She would like to engage others to help her increase her perception but says that she is not around enough people who can have that conversation with her on a regular basis, as she and Jennifer now live far apart.

In Jennifer and Karen's book, Jennifer writes about her exhaustion from the need for African Americans to continually teach whites: "I got tired of wondering why Karen couldn't just acknowledge certain things . . . Why does Karen have to be taught how to relate to African-Americans? . . . Why do African Americans have to keep teaching White people how to relate?"[9]

Just like Karen, I depended upon one of my Black friends to help me see the effects of race and racism on relationships. Recognizing this is precisely what has led me to believe that white people really need to help each other develop the capacity to develop our own antiracist white identity and practice. We so often depend on people of color to help us with this work, and when this guidance becomes expected we further enact the privilege of assuming that another person, usually a person of color, will come and help us fix our own problems.

Part of Karen's challenge is that although she has spent years facing issues of race, the idea of focusing on what it means for her to be white is still a very new concept. Although she is able to dialogue extensively regarding the economic and social privileges that come with white skin in our society and the racism people of color have faced, she still has difficulty naming what it means for *her* to be white. Here is what Karen had to say when I asked her what being white meant to her at our first interview:

> You know, to tell you the honest truth, I very rarely think about it. I think about Blackness. I'm trying to understand Blackness. Maybe until I figure out blackness I won't be able to really understand whiteness. I don't know. But what it means to me is that I am very lucky in terms of this society and this world— well, this society, let's say—that I was born white and with all the—because it's the dominant group in power—with the wealth, wanting to sustain itself, wanting to support itself, I had every opportunity. Now I was not rich. It wasn't a socioeconomic thing or a class thing. But I never was discriminated against because I was Black. So everywhere I went, I was never followed around. Everywhere I went there were white people. We were all white and nobody ever looked at me funny.

One of the things that makes Karen's example so helpful is that through her story we can see the enormous growth potential that awaits us if we make significant efforts to grapple with issues of race, working intently with messages from our cross-race partners to recognize the ways white skin bestows privileges in our society.

The second woman interviewed was Katie Gottfred. She is a white woman who lives in an exclusive, predominantly white suburb north of Chicago, Illinois. She is the founder of LEAP Learning Systems, a nonprofit organization specializing in language development. I met Katie through a family connection several years prior to the interview process. I asked her to participate in the project because I was impressed by her twenty-year commitment to people of color in Chicago's Cabrini Green housing project, helping parents to code-switch, preschoolers to increase their language skills, and adolescents of color to move into top college-preparatory high schools. I was also impressed by Katie's thirty-year friendship with Lorraine Cole, who was then the president of the Black Women's Health Imperative in Washington, D.C., and who is now CEO of the YWCA USA.

Of all those participating in the project, I know Katie best. We enjoy both a professional and familial relationship. At the same time, Katie and I approach things from very different points of view. For example, whereas I have experienced a sufficient degree of personal torment over dealing with class disparity, Katie focuses her view of class as being primarily about manners and etiquette, seeing economic disparities as practically inescapable.

Yet Katie has also been working at understanding race dynamics for decades and therefore she is an elder to me in this regard. Perhaps because of all this, our interviews were less about me asking questions and more about us having deep, challenging conversations. Ultimately, my relationship with Katie has been instrumental in forming my views, sometimes with me following her lead, other times reacting against her stance. Either way, I have found the push and pull essential in forming the more solid base upon which I now stand.

All that said, conducting the conversational interview with Katie allowed me to learn more about her upbringing than I previously knew. Katie described her maternal family as "socialist" with an attitude that "we should take care of everybody," that there is "no differentiation," and that "all people are all in this together." Katie spoke at length of her mother's influence on her life:

> She felt absolutely obligated to volunteer her time in the summer, and whenever she could, to help others less fortunate. So she gave every summer . . . working for the Mexican migrant worker camps . . . I was six years of age and she was a first-grade teacher and we went and she took me along to play . . . And as time went on and the suburbs moved out [and] the Mexican migrant worker camps disappeared . . . she would turn around and we would go into the [inner] city . . . and work with African Americans.

Her first recognition of discrimination based upon skin color and race came when she visited her paternal grandmother along with her Japanese American half-sisters. One of these sisters was "crying one night and she said 'Why does Gramma love you but not me?' and [Katie] immediately knew it was because [the sister] was Japanese." Katie recounted the realization she had in that moment:

> But it hit me in the face that I immediately knew why our grandmother favored me so drastically and it was horrifying to me that your flesh and blood could discriminate against you . . . realizing that my grandmother was prejudiced against her own flesh and blood because of racial differences.

This early recognition did not prompt Katie to create an identity around being white, however. Katie said, "I feel very ethnic myself because of being raised by my [maternal] grandmother who was so Norwegian." This gives her "a cultural identity." She said,

> Well, one thing that I've always said is that I have a culture too. But it isn't white culture. It happens to be Norwegian. My hang-ups happen to be the politeness issue. I was also raised in a situation where I felt that people of

Norwegian heritage were much different than people of Italian heritage and etc. So the different European cultures seem very different to me. Just like you won't get a Nigerian to say, "I'm African." He'll say, "I'm Nigerian." You don't define yourself as a continent, except if you are Australian, and it is a continent . . . Asian Americans don't say, "I'm Asian." They say "I'm Japanese" or Korean or something like that or the other thing. So, and they are different. There are different cultural values within those. So I think it's important to see things as not just Black culture or white culture, but the nuances.

Katie was raised to take pride in her cultural heritage. Her mother and grand-mother instilled a sense of being Norwegian that allowed Katie to avoid having to do an extensive search to resolve the type of identity crisis that so many other white people experience.

Katie's concentration on her ethnicity, as well as her recognition that there is a lot of diversity among different cultural groups lumped together within the white group, makes it hard for her to consider herself "as part of a larger white group." Katie simultaneously can say, "I'm part of [an] upper-class, upper socioeconomic group, privileged white people. I see the diversity of the white world too, and I'm really not a part of it. Not that I don't want to be, but I'm not." Then, in later conversations she easily discusses what it means when people say someone is "acting white," "the assumption of white America is that the justice system is fair," or noting that as a woman she was not "equal to the white, male supremacy in America." In this way, Katie sometimes uses broad strokes to speak about the larger white group, but she retains a focus on her individual heritage when speaking of herself.

This left me curious, however, and so I asked her about what she considered to be the meanings of whiteness. At that point, Katie said that she does consider herself a WASP, a white Anglo-Saxon Protestant. She named her stereotypical images of what that means as "being reserved, having a lack of a sense of humor, being somewhat rigid." Although these meanings exactly match those presented in the previous chapter regarding the development of the white, American self, Katie related those images of being a WASP as perhaps being a reflection of what it means to be Norwegian.

Since to my way of thinking Katie's perspective seemed to draw a lot from the replacing race with ethnicity approach that many whites use to avoid taking race issues seriously, I wondered: To what degree does Katie really face race issues? And what does it mean for her to be white at the same time that she doesn't see herself as part of a white group? Talking with Katie along with her friend Lorraine helped answer these questions.

Katie spoke of the way that her friendship with Lorraine offered her a radically different lens through which to view the world:

> But it was really Lorraine who was my [first] deep friend [of color], and we would talk about how it felt, what it felt like. "Gee, this feels like this to me and why does it feel different to me than you? And what does that mean?" ... I don't think I would have been here without a deep close friendship where I could talk about this. It's not something that I could read a book about ... Understanding my own perspective and realizing that my own perspective was from my ... not having to deal with being of color in America.

The altered perspective gained within the friendship has had a profound effect on Katie, her work, the success within it, and how she sees the world.

In fact, Lorraine believes that her influence inspired Katie's work in some way:

> You know, we talked about our different experiences constantly. And interestingly enough, my doctoral dissertation was all about language acquisition in African American children and because we talked constantly about everything, including our research, I often credit her interest now based on her living with me all those years, working in those areas. And it's ironic that that's where I thought my career would take me.

For Katie's part, she also knows that her mother was a strong influence in her decision to do the work she does. And yet, Katie readily admits that Lorraine is a main contributor to her ability to do the work well: "I don't think I would have been as successful because I wouldn't have been able to see things from the other side as much. So I would not have been as successful because I would have still been coming from my view as a white woman." Here, we see that although Katie really honors her cultural heritage, she can readily admit that being white shaped her worldview. Only through the years of dialogue and listening did Katie develop the skills she would need to be able to "see things from the other side," the side not marked by whiteness.

Another profound change for Katie is the degree to which she now thinks about race. Prior to meeting Lorraine, she did not consider the racial divide with seriousness. Yet the learning she received through her friendship with Lorraine is evident as we discuss how often Katie now sees issues of race. Prompted by a discussion with Lorraine concerning how often Black women think about race, Katie spoke about how much race is now a consideration for her: "Daily at least, if not more. I mean ... for me, I've made it a mission. And maybe I've made it a mission to some degree because of Lorraine making me conscious that part of the problem of class warfare—at least in Chicago it's warfare—is racial."

Hearing Katie and Lorraine speak, it became clear that Katie's concentration on ethnicity is not used to avoid issues of race in our society. From Lorraine's perspective, she believes that Katie's understanding is unusual and that Katie is a "different sort of white person." Lorraine speaks of a conference she recently organized to illustrate:

> The focus of the conference was on outreach to African Americans and the participants were all white representatives of predominantly white organizations . . . who wanted to know how to outreach to African Americans . . . And just listening to the conversations [of] these people from all over the country and how they thought about race, it was apparent they were coming to this scenario naive. This was like truly the first time they were confronted with questions of race or the questions of interactions with African Americans. If you asked them this question—and I'm considering these typical white folks, as opposed to "different kind of white people"—I would say they think about it very, very rarely, certainly never sat to contemplate it, because in the one-day conference it was a life-transforming experience for many of them, again because they were hearing things they had never heard before. They heard the "r" word discussed, racism, and discussed it . . . I mean they never had to think about racism before. You know. Their daily existence did not give them a reason to think about it. The conference provided the special immersion experience on race.

Lorraine clearly sees Katie as someone who takes issues of race seriously and does not shrink from difficult conversations and understandings. Hearing from both of them taught me that each of our identity processes is different and that much room needs to be left for each of us to construct the various meanings that make sense to us. The key for me is that whatever we come up with, that it helps us retain the desire to take responsibility for continuing our learning and growing process so that we can be increasingly active in justice efforts. In my mind, Katie offers a great example of someone who has constructed meanings that might be very different from my own, but that keep her actively working for equity and justice in productive ways.

The final white woman interviewed was Cayce Calloway. Cayce is a white woman who lived in Laurel Canyon, the hills above Los Angeles, at the time of the interview. Cayce is a photographer who taught radio production for youth programs serving students with gang-affiliated backgrounds. Cayce's friend Amanda, a Latina, referred me to her. For all of Cayce's affluence, Amanda continues to struggle to survive economically. Amanda is a former prisoner who now uses her earlier experience to teach life skills to parolees through her organization, Adelante. Amanda befriended Cayce when they worked together on a project to get youth removed from the Los Angeles police's gang database.

Cayce and I met for the first time at her home. We sat in her small kitchen overlooking a steep, tree-lined street. She appeared younger than her forty years, very energetic, lively, and humble in regards to her life. Yet for all of her dynamism, we began slowly, with Cayce carefully choosing her words. Her manner betrayed her recognition of the importance of these topics and she moved through the interview very thoughtfully.

Cayce told me that she grew up in a small southern town in Georgia and she refers to her upbringing as "idyllic" in a lot of ways, having "parents still together, two brothers, the dog." Although she never had a close African American friend growing up, there were several African Americans who came over to the house as family friends. She reported proudly that her father, who was once in local politics, was also known as a bridge-builder in the community. Cayce attended "some of the earliest integrated schools in the South" and recalled her experience:

> There had been so much going on in the Civil Rights movement that people were kind of like walking on eggs and so as a kid we didn't really notice that there was anything awry. There was a Black part of town, like there is here, and most of the Black kids lived in the Black part of town. But it wasn't like we couldn't go there. It wasn't a scary place.

She did not recall any racial tension at school, but she imagined that might have something to do with her being in a small town. Yet, she noted, "I certainly grew up hearing racial jokes. That had not gone away."

In sum, Cayce said, "I would have thought growing up that I didn't have a lot of prejudices." But since then her perception has changed: "I probably grew up in the kind of 'Yeah this race thing is behind us' . . . That was probably more my feeling . . . We need to just be colorblind and just look at each other as people. And it wasn't until the last ten years when I realized, no, it's really not that way." Cayce's perspective shifted in response to the events surrounding two key events, the Rodney King beating and the O. J. Simpson trial. These events made her aware that she "didn't live in the city that I thought I lived in." She says that they were "real wake-up calls for me" and that she had not realized that "everyone was so unhappy." Cayce said, "At first I was just kind of blown away with how could this possibly be happening? And then what I decided I was going to do is figure out what city I did live in."

Cayce sought out experiences that both confronted her with the segregated nature of Los Angeles as well as her own unrecognized prejudices. Cayce talked about what she learned.

> So just an understanding of holy shit, if you just look at a map of Los Angeles and you look at how much of it is occupied by places you've never been and how small, actually, the ruling, privileged, elite of Los Angeles live in a very small portion of the city. And that was really eye opening to me. It was like "wow." Then I have done a couple different projects that have had me in a lot of different areas and in a lot of different people's homes. And this is one of those prejudices that I didn't realize that I had where I assumed that people who were poor were also sloppy, or whatever. I don't know if I'm saying this right. But I was kind of blown away when I started going into people's houses. I was doing a project called Community Voices Project for a while where I worked with kids . . . So I would go and people would write these little blurbs about themselves and I would go and record them and put them on the radio.

Interacting with progressive whites also taught her about how even in the attempt to be sensitive, white people who are as-yet unresolved about their own whiteness can operate out of racial prejudices in offensive ways:

> That was another thing actually. People said to me, when I started this project, "You just need to go interview them and then edit together. You can't ask them to write anything. That's a white person's way of thinking." And what I found out, no, that's a white person's way of thinking, the assumption that these people can't write their story, because sometimes they were really good. Even some people who were not terribly literate, when asked to focus their thoughts in a couple of paragraphs, wrote amazing things. So I decided that instead of having people come to me, or the station, or doing it over the phone, that anybody that I worked with on Community Voices that I would go to them. So I just went to a lot of different places in LA and I would go into these houses that I had seen from the street, these little tiny houses, and they were immaculate. And they were decorated and they might have three sons in prison, but they've got family pictures everywhere. And everything is in place and that was a big one for me, realizing that poverty and . . . sort of a lower level of living physically were not one and the same. And it wasn't like people had the most expensive furniture, but it was everybody had put-together houses, in some cases, more put together than some of my friends who were kind of transient, college-graduate-school types.

Cayce's newfound recognition regarding the flawed nature of the colorblindness approach led her to see that the movement forward is "about redressing some serious, deep prejudices and wrongs." She said that:

> It fucked me up for a couple of years, actually. It was really hard because I had just come out of Warner Bros. making this film and I'd been there for four

years, actually it was before that that this all happened, but it was still being there in that environment and learning all this other stuff at the same time, it was hard. At that point, I went through that thing of questioning how come I've got so much and these people have nothing and feeling bad about who I was and trying to downplay who I was . . . so I had a hard time living in my own skin for a couple of years. And interestingly, I can probably bring it back around to Amanda in it. She was probably one of the people who helped me realize I am who I am. The best that I can do is live consciously and not try to kind of pretend that the world is not [as it is] . . . to see truth. But she was probably really helpful in that . . . To me, I've come to terms, I think, with that, that that is the point of who I was born. I think I've moved beyond the feeling guilty about it.

Cayce's sense that the point of her being born as a white person is to come to terms with race issues is in some ways similar to my own belief that the work I am meant to do in the world as a white person is to become as aware of these race issues as possible so that I can do something about them. Cayce went on to describe how Amanda helped her move out of her sense of anxiety over her whiteness:

She did it simply by accepting me, and everything about me. It's like she knew who I was and where I came from and she wanted to be my friend anyway. She's the one who kept pushing the friendship . . . She helped me understand that we are who we are and we can work at being the best version of who we are, but that we don't need to denounce ourselves.

Amanda's acceptance of Cayce, an affluent white person, as a worthy human being in the world prompted Cayce to develop a positive sense of self.

Yet even though this resulted in a reduction of guilt, Cayce went on to talk about how her learning also prompts her to continue immersing herself in social justice issues. In other words, she uses her positive sense of self in order to become more responsive to race issues, a stronger witness, not to turn away from the work.

In some ways, Cayce's experience is not unusual. White people struggling with guilt often find personal validation within relationships with people of color, just like I did with those working in Watts and Inglewood. What is different, however, is that Amanda's unconditional acceptance of Cayce does not depend on Cayce seeing herself as a "different sort of white person." Cayce sees her whiteness and its relationship to social justice, yet she does not separate herself from other whites in order to accept herself. Instead, she works toward being the best version of who she is by continuing to challenge herself to become more aware of her own deep prejudices and how they play out in the world.

Further, Cayce sees that her entire relationship with the world has changed both in how she sees others and how she sees herself. Cayce spoke about how Amanda helped shift her worldview:

> Hearing Amanda tell her story and seeing what a struggle it's been for her to try to reconnect with her children and I'm way more compassionate. I have a lot of compassion for people. Not just not making a snap judgment but being more compassionate, knowing that you never know what drives people to do what they do and really intense pain drives people to do some really horrible things. And it doesn't mean they're bad. It doesn't mean they're evil. It just means they've made some really bad decisions . . .
>
> A lot of the social justice movement allows people . . . [to] only meet other activists for the most part. Amanda was one of the people who introduced me to all the people that all this stuff was all about and showed me that they were real people. That's been really important for my own growth . . .
>
> I just look at people differently. I look at the world differently. I read newspaper articles differently. It was a matter of the "Don't judge a book by its cover" thing. I don't think most of us realize how often we do and she really showed me, "You don't do that. And this is why you don't do that." And she introduced me to a lot of different people whom I might have judged based on what I knew about them. And she really sees people as people, on both sides. Her interest and willingness to be friends with me is also because she sees me as a person. She doesn't see me as a stereotype.

Not only does Cayce credit Amanda with helping her become a better version of herself, but she also extrapolates from her experience to generalize about the benefits of being in cross-race collaborations with people who can accept each other's full humanity. Cayce said:

> I think we both also understand that we each have something to teach the other. Or maybe what we understand is that we each have something to learn from the other. It's probably more that even, and so we really respect each other's point of view . . .
>
> I think it is true that we see things in different ways because our backgrounds are so vastly different and our cultures are different and all that sort of thing. We do see life differently and I can say something, have a quandary about something, and she will come up with something that will be just, "Huh, I hadn't thought about it that way." And that's where I really feel like multicultural relationships can really help each other if we understood that there are strengths and weaknesses and that we can fill in each other's gaps.

Cayce's journey allows her to see deeply into her own whiteness in a way that many others cannot. As she now operates from a place of resolution, beyond paralyzing guilt, her voice is strong and offers us important direction.

THE LONG ROAD

The men and women introduced in this chapter have all begun their journeys into witnessing. Overall, we saw the distinctiveness of each individual's journey and the important lesson we can learn from them. And yet, even as I argue that white people need to take up the burden of opening each other's eyes to begin witnessing our own whiteness, we also have to acknowledge how many of us have benefited from people of color who raise our consciousness. I could have never begun the journey toward writing this book without the guidance of a Black friend who helped me understand myself from a racial point of view. Not surprisingly, several of those interviewed also experienced this type of learning process wherein the ability to see the effects of race develops within a friendship with a person of color.

Questions to consider at the close:

- In what ways can you identify with the stories of the people in this chapter?
- Have you experienced any radical shifts in your thinking about race during your life?

As we move forward it should be stated clearly that recognizing that it is *meaningful* that we are white is not exactly the same thing as knowing what it *means* to be white and how it affects our lives, relationships, and institutions. Even with Hecate's powerful guidance, there is no magic formula that offers clarity in an immediate or comprehensive way. Understanding how whiteness shapes and affects us takes work. For this reason, the next chapter gives insight into what our guides have found through their journeys.

NOTES

1. Meade, M., *Men and the Water of Life* (New York: HarperCollins, 1993).
2. Rodriguez, L., *Always Running: Gang Days in L.A.* (Willimantic, CT: Curbstone Press, 1993).

3. *Road to Return,* directed by L. Neale, documentary film produced in 1998.

4. Roberts, R., *My Soul Said to Me* (Deerfield Beach, FL: Health Communications, 2003).

5. Roberts, *My Soul Said to Me,* 10.

6. *The Color of Fear,* directed by Lee Mun Wah, Stir Fry Seminars, 1994, http://www.stirfryseminars.com/pages/coloroffear.htm.

7. Obidah, J. E., and K. M. Teel, *Because of the Kids: Facing Racial and Cultural Differences in Schools* (New York: Teachers College Press, 2001). This is a good text for examples of how a well-meaning white teacher can be party to the disengagement of students of color due to a lack of race consciousness

8. Obidah, J. E., and K. M. Teel, *Because of the Kids: Facing Racial and Cultural Differences in Schools* (New York: Teachers College Press, 2001). This is a good text for examples of how a well-meaning white teacher can be party to the disengagement of students of color due to a lack of race consciousness

9. Obidah and Teel, *Because of the Kids,* 90.

Chapter 5

Clearing the Way

Whiteness in Sight

By the time I was twelve years old I recognized that being "normal" was uncool and confining. So much so that in the 1980s when Burger King began an ad campaign portraying random customers looking for a guy named Herb, described as "a strange man," I had my father call me Herb for months. In the same spirit, the most annoying and repetitive argument I had with my mother occurred every year while shopping for school clothes. "Everyone's wearing this style right now," she would say, as though that would make me want to wear the outfit.

The underlying issue ultimately was about freedom. Somehow I intuited that following the crowd without question would require me to give up something of myself. It was important that I be able to think, feel and act out of my own understanding of the world. Looking back, it makes sense that it was around this time that I became fascinated by psychology.

I know now that what I was challenging at that time, in my own very limited way, is what Carl Jung called "collective consciousness." The term essentially refers to the fact that as we grow up, our dominant culture attempts to train us to take on certain beliefs, values, and ways of being so that we will fit in to mainstream society. What we end up with is a consciousness (a way of understanding the world) that is collective (in agreement with a group) that maintains the status quo. From Jung's point of view, becoming a full individual who can freely make choices requires the questioning of our various groups' values and beliefs.

As part of the dominant racial group in the United States, white people have generally not been either inspired or forced to question the ways that race has shaped our attitudes, beliefs, and actions. This limits our freedom. We don't recognize our own patterns, and therefore we are unable to decide whether or not these patterns are beneficial for our lives and relationships. Allowing a new vision to challenge ideas developed over the course of our lives is therefore a move toward personal liberation.

Here we can call again upon Hecate, with her lighted torch, to reveal the dark truths of the psyche so that we can clear a path toward a new vision. Whether or not we feel every word of the messages from our fellow travelers to be true for our own lives, if we have the courage to face what they convey to us, this other way of seeing the world might free us from blind participation in hurtful race dynamics.

Like peeling back the layers of an onion, the meanings attached to being white continually reveal themselves if we repeatedly ask the question "What does it mean to be white in the United States?" Before we delve into this question, however, let us first recall that everyone's experience of what it means to be white differs. Our experience of our racial identity is interconnected with our other multiple social identities, such as our gender, socioeconomic class, family background, citizenship status, and sexual orientation. All of these things, and more, make up who we are and how we experience the world.

A white, college-educated, heterosexual woman experiences the world differently than does a white, homosexual male without a high school diploma. A white, working-class woman has a very different experience from a white, affluent man. However, just as there are some experiences that are shaped particularly by our gender or class position, for example, there are also ways that our racial position influences our lives.

Understandably, the opinions of the people speaking in this chapter might not match those of some readers. And yet, my hope is that when we look at the diverse group of meanings associated with whiteness, we might become better able to create a visual of the whole. I want to create this rather elusive and uneven big picture because seeing the broad view has important implications for our effort to become effective witnesses and better relationship partners.

Before we turn to how the people interviewed see whiteness, let us take a quick glance back to the terrain already covered. Recall that in Chapter 1 we saw that some people view whiteness as a way of being, a culture. Some common meanings include being just normal, achieving middle-class status, and living a segregated life. Chapter 3 detailed particular aspects of the history of the white race and how various associations with whiteness developed. This included whiteness as meaning American, Christian, Western, modern, innocent, free, individualistic, ambitious, and rigid.

These are some general ideas, a foundation from which to start. Important to note is that this chapter does not offer an exhaustive list of what it means to be white. These people's perspectives are a place from which to begin. So although we are looking for a composite picture, we must also see that there will be holes in our vision still to be filled in through continued inquiry.

We also have to be honest about this. White people have not generally had clear vision in regards to this subject. The insights of the people of color are therefore essential. Their insights help us fill in some of the gaps left open by the white people, as well as help us see what being white looks like from a different vantage point—one outside of the collective white consciousness. As Bob noted about his experience living in Germany for several years, going outside of our culture helps us better understand the very place from whence we come.

WHITE CULTURE?

Let us acknowledge from the start that the broad view that speaks of *white culture,* a *white way of being,* or *white thinking,* never fully encapsulates the fullness of anyone. But let us venture forth with a sense of curiosity and appreciation for challenging messages in order to learn what is meant when people use these terms and be open to the possibility that we are related to their meanings.

Recall from Chapter 3 that "Western culture" and "white" are often considered related terms. Speaking from this point of view is Lee Mun Wah, who admitted that he uses white and Western synonymously. He said,

> I don't think that we're ever seen as Westerners. I think that we can even still be born here and be here all of our lives and people would never be considered a Westerner, or white, or American per se. In fact, for European Americans it's very integrated and established in their Western ways so that they don't know it. They don't know what values they have that are very Western and imposed on the rest of the world. And I say that in a way because I think that quite oftentimes people of color are always adapting to white folks and accommodating to them and I don't think the white folks, until they have to travel, ever do that.

This single quote alludes to two important issues. First, we see how even in our contemporary society being white remains linked with being American. Exclusion occurs even if Lee Mun Wah takes on American, white cultural forms of dress and manner. Although born and raised in the United States, white people continue to assume that he is an immigrant. This does not happen to white-appearing people.

Second, Lee Mun Wah highlights that there is a culture that most white people fit into, *white culture,* and that this is a culture in which most people of color have to consciously try to fit in order to maneuver successfully in this society. White people generally do not constantly wonder how we might need to modify our behavior in order to move through our environment safely or successfully. A feature of white culture, therefore, is an expectation that people ought to shift as needed in order to fit within white norms of behavior, dress, speech, and manner.

But this is not the only way that people link white culture with a broad philosophical approach. Bob, the white man from New Orleans, spoke of white culture by identifying what appears lacking in the United States in comparison to traditional, tribal societies. Bob defined white culture as "European culture, a culture that is further away from the indigenous world than say African or Mayan or Native American cultures, a culture that quit initiating its children long before other cultures did and so are further away from what is today still understood by indigenous people." For Bob, whiteness involves the movement away from a worldview he respects and admires, a worldview historically considered developmentally inferior by Western society.

As mentioned regarding the building of a broad picture, if we shifted into the exact details separating Western from Eastern or indigenous, these distinctions would assuredly break down somewhere. What might be generally true may also be false in particularity. Certainly, white culture is not always seen from such a wide lens.

Narrowing our vision just a bit is Dr. Shirley Better, an African American author. She concentrates on the different cultures that have been bred in the United States. She said:

> Whiteness is a culture, just like African American is a culture. I don't have to think about it a lot because everybody is raised in white culture, whether you're white or not. Everybody is raised within American white culture because it's the dominant culture. So it is as much a part of me as it is a part of you in the sense that I know all of the nuances of what is American culture. American culture is white, European culture added with a mixture of what we have here. So I don't have to think about it as separate. I'm aware of it as a difference. Everything that we have operating in our society is whiteness. All of that is white culture, the language that I speak. But everything in our culture is white culture in the sense of how we mean it. We mean it as European based.

Linking Western with American and seeing them both reflecting white culture presents challenges, though. Luis Rodriguez, a Chicano man, described how Western culture is perceived as white even though it is truly a hybrid:

> My feeling is that Western culture isn't really just European or white. It also draws from all the world's cultures. We can prove that the trajectories of

African, Native American, Mexican, Asian, and Jewish and many other cultures have made up our Western culture. But I think there is a sense that the rule of it is very white, European.

I think that is why it is hard to separate those dominant, even racial things that come up in Western culture. Because then you have people like Pat Buchanan, who defends it. "Western culture is the best culture," he says. Western culture is the best because white people have framed it and set the basic parameters of it. Yes, other people have been involved in it, but they are not acknowledged.

In recognizing the influential contributions made by the diversity of groups, Luis does not have a problem seeing himself as a part of Western culture. And yet, Luis also says that "whiteness is a way of being in the world." Jennifer, an African American, also said, "There is a white way of doing things." But Jennifer also questioned the role that class plays: "Those looking in see it as so radically uniform that it is defined as a white way of being, where it might be a white way that is significantly influenced by wealth versus a white way that is significantly influenced by being white." This is an important point. Distinguishing the effects of race and class can be really difficult, but Jennifer reminds us that white culture is often associated with a middle-class or affluent life.

This can help explain why working-class white people often reject the idea that they benefit from white privilege, feeling outside the loop of many of the benefits that whiteness bestows. The implied meaning of the oft-used term "white trash" also starts to become clearer. The middle-class status of the large proportion of whites makes some whites the ill-fitting "trash" of the white community. If we speak of people as "white trash," we essentially state that we would prefer to throw away those less "educated," "cultured," or "affluent" and cut them out of our group since they do not represent the meanings we hold for what it means to be white.

The ramifications of the economic connections to these ideas are far reaching. Luis also spoke of how economics affects racial identity within the Mexican American community:

It's really weird, huh? So, then you get "white" as transforming to mean, not really race anymore, but power and economics. So, if you hold an economically powerful place you could actually be white.

Luis' statements align with a *Los Angeles Times* news article reporting that large numbers of immigrants who feel increasingly economically prosperous racially classify themselves as white.[1] Additionally, this reminds us of the legal history we saw in Chapter 3 in which Mexicans were often legally considered white even though the classification does not resonate with the opinions of the general populace.[2] This can help us to understand why people of color who achieve middle-class status often begin to be referred to as either becoming white or as selling-out by the people in their home communities who are quite often less economically well off.

Overall, Lee Mun Wah, Bob, Shirley, Luis, and Jennifer offer broad ways of seeing that bring being white to the level of culture. This is in contrast to those who resist defining white or whiteness in any sort of general way, favoring instead a view of the diversity within it.

Only a few of the people spoken to resisted naming whiteness as a broad idea. When speaking about white culture, Perry, an African American colleague of Bob's, quickly stated that "you have subcultures within subcultures" even within the white community. And Luis, while speaking about whiteness as "a way of being" above, also said that he tries to avoid seeing white people as a "monolith" so that he can relate to people on an individual level.

More insistent, though, was Katie, who never made a generalization about the meaning of being white. Katie attributed this resistance to define whiteness to her upbringing, wherein she saw differences between people of various European cultures: "Just like you won't get a Nigerian to say I'm African. He'll say I'm Nigerian . . . There are different cultural values within those. So I think it's important to see things as not just Black culture or white culture, but the nuances." The only way Katie could speak of her belonging within white culture was to narrowly define herself as a white, Anglo-Saxon Protestant (WASP).

The choice to generalize versus narrowly focus is a tension that pervades the academic work on whiteness as well as our common everyday speech. The message offered in an essay speaks of the tension. John Hartigan writes that no matter how much we are able to see whiteness from a large view, that when we try to trace whiteness down into something specific or consistent that we can never really arrive at defining a succinct white identity that is common to all white people.[3]

So as we shift into the particular meanings related to what it means to be white, we understand that as these large associations capture something essential, they also lack consistency and cannot be used to automatically brand any particular individual. In this way, this offering *does* generalize what it can mean to be white—yet the intention is *not* to create a stereotype. In reflecting on the generalized meanings, it can be helpful to ask ourselves: to what degree do our lives reflect what is described as "white culture"?

BEING WHITE MEANS WHAT EXACTLY?

Sifting through the various responses from those I spoke with, several meanings repeated often enough, or related closely enough, to call them themes. Some were long ago overheard ideas, while others expanded my own vision.

This offering just scratches the surface, but at least we have a place to start. We start with the most common association: *white privilege.*

Being White Means Unearned Privileges

For those who see race as continuing to make a meaningful difference in our lives, far and away the most common meaning associated with being white is privilege.

Lee Mun Wah:	Probably Peggy McIntosh in "Unpacking the [Invisible] Backpack" probably best illustrates what whiteness is, and not just as a power paradigm, but just in everyday experience of what white means to me.
Bob:	It's a given. It's true. Being white is having privileges . . . No law can change that.
Shirley:	Whiteness is unearned privilege.
Spencer:	What whiteness is? Privilege. That's all I've got to say, privilege.
Jennifer:	It means privilege, whether assumed or in reality. Poor white people have that privilege.
Cayce:	It is an absolute point of privilege really. There's no other thing that you can be born, with the possible exception of if you add man to that, being born a white man. There is no other more privileged place to be born into, period. Even the poorest white person in most circles is given more consideration than certainly your everyday person of color.
Lorraine:	The first thing that comes to my mind is privilege. I have a hard time answering that question outside of the context of my everyday world that I am totally immersed in because I'm dealing with, my professional life has been dedicated to, eliminating disparities and everything that I'm reading constantly just reinforces the gap that exists between white people and Black people and particularly when it comes to Black women. We are at the very bottom of every index compared not only to white women but in many cases to Black men. So, you know, when you ask me what that means, it means access, it means less stresses, it means a totally different existence.

Knowing that most whites do not automatically understand what the term "white privilege" includes, our fellow travelers expanded and clarified. They then offered a variety of particular contexts wherein white people receive unearned benefits simply by being part of the dominant racial group in our society. Again, this is but a small snapshot, hardly inclusive, simply a place to start.

Being White Means More Opportunities

Being white can be seen as conferring privilege in terms of education, economics, housing options, and employment opportunities:

Jennifer: It means opportunity, because most of them I interact with have some power.

Spencer: It's the privilege for being hired, getting a better house, living in a better neighborhood, getting a better education, getting a better seat at a restaurant, getting a higher-paying job, that's privilege.

Karen: I have anything I want. I can have anything I want . . . all opportunities are open to me. I can choose to do whatever I want and know that I'm not going to have barriers put up because I'm white. I might have barriers because I'm a woman. But I'm not going to have barriers because I'm white.

Worth noting is that along with Karen, Spencer talked about the role that gender plays. He asked me to be sure to mention "male privilege" in addition to the advantages bestowed by race. This reminds us of the multiple social positions we occupy, how they interweave, can complicate, and are sometimes contradictory, overlapping, and shifting.[4] Paying attention to this helps us clearly recall that one can be simultaneously advantaged by one form of privilege while feel disadvantaged by a different aspect of our social identity.

Two of the people of color within this group, however, voiced specific charges concerning the role that economics continues to play in terms of systematic privileging related to being white. Luis spoke of what the economic divide allows in terms of spatial and relational experience:

The big divide is really economics . . . white people have economically removed themselves by moving away from the inner city, or whatever it might be—they moved away from some real issues about cities and poverty and pain.

Shirley focused directly upon the economic advantages of whiteness, using language taken directly from a book by George Lipsitz, *The Possessive Investment in Whiteness,* to discuss the way white privilege remains institutionalized: "Until whites are willing to give up that economic advantage that comes from the possessive investment in whiteness, all the integration and individual friendships [are] not going to change the central nub of that."[5]

Lipsitz' book chronicles the various ways that white people economically benefit from being white. Picking up that book for the first time, I only made it through the first fifteen pages before putting it back down, so strong was my dismay at my own ignorance and desire to escape from the facts outlined in the book. While true that plenty of white people live in poverty, there are still a disproportionate number of whites who do not. This feature of white-ness, the systematic economic advantages, is one of the most concrete and measurable, although often unrecognized by whites, and it has a tremendous impact on our systems and institutions.

Being White Means Feeling Entitled

William, Katie, and Spencer specifically identified how white privilege relates to a sense of entitlement. Understanding what it means to "act enti-tled" is often a difficult issue for white people, especially in a culture where white people regularly receive messages that we deserve to be treated well. Children in my predominantly-white neighborhood were raised to expect that doors would be opened for us as long as we put in enough effort. Nothing was to be considered out of reach and our voices were considered valuable by the majority of authority figures in our lives.

While these attitudes benefit us in myriad ways, quite often, these mes-sages are neither conveyed nor reinforced enough in the lives of many people of color, especially students of color in inner cities. In fact, the enactment of this entitled existence can actually cause white people to act in ways that are infuriating to people of color. We might ask ourselves how we enter spaces where conversations are already occurring and the degree to which we speak in ways that assume correctness. We might also stop to imagine when there might be moments when it is important to take a step back and ensure that others have space that does not include us.

For example, William, an African American, spoke of his experience see-ing groups of whites entering a situation that would have felt unapproachable to him had the situation been reversed:

> There is also a sense of privilege, a sense of entitlement. And . . . you think about the Million Man March. This was a day of atonement, everybody asked, "Please let us just have this day for ourselves and this is something we need to do." Then you watch CNN or CSPAN . . . and you see some white people walk-ing in there anyways.

For William, although legally allowable, white people entering that space was inappropriate and can only be described as the enactment of privilege. Even if the white people's intent was to show their support, we should wonder, did they ask whether or not the African Americans who planned and participated in the event desired the support? If we do not see that our everyday behavior often carries a sense of entitlement we will not ask questions about its effects. For this reason, just knowing that we need to ask the question is an important step.

Katie recognized how a sense of entitlement affects her as a white woman. Katie described a time when she was one of the only white faces at a conference primarily geared toward Black speech pathologists:

> I thought, now this is interesting, I could come in here and sit and I'm assuming you're going to accept me into this. I'm OK. I'm free. Whereas if I had been one Black in [an] all-white [place] I would have thought, "Well, how is that? Is this OK? How am I acting?" But I was just, "Hey, I am OK." . . . But that freedom and privilege and access allows me to say, "Oh, I can pretty much be who I want to be and assume that I will be accepted."

For Katie, the ability for whites to feel free to enter any space regardless of its makeup or intent symbolizes the entitlement bestowed by a racially dominant position. The problem is not that being at events filled with mostly people of color is wrong. The point is that the freedom to feel comfortable going anywhere without any consideration of our manner of approach is a privilege that white people receive but that people of color regularly go without.

Spencer spoke about a different type of entitlement. He described a way of interacting in the world that assumes a certain quality of treatment:

> I am highly aware all the time of the privilege of walking into a restaurant and feeling, really feeling like I deserve the best seat, and not having to think twice about it . . . If I go out for a job and I know I am the best person for the job and I don't get it, I feel totally justified to get in that guy's face. "Who the hell do you think you are?" Most people, I have found out from my friends of color, would hold back because then they would be the "ugly" person of color making waves.

When Spencer brought up the idea that people of color do not feel the freedom to lash out when their personal interests go unmet, he also spoke to the lack of fear among whites. Being conditioned to see ourselves only as individuals, we do not generally worry about being viewed as representatives of our race.

A woman I met recently at a book club told me a story where this idea emerged as well. This elder, white woman recounted a time when she and a Black girlfriend were fooling around decades prior. This white woman had dressed up as a Black person, including black makeup and an Afro wig, to accompany her friend out shopping. The two young women did not intend to run a social experiment. According to the story, they were simply out having fun, dressing to avoid display of an interracial friendship during a time in our history when that was not yet the norm.

Within moments of the pair entering a store, the white woman (in disguise) noticed she was being followed around the store. As she proceeded to the rear of the store where knives and other arms were sold, she noticed glaring looks on the faces of store clerks and she began to be spoken to gruffly. She found herself glaring back, even overplaying her interest in those items as she recognized the anxiety and upset it was creating in the store clerks. She did it purposefully, recognizing how angry she was at the treatment she was experiencing.

There is a key element of this story related to our theme of entitlement. Notice how rapidly this disguised white woman became incensed and altered her behavior as a way of challenging white people treating her badly. Decades later while telling this tale, the woman remained amazed at the deep level of anger she had experienced, how rapidly it had arisen, and how it was her Black friend who calmed her and got her to leave the situation without provoking the clerks further. Can we imagine how we'd respond if we were treated that poorly on a daily basis? What if that level of insufferable rudeness were the norm? Worse, what if each time we tried to call attention to it, the experience was dismissed as our imagination?

Linking these last two stories highlights that with few exceptions white people are entitled to behave very badly without adversely affecting other members of the white group by association. We can pretty much behave as criminally as we want and never hear anyone say, "Oh, those white people, there they go again." Further, when white people are the majority of perpetrators of a crime, we rarely hear race discussed as an issue. Take, for example, the vast number of serial killers, school shooters, and corporate swindlers who are white. White people have yet to start questioning what is going on with us as a racial group to make us susceptible to enacting these awful crimes. Unfortunately, many whites have regularly made use of examples of people of color to justify broad, sweeping generalizations.

Being White Means Being Normal

Our privilege to avoid being named as a representative of our race exists because of the way white identity remains invisible to many white people. Since seeing whiteness as "normal" is an identified pattern, I sought out only people who consider race to be an important issue within the United States.[6] Not surprisingly then, those I spoke with recognize, and are critical of, whites who see being white as normal or invisible. Shirley notes, "What I'm trying to move to is finding another term to get away from the term whiteness because white people don't call themselves white. You don't say, 'my white girlfriend.' It's normalized."

Karen and Katie recognized that sometimes they continue to operate from the point of view of white as "normal." Karen saw it in her own relationship with her home environment and Katie even identified a moment when it hit her, literally, in the face:

Karen:	I think I am so attuned to, conditioned, to my own environment and the way things work in my own environment that I just assume that it is happening everywhere else.
Katie:	I remember the other experience that day [at the Black speech pathologist's conference]. I was going into the bathroom and looking in the mirror as I washed my hands and thinking, "Oh my god, what happened to me? I look . . ." And I realized that I had gotten so used to looking at color that I looked sick. I thought, "Oh, I must be getting sick because I'm looking so pale today." I didn't look normal. And that was an interesting thought for me . . . because suddenly I saw myself as not looking healthy and that something was wrong with my face because the norm for those two days had become looking at all sorts of colors of darker faces.

This begs the question, what are we conditioned to see as normal? How might our perception change if our world asked us to interact meaningfully with a diverse crowd on a daily basis in ways that appreciated other cultural ways of being? Additionally, this normality is linked to privilege and entitlement, as this exchange between Karen and Jennifer makes clear:

Jennifer:	Having everything you want for white people in this society is such a taken-for-granted thing, to name it "white privilege" connotes something negative and they've never perceived it or lived it as negative.
Karen:	It's normal.
Jennifer:	It's normal. So it's a normalized sense of entitlement, if you will.

Essentially, this takes us back to the fishbowl analogy offered by Shirley in Chapter 1. White people are so used to being part of a society that does not prompt thoughts of racial identification on a daily basis that we do not see that most people of color experience the world very differently than we do. This obliviousness is also a feature of our privileged position.

Being White Means Being Unaware

A significant feature of white privilege is that white people tend not to be conscious of our privileges and how the dominance of whiteness affects other groups.

Lee Mun Wah:	I think it's what I could say about most white men, from my experience, a lack of awareness.
Jennifer:	Part of whiteness is the unconsciousness, the believing in meritocracy that you work really hard to get everything you have and so you are lucky and you deserve it. So when you say whiteness and privilege, it sounds like somebody gave it to you without you earning it. And for white people who had to work, that notion is so offensive, but they don't interrogate what happens.
Cayce:	Being in that privileged place, being of that elite, often carries with it a lack of understanding . . . I think when somebody says, "Well, they don't act white" it means they're not totally unconscious of the fact that their race gives them and us a privilege that we wouldn't otherwise have and also an understanding that it also gives us an ignorance.
Shirley:	I think the difference between whites and nonwhites is that all the nonwhites who have lived in this country are very aware of it and sensitive to it and relate to it. It is whites who don't see it. It's sort of like being right-handed, which is what I say in my book, it's there, you never even think about it, the privilege and that everything is based on being right-handed.

This privilege to be unaware also plays out in many white people's ability to remain removed from difficult situations, whether mentally or physically. Spencer still grapples in some ways with the learning that took place during his friendship with Lee Mun Wah. Spencer now recognizes that his choices of what to pay attention to are part of his racial privilege: "With this knowledge I could never turn back to turning a blind eye ever again because I've got the privilege to do that. That alone is sad, that because of my color, I have the privilege to see or don't see. I choose to see." It is also clear that this topic is of utmost concern to both Luis and Michael, as this pair spoke extensively on this issue.

Luis:	I mean the privilege that they can walk away from people, Mexicans or otherwise. You don't have to know them. There is a privilege that you can choose who you want to connect with . . . But some people have the privilege to ignore what they want to. They can ignore a vital and large segment of the population. It's a privilege. I can't ignore white people.

Michael: It's a tremendous ignorance. And I mean ignorance exactly. Some of it is people do not know, like Luis said, they know some of the history of African American and Anglo Americans, of slavery. They don't know anything about Mexico. They don't know anything about the war. They don't know anything and they're all right with that. I don't have to know. I don't have to take it on. So ignorance is part of it . . . That's privilege, I don't have to adjust myself to understand.

This is as specific as we got regarding the privileges that come with whiteness. If you are interested in investigating this aspect more fully, an Internet search for Peggy McIntosh's "Unpacking the Invisible Knapsack" offers immediate access to a list of over forty additional unearned privileges white people receive in our society that people of color cannot claim.[7] Overall, though, we would do well to ask ourselves the degree to which we recognize the way social and economic white privilege is enacted systematically in our social, school, and work worlds. Keeping our ears open when people of color speak likely can add additional insights as well.

Being White Means Dominant, Valued Images

What it means to be white also means seeing images of people who are of the same racial background as ourselves. The people of color I spoke with noted the pervasiveness of white people within the cultural atmosphere, especially in terms of media representation. This includes movies, television, magazines, and advertisements. But this also includes other environments where people are portrayed, including churches, gift card stores, and book illustrations.

Jennifer put it succinctly. She said of whiteness, "It means magazine ads that look like them, a world we move through that reflects them." Lee Mun Wah spoke similarly: "What whiteness means to me is . . . to see images that look like you every day of your life . . . to be yourself and see varieties of yourself." The earlier discussion of normality and lack of awareness also relates to this experience. Luis discussed his impressions of whites in terms of the media:

[My wife] and I were thinking about how white people love each other. And I know white people don't say this. But when you are looking from our end of it, they are always putting themselves up there. In the movies, it's them. They love to see themselves. I mean, it's not a bad thing, but when you're coming from our perspective it's too much. They aren't even aware they're doing this. They think they are telling universal, human stories. But all the characters have their faces, their ways of doing things.

Luis' last line is particularly important. Many of us are so accustomed to seeing media images that confirm and support our way of living in the world that we do not understand why people of color might feel disconnected from stories featuring whites.

Stories are told from a cultural point of view. White culture pervades all stories featuring predominantly white casts. The desire to see people who reflect one's own cultural values has massive implications for the entertainment industry and links to critiques that white adults, for the most part, only watch shows featuring people of color if they are exemplifying white norms. This, then, might have an effect on the portrayal of characters of color as each show pursues the largest audience share it can muster.

The experience of the media also depends upon our orientation. Within hip-hop culture, alternative media, and other less-mainstream cultural forms, different messages may be conveyed regarding race and the meanings of whiteness. We should be careful, though, to not assume that just because white faces do not dominate a particular media event or show that deeply affecting images of what it means to be white are not being conveyed. No matter where we receive our media messages, we need to critically interrogate what is being shown to be beautiful, valued, and respected.

Being White Means Being Knowledgeable

There is a pervasive perception of white people as experts in our society, which goes hand in hand with a regular dismissal of people of color. Through first-hand experiences, William developed his current belief that there is "an assumption of authenticity and an assumption of being correct" in regard to white people. Growing up with middle-class parents attending elite, private schools, William grew up believing that his words would be just as valued as anyone else's. William spoke of his current perspective, developed after bearing witness to other professors' experiences during college and medical school:

I think if you put . . . two teachers in a room and one was white and one was African American, and they taught the same thing. I think if you polled the class[es], I think the class here . . . would believe more in the veracity of the words [of the white teacher], whereas here [students with the African American teacher] they would be either questioning more, trying to assert themselves more, trying to challenge more. The first time I ever had an African American science teacher was at CSUN and this guy was just like hammered all the time, just questioned all the time. And it wasn't that he was a bad teacher. He was a good teacher. I mean, they just peppered him compared to the other professors we had. Same kids, same class. They wouldn't pepper these [white] . . . teachers at all. And then I experienced that when I student taught or later on when I was a resident as well too.

Similarly to William, Spencer realized that people often do not see people of color as valid holders of knowledge. Spencer spoke of his recent experience raising money for a high-tech venture he was working on and said, "I realize that if I went in there as a different person of color in that room . . . I would not be listened to as well." If this is true, what might it mean for those of us who attend classes and meetings led by people of color?

Actually, this pattern of privileging white voices is so well-known that some people of color working with nonprofit organizations or service projects occasionally bring a "buffer" to meetings with institutional decision makers. The buffer is a white person who acts as the spokesperson for the group and appears as the leader, even if the person in the top position is actually the person of color sitting to the side. Many people of color know that no matter how good their ideas and plans, a white person saying the exact same thing is very likely be seen as more trustworthy and more knowledgeable than the person of color. This can lead to the belief that the search for funding might be more successful if a white person appears at the helm.

Sadly, several examples from my own experience are easily recalled where this played out during efforts to promote programs to offer counseling services within elementary schools, mentorship opportunities, and other after-school service programs. Although most people would claim that they would *never* see a person of color as essentially less knowledgeable than a white person, the messages given and received that this *does* occur cannot be ignored. Many, many people in powerful positions subtly reinforce this pattern unconsciously on a regular basis. The trick is that we cannot do a thing to disrupt it if we cannot notice it and name it.

Being White Means Isolation and Emotional Superficiality

The meanings associated with being white previously discussed are the more evident and visible in my opinion. A number of books written on whiteness allude to them to one degree or another. This next piece, however, strikes at the core of the dis-ease that many white people face. These next two meanings resonate with my personal experience so deeply that I was struck at my own surprise that they emerged as a theme.

My academic work did not often speak of these ideas, and yet they surface regularly when I am in conversations with multiracial groups of friends and colleagues. Looking closely, we find that the following associations with being white in some ways mirror the meanings described in Chapter 3 regarding the development of a new, white identity, characterized by emotional restriction and the isolated, self-contained individual.[8]

Admittedly, these meanings are heavily loaded and may not resonate with all readers. But we do ourselves a disservice if we dismiss them too quickly. Let us keep in mind that checking in with ourselves regarding these generalized patterns in no way suggests that only white people face isolation and surface-oriented relationships. There are certainly many people of color who face similar challenges. In fact, *Bowling Alone,* a book by Robert Putnam, investigates how American society in general has moved through many phases in terms of our social engagement during the past hundred years. He acknowledges that during the past few decades all racial groups have lost what he calls "social capital," referring to social relationships and civic engagement.[9]

Here we have to recall that what people consider "American culture" and "white culture" are so entangled and variable that it is hardly surprising if many people of color are swept up into the meanings and associations as we try to speak of our experiences. For this reason, we should not be surprised that some people speak of white culture in ways that might rightly also describe lives led by many people of color. That said, isolation and superficiality arise as identified patterns by many in relation to being white, and my suggestion is that we concentrate on ourselves as we consider what this might mean for our lives and relationships.

This section offers these ideas as two aspects of one larger theme because teasing them apart is difficult. Ultimately, the image of a cross is a connecting visual that can allow us to see their actual distinctiveness with clarity. Imagine a cross with one arm outstretched to the horizons and the other reaching simultaneously upward to the sky and downward toward the earth. Notice how the arms of the cross connect while representing different movements. This is true of the following meanings. The horizontal arm of the cross extends the various meanings associated with disconnection and isolation, the ways that we interact with others within our world. By contrast, the vertical arm holds the image of depth and surface, the *qualities* of those interactions. The meeting point resides in their mutual interest in relationship.

Disconnection and Isolation

The arm of this cross extends quite a distance, for this category encompasses much. To those I spoke with whiteness can be associated with isolation, dissections, and disconnections.

Amanda: Well, my first husband was half-Irish and I lived with his family . . . So I got to see how they raised their children and I've been in prison and was raised with white girls there too.

	So I got to see a lot of pictures from poor whites to affluent whites. So I've seen that there is a disconnection. I mean, feelings are covered.
Michael:	One of the ways of sustaining cultural whiteness is isolation, like old Descartes. It's not a plot, just the resonance of bad ideas. Isolate the individual rather than see the individual as the contributor back to the collective. And the carpool lane is empty and there are four lanes filled with one person in each car and that's white culture pouring down the road, each isolated inside and hearing the news that reinforces the ideas of isolation and whiteness.
Cayce:	And white people for the most part have kind of isolated themselves . . . there is like a boundary around white people that a lot of times people of color drop when they are together and white people don't always drop when they are with other white people. There's not this sense of community.

I would love to say that the above characterizations do not reflect my life, family, white friends, and their families. Unfortunately, there is a lot of it that seems right on. True, on some level these descriptions might reflect the general trend toward decreased social engagement.[10] Yet over the past decade, I have spent a lot more time around people from different cultural and racial backgrounds. I am very sad to say that this sense of white people as being less emotionally connected, more isolated, and more guarded *even when we are with other people* resonates.

The pain that comes with admitting this is all the more intense because this is something that I have known deep down for quite some time. The patterns are so ingrained that serious effort is required to break out of habits that keep me alone when in pain and nervous about sharing difficulty with family and friends. I wish that this did not characterize a broader struggle. Unfortunately, there are too many white people who exemplify these characteristics. The significant numbers of whites who seriously battle depression and a sense of aloneness in the midst of seemingly comfortable lives and intact, loving families are too great. It bears repeating that, of course, white people are not the only ones who face these issues. But that does not mean that it is not a pattern characteristic of white people worthy of honest investigation.

Moving into broader territory, for some whiteness also brings to mind the dissection of Latin America, the raping of Mother Earth for resources, a sense of separation from nature, and a disconnection from prior generations, our ancestors, and the sacred. There is also a collective sense that being white means having a wall built up between people, having something killed off inside that is required for holding a false sense of superiority, and an unwillingness to cross racial boundaries. Here are a couple of representative statements.

Amanda: When I think of countries like Latin America being dissected, I think of white. When I hear of Mother [Earth] being raped and resources being taken out of her, especially her resources, I think of white. So I know it's not only white, that power and money comes in many colors. Politicians, always all white. Honestly, that's what we see.

Lee Mun Wah: In the Western thought, it's almost always, well, you wound your environment but there's no connection to your environment. "It's useful this moment, and if it happens to break down we'll figure it out." Or like George Bush or Ronald Reagan. "Well, if we ruin all of the clouds so there is no more rain, we'll just pour tons of salt on the clouds to get it to rain. Or we'll plant lots of little trees to make up for all the forest we've destroyed." But it's never the sense of interconnectedness. It's always isolation, even if it takes 500 years for something to grow back. But there's a sense that I'm connected to the trees and to the person and to the words and to the actions and to the generations that come. There's a sense of evolution and continuity, whereas I don't feel that in the Western culture and so when you ask me about my race and my culture, I think to me a Western thought is that they are separated.

From a big-picture point of view, this characterization may be fair. Western, white culture is linked with the Industrial Revolution, technology that allowed for increased use of both natural and human resources, and the purposeful destruction of communal forms of living within indigenous populations. Our history is rife with movements that led us to become a highly individualistic society dependent upon the existence of exploitation.

Taking Lee Mun Wah's approach for a moment and using whiteness synonymously with Western culture, most of the associations are also located within Tarnas' book, *The Passion of the Western Mind*, discussed in Chapter 3.[11] After analyzing the development of Western consciousness over its two-thousand-year history, Tarnas argues that, ultimately, the deepest passion of the West's masculine consciousness is to reunite with the whole, with all that it has separated itself from, including nature and femininity, and to transcend human alienation. This is no small critique. What these associations suggest is that being white is fundamentally related to being disconnected on a number of levels.

Further, the entire project of our Western, white civilization cannot be completed until we heal from these various disconnections and make use of whatever this separation has taught us in order to become more conscious.

In other words, to follow Tarnas' logic, those of us raised within the Western cultural matrix likely require a sort of radical healing that reconnects us with spirit, soul, self, other, nature, the feminine, and so on if we are going to live in a way that is more holistic and promotes a sense of widespread connectedness.

Emotional Superficiality

Many people I talked with also used language that linked whiteness with life on the surface of emotion. Stories regarding surface and superficiality came with images of ease, cleanliness, and sanitization. Conversely, descriptions of depth brought associations of difficulty, struggle, and conflict. Bob and Karen both recognize how the avoidance of depth within relationships plays out. In his memoir, Bob wrote: "To my friends and me, friendships mostly meant being polite. Getting angry with a friend would almost always mean an end to the relationship."[12] Karen commented on the conflict she and Jennifer had recently passed through: "Just because there are conflicts, then that means that it's not going to work out. And we were having a conflict that made me think that our friendship isn't going to work out." The fact that both Bob and Karen feared the ending of relationships when faced with conflict accentuates the serious nature of the desire to avoid discomfort.

Lee Mun Wah and Jennifer both see this avoidance of difficult emotion as being a particular feature of white culture. Lee Mun Wah spoke of a general avoidance of discussing feelings:

> I think a cocktail [party] is actually my same experience of most white people around the country . . . I don't think that the white folks talk about how they feel. I don't think white males talk about how they feel up front. I don't think they deal with it too often. It's what they do or what they're thinking or sharing information. But it's not always how they're feeling.

Yet Jennifer went even farther. She said that whiteness "means Kum-ba-ya. Only poor white people or white people who have had a major struggle in their life are open to talking about conflict."

Certainly, then, there are plenty of whites that enjoy very open, deep relationships. However, the tendency to avoid conflict on a large scale has serious implications for cross-race relationships. What do we believe about conflict? Can we transform our understanding so that we see how conflict can be beneficial and be more honest with our friends and family? Or will we continue to respond by shutting down, fearing the breakdown of the relationship?

Jennifer discussed her own relationship to the emotional ease she experiences when visiting white spaces with her friend Karen. Jennifer said, "I love the life [Karen] leads because of the ease of it. But the ease of it is a trap as well." Jennifer went on to explain, in two particularly illustrative sections, how this avoidance of difficulty proves problematic.

> You don't discuss tough issues. You can talk about plays and dinner and the last meal and the last movie and good, good things that happen to you. But bad, bad things that happen to you, you don't get the impression that anyone would want to hear it and sit with it. So it's very esoteric, very sanitized . . .
>
> It seems that white, middle-class to upper-class Americans have a persona, or a way of being, that does not include conflict or discomfort. So that means that language is censored. Behavior is censored. Ways of being are censored and censored sometimes to the detriment of those who enact these things, and because the investment in normalcy far outweighs the investment in the human condition in all its complexity, the human condition gets sacrificed.

This last part of Jennifer's statement is really striking because it asks us to acknowledge that this surface approach might injure more than only the white people involved.

It is one thing for me to reflect on the myriad ways that my family rests stoic in the face of challenge and withholds information to protect younger members from anxiety. I even remember my father telling me that I did not have to go to my grandfather's hospital bedside because he thought it might upset me. My grandfather died, and my father then questioned whether or not I should go to his funeral. I was sixteen at the time, and all too socialized to accept this caretaking, excuse-making allowance to be self-centered.

But I had never thought about what it would be like to be involved in that type of "sanitized" and "protected" space for people who are used to really digging in to the difficulties friends and families face. It makes sense that the same level of attention to discuss challenging topics would also arise in cross-race relationships in our social, school, and work settings.

If our friends of color push us to alter our patterns and really speak openly and honestly about difficult topics, we might scapegoat them as the problem in the situation, see them as the instigators of conflict, and minimize their concerns in order to support a false sense of emotional calm. If our fellow travelers are right, that white people tend to avoid hard conversations more often, this pattern is highly destructive. People of color can end up being demonized and shut down, and white people can move ahead without even knowing that they played a role in damaging relationships. Being able to witness moments when this occurs and naming it would be a very valuable skill.

Cayce also questioned the relationship white culture has with conflict and difficulty. Her analysis of the situation relates to Jennifer's in that she sees how whites often avoid tackling tough emotional issues:

> I feel that among white culture and white friendships a lot of times there is not a depth, that you don't have the depth of emotion. People stop before they get to the part that is scary . . .
>
> So for me to be in the midst of Amanda's family, going just about as deep as I'd seen family members go with each other, not just feeling emotion, but being honest and really working with each other, that is something that, to my mind, white culture has to learn . . . And I think it's one of the biggest problems in white culture, that we don't do that. We support each other, but tidy, clean.

Cayce critiques what she sees within her own family, a tidiness and lack of depth that inhibits honesty and a real working through of familial problems. I would love to say that I believe that this is isolated to Cayce's family. However, her description sounds a lot like the way my family handles difficulty, and my white friends and colleagues often admit the same. Of course this does not characterize *all* white families. But if we do find that this is a fair assessment of our individual and collective selves in some way, we really have to spend some time reflecting on what else this might mean in terms of our ability to form healthy relationships across race.

Cayce also links the ideas of being disconnected and superficial with the way white people deal with our U.S. history.

> My theory about why we're this way in America is, how can you possibly live in a country where for 200 years you're enslaving a huge portion of your population and not have some kind of emotion? You have to put a lid on it. Otherwise, you couldn't be human and stand it, right? So I think that in this country we've learned to cover the bad things with really pretty things and that we don't show it when we fall apart.

Cayce's analysis fits with my earlier study of psychology. If people in a society must renounce their perception of injustice in order to avoid danger to themselves, the effect is "percepticide," the killing off of one's own perceptions and knowledge.[13] Our society generally reacts harshly against those who offer damning critiques of our country. Some white people choose percepticide in order to shut down the cognitive dissonance of living with contradictions that we simply cannot resolve.

When those in our surroundings cannot witness, cannot tolerate seeing the pervasive injustice around them, and cannot hear our testimony, our own perceptions become silenced and pushed into the shadows. Michael also spoke of this defensive position.

Imagine the ignorance of a culture that can take pride in not knowing and not learning, the damage done inside the oppressing people and their families. Because in order to sustain these ultimately nonviable ideas, something has to be killed off in those who continue them. People can only hold a false sense of superiority by remaining undeveloped and unrealized inside themselves.

Cayce and Michael's comments raise two issues. First, has our collective history left white people less able to deal with our emotional pains openly? Have we shut down our perceptions in order to live within a racist environment for so long that we have become numb in general, habituated to covering over the pain residing just under the surface?

Second, how does this affect our approach to historical knowledge? It seems to me that the idea of acknowledging the fullness of past traumas sparks fears that our country might not survive the process intact. No wonder, then, that white society generally avoids looking at the past. It also starts to make sense why being white is associated with an orientation that privileges a view toward the future.

Lee Mun Wah notes, "Western thought doesn't think of the past. It only thinks of the past if it is relevant or useful for the future; otherwise, it is of no use to them."

Michael sums up how the consistent striving of whiteness, the avoidance of anything that might get in the way, complicate, or delay progression, results in an inability to value difficult, conflict-ridden, and deep emotional understandings:

> in trying to speed ahead, it attempts to distance from the past, which is imagined as primitive, rather than primal, ancient, resourceful, and deep. Thus, "white culture" remains surface-oriented, superficial, obvious, lacking shading and soulful nuance. In avoiding the natural drops into the primal, it becomes primitive and brutal just when meaningful change might occur.

This consistent movement forward also plays a role in what is sometimes called historical amnesia. This is related to the contemporary approach to our own legacy that seeks to deny the continuing effects of historical and contemporary racism.

These aspects of whiteness, both the isolation and superficiality, figure prominently in the minds of many of those interviewed. Clearly, this is a tremendous critique, a painful one at that. These deeper, more personal meanings are important. We cannot simply attend to them for the sake of our relationships with people of color. In order for our vision of how being white affects us to become consistent and penetrating, we have to honestly ask ourselves, to what degree are our lives characterized by feelings of isolation and disconnection and an effort to avoid difficult dialogues?

Symbolic Meanings of Whiteness

James Hillman is a contemporary psychologist who has written about the fallacy of white supremacy.[14] In a lecture by Hillman, Bob learned about the history concerning how the use of colors as symbols came together with the unfortunate laying of those color symbols onto human beings in ways that resulted in the devaluation of dark-skinned peoples.[15] Once he learned of this, Bob began to reject much within our common vernacular that unconsciously builds upon symbolic imagery linking blackness with things our culture rejects and represses.

Bob talked about how he and a friend responded to this new knowledge:

> Because in all these cultures the color black was associated with evil and dull-ness and so on and the color white was purity and intelligence even in African cultures. But it was always, the colors were always cast upon archetypes of evil, not human beings . . . And so all these archetypal images of black were suddenly projected onto a race of human beings. And if that were true and all the images belonged to those human beings, then of course there could be racism and of course there could be invasions and colonizations.
>
> It was very interesting . . . We were in a conversation one time and I had just heard this at a lecture by Hillman. Malcolm [a Project Return cofounder] was still in prison . . . And when I told him about this thing that Hillman said, he told me, "Yeah, I used to be called the black sheep in the family. I was the black sheep." So, we kind of agreed, we didn't use that term anymore just to discipline ourselves from that kind of thought. To get away from it, we didn't use black to describe anything.

Bob told me that his conscious avoidance of using the word *black* to mean anything that might carry a negative connotation lasted for a significant period of time. He said that recently he found himself "beyond all of that" in certain areas. For example, he again uses the word *black* in a particular poem he likes to recite. For years, he replaced the original word *black* with *dark*. He believes that to some degree blackness has returned to the mythic, symbolic layer in his thinking, but not fully. This is something that continues to plague him.

Michael's discussion of the symbolic meanings of the term *white* also builds upon the work of James Hillman, and Malcolm X as well. Michael helps us see the way that religious images and symbols involve the mistaken use of the color white as a descriptor for a human being.

> Well, I remember Malcolm X writing of when he was in jail and started to study the meaning of words like *white* and *black*. White means pure. White tends to mean clean. It can mean high and bright, up where the light shines . . . He started working at racial ideas from there.

James Hillman has a good essay on that, the fallacies of white supremacy, the danger of identifying with whiteness as a natural indication of supremacy. The angels are depicted with white wings, so someone declares that their kind of white skin makes them an angel and the devils can be identified by their darkness, the incredible fallacy of taking things on the basis of appearances. White appearance is taken to mean being elevated and chosen by the light and Lord and heaven. Then, the most powerful person in the land lives in the White House. White is elevated, on top and in charge.

It's interesting, philosophically and in the history of symbols, that white often does have superior qualities attributed to it. In many parts of Africa, white means ancestors and the ancestors are the source of dreams and meaningful visions. But when they married the symbolic idea of white as elevated, pure, clean to the appearance of certain people, a historical literalism became the basis of opportunism and colonialism.

We live with the continuing complicated effects of those erroneous ideas. It's part of the disease of literalism and the people who have the worst case of it are those who believe in self-serving simplicities that make things "black and white." Claiming to "be white" makes them the elect, superior, chosen children of God.

If we reflect on this last part of Michael's statements, it is likely that this history of symbolism and the way avowed racists link purity, goodness, and whiteness together also feeds white people's tendency to avoid naming ourselves as white. With so many meanings of whiteness conveyed explicitly critiquing white culture, it is not hard to understand our reticence. This is precisely why it is helpful to create an explicitly *antiracist* white identity that serves social justice and works against oppression. Since is seems clear that being white has not been associated with antiracism and equity in the past, this approach can give us room to develop a completely different way of being white.

A CLEARER VISION, A DEEPER CONNECTION

White people in general are not known for questioning (1) how we receive unearned privilege in our daily lives and (2) how whiteness marks our environments. For this reason, people of color are often rather surprised, if not shocked, when encountering white people who are adept at (1) naming white privilege and other manifestations of whiteness and (2) speaking clearly about how and why it continues to play a role in institutions.

Let me restate more clearly, the purpose of becoming better witnesses of whiteness is not to ingratiate ourselves with people of color. This is not about being redeemed or validated. Instead, people need to be clear that when we can witness the whiteness present in our surroundings, we let people know that we can be a part of conversations that most white people generally avoid, defend against, or deny. We take a step forward in our individual and collective healing process by being more available for deep, honest dialogue. We enjoy a measure of freedom previously unavailable; we choose how to relate to our whiteness.

If we choose to challenge prior patterns and begin to connect more deeply with exiled feelings, challenging whatever tendency we might have toward disconnection or superficiality, we increase our capacity to create more open and honest relationships. In some ways, our ability to witness white privilege may offer validation for the experiences of the people of color in our lives. At other times, our increased vision may help to build trust, connection, and mutual sharing. In either case, when white privilege can be named and discussed as a real factor affecting people's lives, the doorway opens for an entirely new ability to relate.

To imagine, however, that this path is easy would be a mistake. At some point we are likely to find ourselves at a crossroads where we are called to make significant breakthroughs if our relationships are to deepen and our understanding of self is to be enhanced. The next chapter explores conflict and the challenges we face when confronted with remaining blind spots.

NOTES

1. Moore, S., and R. Fields, "The Great 'White' Influx." *Los Angeles Times Online,* July 31, 2002, http://www.uwm.edu/%7Egjay/Whiteness/latimesarticle.htm.

2. Haney Lopez, I. F., *White by Law: The Legal Construction of Race* (New York: New York University Press, 1996), 96.

3. Hartigan, Jr., J., "Locating White Detroit" in *Displacing Whiteness: Essays in Social and Cultural Criticism,* ed. R. Frankenberg (Durham, NC: Duke University Press, 1997), 204:

However whiteness may be regarded at the level of greatest expanse [ideology, for instance], no continuous motivating or informing impulse can be traced down through the various levels of increasing specificity with absolute consistency. Nor . . . can we compile a more or less thorough aggregate of whites, abstract out of them a common condition or an intrinsic set of connections, and have neatly defined by these efforts a succinct, abiding identity—whiteness.

4. Giroux, H. A., "Postcolonial Ruptures/Democratic Possibilities," in *Border Crossings: Cultural Workers and the Politics of Education,* ed. H. A. Giroux (New York: Routledge, 1992).

5. Lipsitz, G., *The Possessive Investment in Whiteness: How White People Profit from Identity Politics* (Philadelphia, PA: Temple University Press, 1998).

6. Vanderryn, *A Qualitative Analysis of the Meaning of Being White American.*

7. McIntosh, P., "White Privilege: Unpacking the Invisible Knapsack," in *Peace and Freedom* (Philadelphia, PA: Women's International League for Peace and Freedom, 1989).

8. Cushman, P., *Constructing the Self, Constructing America: A Cultural History of Psychotherapy* (New York: Addison-Wesley, 1995).

9. Putnam, R., *Bowling Alone: The Collapse and Revival of American Community* (New York: Simon & Schuster, 2000), 280.

10. Putnam, *Bowling Alone,* 359.

11. Tarnas, R., *The Passion of the Western Mind: Understanding the Ideas That Have Shaped Our World View* (New York: Ballantine Books, 1991).

12. Roberts, *My Soul Said to Me,* 10.

13. Lorenz and Watkins, "Silenced Knowings, Forgotten Springs," 3; their use of the concept of "percepticide" is taken from Diana Taylor, *Disappearing Acts* (Durham, NC: Duke University Press, 1997).

14. Jordan, W. D., in J. Hillman, "Notes on White Supremacy: Essaying an Archetypal Account of Historical Events," *Spring* 46 (1986): 29–58.

15. Jordan, W. D., *White over Black* (Baltimore, MD: Penguin, 1969), 11.

Chapter 6

Blindness at the Crossroads

Leaps of Faith

On a warm day toward the close of my first semester of teaching, after hurriedly leaving my classroom, I waited. I sat in my car at the top of the hill and waited. We were to have met at 3 o'clock that afternoon and at 4 o'clock I continued to wait. My friend's phone went unanswered and, for reasons too complicated to describe, I was unable to approach the door and search for him. I moved between worry and anger, yet knew intuitively that his tardiness was not due to any physical emergency. At one point I almost left, my annoyance having reached its breaking point. This was my first year teaching, and the way I spent each hour of each day was carefully allotted. I bemoaned having left textbooks and to-be-graded papers at school, believing the day would be too filled for the completion of that work. I was therefore unable to use that waiting time to prepare the following week's activities and plans.

Righteous anger over my friend's rudeness filled me as I saw him slowly saunter down the path from his house and approach my car, and especially as he sat down in the passenger seat, offered a nonchalant greeting, and waited for us to move. I was incensed. For a while I stewed in my own boiling juices. Not too long later, my critique emerged and along with it came my insistence that I was owed an apology and that nothing could excuse what he had put me through.

This was my colleague, my mentor, and my friend. I was invested in this relationship in important ways. We supported each other's efforts at the school site, shared important insights regarding staff, brainstormed strategies to move forward, and he helped me understand the students and parents. Through what had often been difficult exchanges, I had learned a lot about myself. I valued him immensely and genuinely tried to understand our differences. But this went beyond acceptable treatment.

We fought. Even after an hour of painful arguing, neither of us was ready to let go of our positions. Frustrated to tears, I could hardly contain myself when he linked my felt sense of injury with my being white. After all of this time, after all the work I had done, how in the world could my whiteness have anything to do with this? His critique appeared nonsensical. He was rude, plain and simple. He was late. I was on time. Then he started questioning me about my experience of the situation, what meaning I had made of having to wait, and how that influenced my emotions. All the while, I was seething with the knowledge that at least to some degree he had acted unjustly.

However, once I made the choice to put my need for an apology to the side and dedicate myself to figuring out what merit his perspective held, things began to shift. Slowly, I started to see that maybe he had a point. The truth is that I had taken the lateness as a personal affront. I had privileged the schedule we were to keep over the relationship he was preserving as he kept me waiting. It took some time for it to become clear. But, in the end, I finally came to realize that my cultural upbringing did, in fact, have at least something to do with my reaction.

The importance my culture placed on time, my anxiety over productiveness, and my prioritized values were issues for me. Although I never gave up my sense that at least some apology was in order, letting it go for a time allowed me to see deeper into myself in a valuable way. Now, even though I avoid being late as much as possible and remain as productive as ever, I have a completely different experience when having to wait. There is an internal shift that I can make in order to operate from a different perspective, one that I have come to value. Looking back on that experience, and many others like it, I recall how hard it was to stay in the situation, wanting so badly to escape with my righteous justification. And yet, there is wisdom gained from having stayed to work through the difficulty.

Courageously choosing to engage the journey toward witnessing whiteness entails continually bumping into our blind spots. What do we still not see about ourselves? How are we supposed to respond to critique? Just as with our literal eyesight, there are gradations to our capacity to see ourselves clearly. This can pose serious problems. We operate amidst a sea of relationships and we need to be able to communicate effectively and consider the needs of our friends and colleagues.

Although we might already have some really deep and meaningful relationships across race, it can be helpful to remind ourselves that everyone has different needs and sensitivities. Learning more about some frequent patterns of conflict can help us as we form new and deeper cross-race relationships and collaborations. For this reason, this chapter focuses on the more subtle side of relationship maintenance.

We must first remind ourselves of the general experience of dis-ease that white people often have about race and what happens once we have begun to take up work to come to terms with that discomfort. Oftentimes, white people taking this journey can become haughty with satisfaction, as though there is nothing left to learn. We consciously eschew racism and even act against it, so what is the problem now? When we are at this stage of consciousness, we might become resistant to the idea that we continue to enact problematic behaviors that come from our experience as white people.

The conflicts that then erupt can indicate that we hit a blind spot. We might get challenged within a meeting or in a one-on-one situation with a friend or colleague. At times, we might find out through the grapevine that someone has taken offense to something we said or did. The commentary may appear unfair, characterizing our entire being as problematic. At those moments, we are at a crossroads. How do we take the criticism? What do we do with the information? Do we excuse our need to listen to the critique if we decide that the person challenging us is speaking from his or her own unresolved issues? Do we criticize the approach to avoid the content?

At these moments we might consider stopping to take a breath in a gesture of openness for support. Just as ancient people once erected poles at intersections with three masks hanging from them in order to pay homage to Hecate's all-encompassing vision and ask for her guidance to choose the correct path, we may need to admit that we need help in deciding how to move forward in a way that honors each person's experiences and perspectives, wounds and understandings.

One of the difficulties we face is that our history has left each racial group in a general, but varying, state of distress. If white people expect their friends and colleagues of color to offer perfect explanations absent of emotion in order for us to pay attention, we will continue to make excuses to escape from painful, yet potentially revealing, dialogue. The eruption of conflict is the heat and fire we must learn to withstand. Sometimes the message might come with the clean precision of a welder's tool that can cut through our blindness. More often than not, however, we might find ourselves awash in a firestorm.

The guides presented in this chapter have been in that fire. One has been burned, two only tinged—but each finds a way to either stay in, or reengage, the dialogue. The intent of this chapter is twofold. First, offering these stories is an attempt to illustrate why our ability to remain in deep connection cross-racially depends upon us witnessing ourselves. Second, these stories highlight the need for us to humbly sit in the discomfort of conflict, however it manifests, in order to find the learning we require for our own healing, the continuation of our relationships, and the improved effectiveness of our social justice efforts. These moments of conflict require not only courage but also leaps of faith.

Moving through these relationship crossroads can bring us incredible learning. Yet this work of developing and maintaining cross-race relationships often requires working through issues such as anger, conflict management, feelings of guilt and shame, and personal racism if they are to thrive.[1] The three pairs of friends presented courageously allow us to peer into their moments of challenge. For Karen and Jennifer, the conflict is at its height through the interview process, the narrative capturing the turmoil and eventual healing gestures. For Spencer and Lee Mun Wah as well as Dave and William, conflict related to race issues resulted in years-long separations, with resolution coming only after significant learning took place in each other's absence.

I would like to say at the outset that sitting with these friends was not always easy. Empathy grew within me as I listened to them present their truth and sometimes their deep pains surrounding it. As I pieced together their stories, I took note that choosing sides is not the purpose. Neither is offering a cold analysis that ignores the tugs of the heart, the inevitable compassion evoked when the human heart bears witness to another.

The intention here is to be generously honest about what I witnessed and the sense it makes to me. Understandably, some of my suggestions will differ from the felt experience of each individual. But the intent is to offer the essential bits and pieces of their lengthy stories along with some ideas about how these conflicts can help us emerge out from under the shadow of racism.

"WHY DO I ALWAYS HAVE TO BE THE ONE?"

When I invited Karen (white) and Jennifer (African American) to talk with me, they were in the midst of conflict. At the time, this surprised me. I had anticipated discussions of past conflict but imagined that Karen and Jennifer's history of collaboration and friendship would mean race issues were long resolved. After all, they had coauthored a book several years earlier and facilitated workshops together on issues of racism within education.

But from the beginning Jennifer stated her hope that moving through the process with me might offer them an opportunity to work more consciously through their conflict. When I invited Karen to participate, she readily agreed and appeared to see the same value in the process as Jennifer. I met with Karen first. She spoke of the conflict this way:

> Recently Jennifer and I had this huge, probably the most intense experience in our relationship so far, and that is why I flew down [to Los Angeles], to see if

we could keep this thing going. And she said, "You know, you don't have any other Black friends and we've been working together for ten years and that makes me very uncomfortable." And that's probably the first time she's confronted me about being white and being in this little entourage of white friends and family.

When I talked with Jennifer, she also spoke about Karen needing to expand her relationships with people of color. But, for Jennifer the issue was also Karen's long-standing reliance upon her for guidance:

Karen doesn't do the work with the teachers in her class. She says she does, but, for example, over the years, if Karen has an issue with a Black student in her class, she'll call me instead. She won't duke it out with the Black student. I'll say, "Why don't you talk to the Black student?" and she says, "I will." And she never does. But she thinks by talking to me she's fixed it, which isn't true. Ok, the person hasn't changed. You haven't changed because you haven't gone to them. You know. That's doing the work. Not talking to me . . . The moment you take the conflict out from where it happens, you are not doing the work. That's my opinion. So the universe is opening up all these opportunities for you to duke it out and you keep being polite and keep backing up. So I've become a safety net.

Hearing both of them, it became evident that Karen, like many white people learning about race, struggles with several issues: (1) developing additional cross-race friendships, (2) moving away from depending on mentorship from people of color, and (3) embracing conflict as an important element of developing transformative relationships. Each of these helped the conflict between Karen and Jennifer to develop.

Looking at the first issue, Karen was able to name the fears she has about making new cross race friends. She said:

I think I have other potential friends. They are people I really love being with that are African American. It seems like it is reciprocal and I am going to pursue that. But, I have these worries . . . I worry that . . . they will think I have some motive for wanting to be their friend, that there is something I am after. Why would I want to be their friend?

I understand why Karen struggles with this. On one hand, Jennifer told Karen that she should develop more friendships with African Americans and Karen honestly does want to expand her friendship circle. On the other hand, in taking up this advice, Karen recognizes that there is something self-serving underlying an attempt to befriend people of color in her community. Worrying about that, she then begins to imagine what people of color will think and how they will react if they sense Karen's underlying motivation.

This period of increased awareness and effort, without all the requisite skills, is really challenging for white people. We want to break out and experience the world differently, but our new sensitivities often make us fearful of making errors. We also do not want to use people, and yet we cannot escape that there is something targeted about our approach at this point. I faced these same challenges myself.

Revealing for me was one of my best friends reminding me of a time about eight years earlier when I approached her and let her know, quite directly, that I was concerned about my only having men of color in my life and was interested in exploring what was going on with my ability to build relationships with women of color. She then admitted to me how, at that time, she had thought, "Ok, I guess I can help out this white girl. She seems well meaning."

We then began talking more frequently, found areas of commonality, and are now extremely close. Beyond our friendship, our work collaboration involves teacher-education courses, racial justice, and community-building projects. But there was no vision for this at the outset. I had simply decided to confront my own anxiety and, regardless of my newness to these issues and the rejection that might have come, I took the risk to say it out loud to another teacher at my school site.

Admittedly, I had not realized at that time what important insights I would gain by having a close relationship with a Black woman, far different than those from my friendships with men. This additional level of consciousness-raising has been really important for me. And yet, what serves us well is that my friendship is not primarily about her mentoring me. We have a truly reciprocal relationship, one that has been strengthened by the fact that my race work is done in a community of white antiracists, which allows me to learn lessons without depending on my Black friend to be my constant and sole mirror.

This leads us to the second issue facing Karen and Jennifer. A mutually reciprocal relationship has been harder for Karen and Jennifer to develop, in part because Karen depends primarily upon Jennifer to act as a mirror and make Karen conscious of her own actions. Karen spoke of it this way:

> Jennifer was losing patience with me and I didn't understand that. But, I do now . . . I wasn't looking at myself the way she was. "Well, if you want to do these things, why aren't you doing them? What is taking you so long? Maybe you don't really want to do them." But I think I'm just very cautious . . . and I don't want to lose what I have. And I think I am afraid of losing what I have, I think, replacing it maybe with something better. But I don't know that. But she's my conscience in a way. And I feel like African Americans who are my friends, if I have more African American friends, my conscience will be more . . . I'll be more aware of it.

For Jennifer's part, she has always recognized that their conflict has a lot to do with Karen's lack of a regular mirror. She described it this way:

> For me, Karen's life doesn't really include racial conflict. Like she has a life with her husband and family and where she lives, that she could, like many white people in America, avoid dealing with race forever. And so it creates blind spots. And so when she's with me and I find that something she says or does emanates from that blind spot, whether or not she's conscious of it, I'm just compelled to react and call it. And because she may not be aware of it as a blind spot, her first response is defense, like "Damn, where did that come from?" Because it's like a mirror that she's not accustomed to seeing and feeling and looking into. I represent that. So that, to me, is fundamentally where the issues I have with her still come.

There are a couple of important pieces here that we can use for our learning. First, Karen's ability to see how race shapes her life was limited because her white world rarely offered her feedback about the lingering racism she carried. Jennifer was the sole mirror in this regard, and this was part of Jennifer's frustration.

Also, Jennifer encouraged Karen's belief that increased involvement with African Americans was a primary way to break through her unconscious racism and speed up her learning process. In this way, Jennifer was not only trying to help Karen learn more rapidly, she was also trying to spread the burden around. Sadly, most people of color do not know white people who are aware enough to help mentor other whites into witnessing.

This unfortunate reality underlies my suggestion that we need to create communities of whites who can become our own mirrors. Only by doing this can we stop making friends with people of color for the purpose of seeing ourselves more clearly. Only then can we build cross-race relationships that do not carry the sense that we are using people. Then, we will also be better able to build the type of alliance cross-race relationship necessary to support the real change efforts we need for our communities and institutions.

Beyond the need for Karen to (1) expand her circle to include more people of color and to (2) decrease her dependence on Jennifer to be a primary mentor/mirror, there is one more important difficulty faced by these friends. Recall from the last chapter that a common feature of white culture is the avoidance of conflict and a desire to keep things calm. This tendency is at the heart of the trouble these friends were struggling with at the time of my interview with them.

With tension mounting between Karen and Jennifer, the catalyst sparking their conflict's eruption was a weekend where the pair facilitated a professional development workshop for a group of teachers. During that weekend,

Jennifer realized that within these work settings she was experiencing increasing amounts of frustration. Jennifer described the revelation she had during one particular weekend:

> I was getting so exhausted because Karen, it was getting so vividly clear, she was always on the other side. She and I were never fighting together in any of these spaces. In these spaces she was always over there and whoever I was with was always over here. What I realized, what she said at BayCES [Bay Area Coalition for Equitable Schools] when we were together was that every time I did that, tried to bring up issues, she felt that she had to protect her friends from me.

This prompted Jennifer to question why Karen was not worried about protecting her instead of protecting other white people who might feel threatened or challenged by what she offered. That questioning led to a significant degree of fallout, hurt feelings, difficult dialogues, and a fear on Karen's part that the friendship was all but over.

The conflict also called into question the level of trust Jennifer could enjoy within the friendship. Jennifer said, "I never trusted the relationship. I never trusted that it could care for me because when we met she was so on the other side of truth." This statement made me ask how much this friendship was based on their mutual work versus seeing Karen as a real friend. In answering, Jennifer suggested that a factor was their differing expectations concerning friendship:

> I was starting to see her as 90 percent friend, 10 percent [work colleague]. But, to me, all of the hard, honest conversation I was having was because of the friendship that I was starting to trust. But friendship to her, I think, means Kum-ba-ya. It means we are all good. We have no more problems. I love you, you love me, the Barney song. Friendship to me means we are now at the space where we can talk about the hard, sad, any difficult issue, and we can overcome it because we are friends.

Hearing this, it seemed clear that Jennifer's disappointment with Karen's racially isolated world and the sense of fighting on opposite sides also contributed to Jennifer feeling a sense of stagnation in her professional relationship with Karen. They were at a crossroads.

It wasn't until several months after those initial conversations took place that I was able to sit with both Jennifer and Karen together. Within that time, significant resolution occurred between them. Karen reported on what allowed this to develop:

> When we got together . . . [Jennifer] came up with this great idea of each of us, for an hour, sitting and talking about how we see our life in the next five to ten

years and how we see ourselves separate from each other and with each other. And that was an incredible process because it was just so clear where we crossed paths and where we didn't and how we felt. And I think that neither one of us really knew for sure what the other one was thinking. So to get all of that out in the open, out on the table to look at, was very, very helpful.

This process that Jennifer suggested helped Karen crystallize her thoughts about their future together and her work independent from Jennifer. Karen spoke of how things shifted:

I know now kind of where my path's going to go and who else I can work with and that's underway. So as far as professionally and the relationship we had around racial and cultural differences, I feel that I am diversifying or whatever. I have other outlets. So now it's now more just feeling like we're friends and we'll just get together on that basis . . . The conflict is so hard, but it really helps to clarify and crystallize priorities.

This diversification of Karen's seemed an incredible advancement over her earlier dependence upon Jennifer. This prompted me to ask Karen about what she did during the months between our conversations. Karen credited her reading of Tatum's book *Why Are All the Black Kids Sitting Together in the Cafeteria?* as partly responsible: "That [book] shed a lot of light on what we'd been experiencing and also what I had been, how my thinking had been evolving and shifting and so I feel like, now, I don't need to depend on Jennifer as much."

It was obvious how much that weight had been lifted for Jennifer. Having mutually decided to create a more significant separation between their work as colleagues and their friendship, Jennifer felt more freedom to resist being a mentor within the friendship. Jennifer now can see herself acting simply as a friend to Karen:

I've looked at it and can say our friendship will last unless she says to me one day, "I don't want to be your friend." But my professional journey is *my* professional journey. It's not *our* professional journey. And having come to that conclusion is just so liberating for me because then, for incidents that come up . . . I'll just treat it like I treat a lot of the shit I hear just walking the streets hearing white people talk. If I don't want to say anything, I won't. And if somebody brings something up and asks a question, I can say, "I don't feel like talking about that right now" and feel very comfortable because it's not my profession. I'm in a friendship situation.

But this freedom was not the only thing that satisfied Jennifer. Jennifer continued to feel gratified that even without her guidance, Karen remains committed to working on issues of race on her own. Jennifer told of how important that was to her:

> There are things that she's getting a lot of satisfaction [from] and dealing with the race issue head on. So she could have had the choice to say, "You know what, OK, I did this stuff with Jennifer. I'm going back to Lafayette and I'll say hi to a Black person when I see them. But I don't need this work." And she's continuing to seek it out for her own self, nothing to do with me, and that I appreciate a lot.

It is likely, however, that Karen's shift will take some time to manifest fully.

Although Karen continued to commit to her work and spoke of groups that can help her on her journey, she still felt a sense of trepidation. Karen shared her continuing fears:

> Now when I'm with this group at Holy Names, there's two Black women and two white women. I'm finding that I feel very strange. And I think it's because I feel like on the continuum they are so far ahead of me. And I'm the new kid on the block. I'm putting it out there, but it makes me nervous because, and I'm hoping they'll jump all over me like Kitty [one of the white women] does. But the other two are not quite ready to do that with me yet.

Karen's new inclusion of white people within her mirroring process is striking. Yet it is likely that Karen will continue to feel overwhelmed by the sheer vastness of what there is to learn if she continues to see the primary work as learning about the experiences of "others."

When I first sat with Karen several months earlier, I noticed that she only spoke of African Americans. I had asked if her increasing awareness transferred to more appreciation for what other people of color go through. Karen responded:

> I just don't believe that I have the energy or the time to really at this point, to really learn as much about the Latino experience . . . I don't have the time because I am spending so much time learning about, reading about, African American history and current experiences and so on. I just can't do it right now.

Months later, it appeared that Karen saw that her whiteness deserves focus.

Karen was then able to reflect and note that the first time she read Peggy McIntosh's material, specifically the article "Unpacking the Invisible Knapsack," she felt that it did not pertain to herself: "It didn't apply to me necessarily. I don't know why, but I think that's what happens all the time. Things are intellectualized, but you don't really see yourself in it or think about it that much." At this point, Karen sees that part of her difficulty seeing her own whiteness involves the life she leads in which there is little opportunity for her to be confronted with her lingering racism or enactments of privilege.

I was struck by the vast difference in Karen's perspective. Whereas a few months earlier she concentrated upon learning about "others," she now appears dedicated to learning how issues of white privilege affect her life. Karen said:

> The conflict we had really had racial implications. It had to do a lot with the white privilege idea and phenomenon. And that [conflict] just doesn't exist [between] my white friends [and me] . . . And I guess I'm learning all the time about myself, about being white and what that means in a multiracial society. And when conflicts come up they are painful, but they are painful in that they are teaching me that I've got issues that I've got to address and to explore and so they're kind of . . . it's not like I have to decide whether I can stay friends. It makes me want to be friends more because I want to change. I want to be different. And [Jennifer] can't be the only one who helps me with that, but she's a very important part of that. And that's very valuable to me in addition to other aspects of our relationship.

If fully embraced as Karen becomes more aware of herself, she may also find an increased ability to relate to all people of color within our society when she is able to operate from an antiracist perspective more consistently.

To help support this shift in focus, Karen might turn to an article written by Andrea Ayvazian and Beverly Daniel Tatum for support.[2] Within the paper, Ayvazian, a white woman, shares what she has learned through her experience of friendship with Tatum. She writes:

> In the end, I believe the issue for me is how I have come to understand social, political, and economic power and my unearned advantage and privilege as a white woman in a racist society. I believe the strongest things that I bring to our friendship, our relationship, and our connection is an understanding of the significance of my own Whiteness. I come at long last to our relationship with an understanding of my Whiteness, something that for several decades, I was helped to not see or to not recognize its significance. It is my understanding of my own Whiteness, not my response to her Blackness, that allows me to interact with Beverly in a way that continues to foster mutuality, connection, and trust.

I know this has been essential in maintaining my relationships with at least one of the Black friends I made during my years at the elementary school. In fact, one of them openly states that I am her only white friend and that she believes the reason she trusts me is because of the work I do surrounding antiracist white identity with AWARE-LA. As a Black nationalist, she feels that she is "coming out" to some of her Black sisters when she admits my role in her life and our closeness. This sense of trust, that I am doing the work I need to do to understand the role whiteness plays in my own life, facilitates our ability to collaborate on many projects.

Returning to Karen and Jennifer, even if this understanding of how whiteness plays its role takes time to fully develop for Karen, the love these two women share, combined with the decreased focus on Karen's progress as part of Jennifer's professional work, will likely support their relationship as it continues. Interestingly, as this book moves into its second edition, one update on this pair is that they recently completed a new book that builds upon their previous work. I surmise that the careful way this pair moved through their conflict, and the resulting shift in Karen's dedication to take up her own learning about her whiteness, aided in the continuation of their professional relationship. Their example offers us much to consider, such as:

- How often does your life ask you to see yourself through a racial lens?
- To what degree do you depend on people of color to help you see how being part of your race affects you?
- Do you value the idea of developing relationships that you know will be growth inducing, but challenging?

Beyond all the particular lessons this story offers, Karen and Jennifer's experience illustrates how living a segregated social life can inhibit our ability to see how being white shapes our lives and highlights that conflict and disconnection are likely if we are not aware of how being white affects our interactions.

"YOU DON'T GET IT!"

My first meeting with William (African American) took place in a crowded courtyard at the UCLA Medical Center during his lunch break. Even with the constant din surrounding us, William was absolutely focused during our conversation. This was in sharp contrast to my individual conversation with his friend Dave (white), whom I met at his apartment. Dave was in constant motion, moving here and there, showing me this and that, all while talking hurriedly about a variety of subjects that could be interwoven with the questions I posed.

The conflict story between William and Dave, which this chapter highlights, appeared as an almost-forgotten aspect of their shared history of childhood friendship. The fact of it emerged within each individual conversation almost in an off-hand way, each simply stating matter-of-factly that they lost contact for several years around college. Neither mentioned that race played a role in their time spent apart, although William recounted that he passed through some difficult times during that period. Hearing this piqued my interest since I had wondered why my earliest cross-race friendships seemed to fizzle out, while my friendships with whites remained strong.

Once I prompted William and Dave to discuss themselves in racial terms over the course of their lives, the way race facilitated their separation clarified. As it turns out, William's early college years involved a radical shift in racial identity with him experiencing intense internal conflict. He spoke of the difficulty he faced:

> But, I do have to admit, there almost was like, and W. E. B. Du Bois talked about this. There is almost like a schizophrenia, a duality, that African Americans have to play a lot of times and I really felt it at that time. And I think I was too young . . . So it was harder for me to be able to reconcile the two faces . . . You live in the African American world and you live in the white world too. And there are different faces, there are different interactions, and there are different perceptions that you have in both. And it's easier to reconcile them as you become an adult. You have more experiences. You have more ways of . . . either confronting or either appreciating, or either ignoring these types of issues versus when you are a child, which I basically was. I was still a child. I was an adolescent.

Even though William's parents talked to him about African American history as a youth, his early schooling suggested that race would play no role in society's perception of him. Once at Berkeley, however, the racism he experienced in high school continued and its effects intensified. Although not consciously deciding to discontinue friendships with his white friends, William experienced a period of confusion and anger and a movement away from previously formed white friendships.

As William struggled with the two "faces" while at Berkeley, he tried to explain to Dave what was happening for him. But, at that time Dave was not as sensitive to issues of race and he could not validate William's experiences. William spoke of the frustration he felt at this disjuncture in their understanding at that time:

> Well, there was one thing that really sticks out in my mind. David and I were walking down the street one time. This was in Berkeley . . . we were both dressed the same. We were both college students. But, the Berkeley cop pulls over, ignores David, goes to me and just pats me down, searches me down, an illegal search and seizure right then and there. He just does it right in front of David . . . And I guess David didn't realize until I pointed it out that he searched me completely, that he didn't search David . . . And I got tired of teaching him,

or showing by example, or showing that these things exist. So I think I became more insulated . . . my friends were African American at that time period.

Dave recalls this period as one in which they moved in different worlds:

[William] got to Cal with the summer bridge program, which to my under-standing was essentially all African American folks . . . So by the time I got to Berkeley and tried to meet anyone, he already had a lot of friends and they were all African American . . . But at that point it was clear that there was a friend-ship and there was this commonality based on race which he brought me into as, "This is my friend. This is my homie." And they were all really friendly. It was not like, "Who is this white guy" Nothing like that. But, still there was clearly an element that that was a circle of friends that was not going to be my circle of friends necessarily . . . He had these good friends and I was this friend from the past and there was this disjunction. We would see each other and say "Yeah! Good to see you" but we were in different worlds.

Although he had an African American stepmother and two stepbrothers, Dave had not yet developed an understanding of white privilege and systemic racism. As a result Dave noted racism when confronted, but he did not yet see it as having anything to do with him and was not able to identify it on his own.

When I look back at my own collegiate cross-race friendships I am sure I was even less sensitive than Dave. Sure, I could listen to my teammates discuss racism. But, I became uncomfortable hearing their frustration. I felt identified with "those white people" who were the subject of complaints. I had no idea how to be in a meaningful conversation about race and I am quite sure that this contributed to a disconnection between us that grew wider over time.

To hear both Dave and William think back and piece events together, there was no major outburst, no particular event that led to their loss of contact, no apology required, no reconciliation needed to pick up again. Looking back, what they recall most is the tension within their interactions over what William perceived and Dave did not:

William: There were limitations. We didn't have the tools to communicate. At least I didn't have the tools to communicate what I was actually going through too. There was no other way other than showing you by example when something would happen. But then again, I wasn't able to admit the pain that I was going through as well too that just wasn't part of being a 17-year-old guy trying to be a man, not be-ing comfortable with who I am and my feelings. But, those were some painful times man. Candie [a mutual high-school friend who is white] and I were really close. For me to lose my friendship with Candie and I lost my friendship with lots of people.

Dave: Really?

William: Yeah, losing my friendships from high school. It was a lot. It was at that time that I think I started becoming a loner. Before I wasn't really a loner. I had a group of people, different people . . . But, I guess what I'm trying to say is, I think I was telling people "these are things that you are not experiencing. And I'm having a much different experience than for you."

Dave: . . . I remember that stuff you were saying about "I'm going through stuff that you can't get" and my attitude was "That's a bunch of bullshit. I can get it. In fact, I do get it." Well, he'd be like, "No. You don't get it." and then we were probably both right and wrong in pieces of it. So, yeah, at that time there was a lot of frustration in our interaction.

Dave and William then lost contact for a good period of time. Looking back at my own experience, although I have never sought out my long-lost friendships with past teammates, I imagine the conversations could be similar to that of William and Dave. There might be tales of frustrating interactions to which I was insensitive, no overt argument, and an eventual loss of contact over time due to a growing disconnect.

But, one thing I am sure of is that if I did not see how white privilege manifests in my life I would not even be able to start that conversation with them after all these years. Dave mentioned that it took him years before a significant change occurred in his racial awareness. Recall from Dave's introduction that this insight began during his graduate school years when he worked at a listener-sponsored radio station known for its ties to social activism.

This experience opened Dave to seeing how race played a role in his life in terms of white-skin privilege. It sparked a deep consideration of what it means to be white and how to negotiate this territory in order to create coalitions with people of color. Having thoroughly invested himself in this new awareness, he now actively commits himself to undermining white supremacy and privilege.

Although Dave is prolific on the subject of white privilege and dedicated to efforts to dismantling racism, he appeared skeptical of the idea that his recognition of white privilege plays any role in the sustenance of his friendship with William. True, the two were childhood friends at a school where issues of race were perceived as almost nonexistent. True, they were friends long before Dave came into a political and racial understanding.

Yet, they also lost contact for several years during a time when William came to understand himself in racial terms. This made me question William on how important it is that Dave perceives whiteness as he does. At first, William said he didn't think Dave's advocacy against white supremacy is really that significant within the friendship:

> I think that if we didn't have that common, that advocacy, that I would be able to talk with him as freely about my research . . . But, I think that at the point that I am in my life right now . . . it would not have mattered if [Dave] was an advocate.

He attributed this to having "reconciled the faces to know where [he] stands," contrasting his current position to his youth when a former professor described him as the epitome of James Baldwin's "angry young man." In this way, William checked himself to see if he needs Dave to be conscious of privilege and found himself far enough along in his own racial identity awareness to know when to teach and when to let an issue go.

Yet, as William continued to ponder the question, he began to note the benefit of Dave's current perspective:

> It's good for me to hear these ideas coming from his perspective, and hearing things that I believe in coming out of his mouth without being prompted, too. And I know that if we were placed in that situation again . . . back in Berkeley, where I was being searched and he wasn't being searched, that I wouldn't have to point it out to him. So, I know that for a fact and I know that we probably would have said something to the policeperson at that time. And now, yeah, yeah, I mean I'm trying to think, is that beneficial? Yeah, it definitely is because it's healthy. It's not like I have to keep part of my life away from David, which I had to do with some of my other friends.

It seemed that William became more convinced about the importance of Dave's perception of whiteness and privilege as we talked. Finally, I asked, "*Do* [your white friends] need to be taking up responsibility [for white privilege] to feel like a really solid friend for you?" William responded, "You know, I guess instinctively now, yes . . . I guess the answer to your question is a simple yes."

A couple of things struck me. First, I began to wonder about my current friendships with people of color who dedicate themselves to their communities. I went home and asked them about their circles of friends. As it turns out, I am one of a very few white friends for most of them. For one in particular, I am her only white friend. Similar to my experience with William and Dave, however, upon initial inquiry none of my friends of color said that our friendship depends upon my ability to see my own white privilege. However, once I started asking more direct questions, the importance of witnessing surfaced. We have more in common because I am sensitive to what they experience.

That made me wonder: Is it possible that white people's ability to witness racism can be important to cross-race friendships even without either friend's conscious awareness? The second thing that struck me was that William's newfound awareness is not one that Dave and William ever shared. Now I needed to know what Dave would think of William's recognition.

Weeks later, when I sat in conversation with both men, I returned to this subject so that we might see what Dave had to say about William's new revelation. Dave immediately engaged the subject with a dismissal of its relevance within their friendship saying, "I don't think my consciousness of it has ever been foundational for our friendship." At that point Dave was up and moving about his apartment and I noticed a look of seriousness cross William's face. He called Dave back over to sit down and speak face to face. William began to talk about how the term "white privilege" emerged over time and then let Dave know how important it really is that he sees issues of privilege as he does:

William: This is an important point as well. Because I don't think there was a term like white privilege, although it was talked about in some books, certainly in Black Rage. But, everything was couched in the perspective as, focusing on what was happening to African Americans or people of color or poverty and then saying what white people had done or whites could do. But, it wasn't the idea that white persons had to be responsible for themselves in terms of trying to figure out what racism has done. It's always been, "white people had to stop doing the racism," which is activities.

Dave: Right. And as long as you were not actively doing it then you were cool.

William: Right. But, not having to account for what you benefited from indirectly from that . . . So, that's what I think was the frustrating thing was trying to point out there were certain things that you were privy to, or getting, that you and I were in similar situations, similar backgrounds, similar reward systems, but things were happening different, man, for whatever reason.

Dave: There was a whole class of things that I didn't have to pay any attention to.

William: And that was freaking me out.

Dave: I remember there were times when you would try to talk to me about it, but I would kind of go off . . . [saying] "I didn't do it."

William: So, what I was saying in my interview is that I have appreciated that idea that you do, or were able, to "get it," that I don't have to go back and try to analyze stuff . . . I don't like feel like teaching it anymore. I got tired of that . . .

Dave: And being told, "No. Aren't you overdoing it a little?"

William: Right, and showing by example. I get tired of that shit. You know,
            why do I have to do this? I'm trying to live my own life too. So, I'm
            not as tolerant as I used to be in terms of my friendships now or my
            interaction with others right now. I'm not even a three strikes and
            you're out person anymore. I might give you like a strike and a bunt.
            Or a foul tip and that's it.

Even though neither of these men imagined that the recognition of white
privilege had anything to do with the sustenance of their friendship, it is an
important part of what allows them to stay connected. For William especially,
he can disclose fully with Dave because of Dave's understanding, which
increases the depth of their relationship.

For William, who is devoted to reducing the damaging effects bred from
racism, hearing Dave bring up white privilege on his own is helpful. This
reminds me of an essay titled *Crazy Sometimes* wherein Leonard Pitts,
Jr. discusses the disparity in attention to issues of race among blacks and
whites. He writes, "It has been suggested—and fairly so, I think—that black
people spend entirely too much time talking about race. That we interject it
into situations where it has no business, use it to explain slights that could just
as easily be explained in other ways. I can tell you why we do: It's because
this thing makes us crazy sometimes. Race, I mean."[3]

He goes on to tell stories related to the infecting and incensing experience
of living with racism and having it overlooked and denied by whites. He
points to the various statistics simultaneously supporting both the position
that progress has been made *as well as* the position that racial injustice has
not been overcome, acknowledging the truth of them both. Then he con-
cludes, "the truth is this: Black people spend way too much time talking about
race. And white people don't spend nearly enough."[4]

To me, this is a key point. My friendships do not revolve around race issues
between us. But, race regularly comes up. It surfaces often because I bring
it up when I see its ugly manifestations. But, sometimes my friends of color
raise the issue as part of venting about their personal experiences. Important
is that when this occurs, they have relatively little fear that I will invalidate
their experience. In terms of William and Dave, Dave's continuing attention
to issues of white privilege also goes against the tendency for white people
to ignore issues of race.

Recall what William said about his exhaustion from teaching, that as an
adult white people will probably only get a chance to mess up maybe once or
twice before he dismisses them. The adult friendship these two men share
depends on Dave being able to perceive what William understands about
the world in terms of race issues. Were it not for this capacity of Dave's, the

separation might have continued. Even though there is little fire to speak of within this example, and seemingly no major challenge in the present, William and Dave highlight for us that sometimes it is the slow burn of unacknowledged tension that destroys our ability to relate. As we come to the end of their story, you might stop to consider:

- Do you have any long-term cross-race friendships that continue to this day? If so, have you discussed what it means for you to be a person of your race and what it means for that person to be a person of theirs?
- If you have never had a long-term cross race friendship, why do you think this is so?

"I NEED YOU TO LISTEN!"

We now continue with another story of what can happen when a person of color turns to a white friend for support and the white friend does not have the basis and background to witness the way race plays a role in the situation. This story also highlights what can occur when both people are simultaneously stretched in new ways.

Essential to make clear is that although this text focuses on whiteness, and particularly the need for white people to witness their own behaviors, we cannot lose sight of the fact that people of color also move through their own phases of growth. Ensuring the health of our relationships involves all of us being attentive to the ways that our partners might be moving through discomfort around race issues. We read now about the deep divide that can result when people are not sufficiently skilled at witnessing whiteness and in giving voice to the racial dynamics present in a situation.

Lee Mun Wah, a Chinese American, and Spencer, his white friend, experienced fiery conflict to such a degree that they went years without communicating. Sitting separately with both Lee Mun Wah and Spencer on the same day, meeting each for the first time, I approached the conversations knowing almost nothing of the course of their friendship. After speaking with both individuals, I noticed that their experience of a mutual conflict years ago, one that led to a fallout lasting several years, was neither clarified nor fully resolved. Their stories about the same event were so divergent that I almost felt as though I were hearing about two completely different situations.

For Lee Mun Wah, the conflict between the two had much to do with him finally speaking out about the racism he experienced after many years of staying silent. With an upbringing teaching him to be sensitive to others' feelings, he had little experience directly confronting offensive behavior, such as racist jokes. Lee Mun Wah explained that, "It happened so many times, people joking about it, that I was probably more used to joking with it than fighting until later in my life." Yet this changed during his friendship with Spencer.

Lee Mun Wah's experience with an Asian men's group, as well as other situations that brought racism to the foreground, propelled him out of whatever remained of his learning regarding conforming to white standards. He recalled his first confrontation with Spencer about the racism he experienced within their friendship. He linked this moment with the period surrounding the production and distribution of his documentary film, *The Color of Fear*. Lee Mun Wah explained, "It was *The Color of Fear*, when it finally came out. Because I knew him way long before the film came out. He did ask me, 'Is there anything that I do that you ever find that's racist?' And that's when I told him and his wife, 'Yeah.' I knew they both were shocked."

After years of friendship, Lee Mun Wah finally spoke about racism and how it related to white privilege. As he attempted to integrate what he learned filming the documentary, he approached Spencer about an incident that occurred during the editing of the music for the film.

Spencer, a music composer, helped an African American friend of Lee Mun Wah's edit the song the man wrote for the film. A few days after the work, the friend returned to Lee Mun Wah and complained about the treatment he received from Spencer. Some of the issues included the quality of the final product, an offer of a meal, and a request to spend the night at Spencer's home studio. Lee Mun Wah explained his understanding of the subsequent argument with Spencer and its relationship to his own newfound understanding of white privilege:

And so I simply brought that up to Spencer and he got really upset with me, didn't think any of that was true, and I told him what it meant for me. It was the first really huge, humongous break we had. And I didn't realize at the time that it was occurring, I didn't realize how much anguish I had. And it wasn't necessarily towards Spencer as it was what he represented for me . . . And it became very apparent to me that whatever I saw that he might be reminding me of, the similarities he might have, he did not want to identify with that. And so it became, and I think it escalated to a point where I got really angry and best as I can remember, I would say something and after he would respond I would just get so mad I'd interrupt him. So he felt very abused by me that I had shouted him down . . . I mean it was so bad that we didn't talk for almost five years. He was really pained about it.

For Spencer, the conflict was not about racism as much as it was about his expectations regarding friendship. Spencer offered his side of the story:

I said, "Mun Wah, we've been friends what—ten? fifteen?—years at that point? You of all people would know if I'm a racist. Have I ever done any of these things? Have you witnessed it?" and he goes, "It doesn't matter if I witnessed it or not. He experienced it, so that must be what happened." I said, "Well, where does my word come into any of this?" and he goes, "It doesn't matter. He's the one that experienced it. You need to deal with it." And we couldn't get past this because I said "Mun Wah, I need you to back me up as a friend . . . You've got to see where the line is drawn that if you have a different experience of who I am in the world, and somebody that you want me to work with, then I feel like, as a friend you have to at least hear both sides. In fact, it's best to bring us all three together to work this out. But I hear that you are backing him up just because he is Black and I am not and where are we going to talk about this?"

I didn't get anywhere. And it just got worse from there until finally, I said "I'm sorry, if this is where you're at and you see all these things and are not willing to at least meet me halfway, then something here needs to shift. You are not willing to come to the table." He got really angry. He started screaming at me. I mean screaming, that I owed it to him, that it was my fault that it was all collapsing. No responsibility, zero. So it just dwindled and went out of the picture. That was what actually happened.

This event and fallout occurred during the postproduction phase of the documentary. During that time, the two had no further contact and Spencer did not see how racism or white privilege were part of either the initial difficulty with the musician or the fallout with Lee Mun Wah. At least he did not see it until he viewed the documentary.

Sometime later, Spencer attended the premiere for the documentary and described it as a life-changing experience:

The minute I saw the film I turned around to the people I was with and said, "I never knew I was such a damn racist." I had no idea . . . That fast. Instant. I mean, I got it. And understand, I brought David into this film and I helped Mun Wah put the whole damn thing together and I thought I was doing my part. I didn't come close. When I saw the film and I saw David, when Mun Wah turned to him and said, "Now, what would it really be like if everything they said was true, if it really was true?" . . . David broke. He completely broke. You know, I broke with him. If it is really that way . . . With this knowledge, I could never turn back to turning a blind eye ever again.

Not only did the film show Spencer how he might enact racism, it helped him understand why Lee Mun Wah was so insistent about Spencer hearing the musician's complaints. Spencer recalled the revelation:

When I finally saw the film, I really got that it was important for me to hear [the musician's] pain about feeling discriminated against that day. I had no model for understanding what that meant prior to that. I needed to hear that. Now whether I agreed with it or not doesn't matter. I needed to hear it. And it still doesn't take away the fact that I needed [Lee Mun Wah] to walk in the door side by side with me when we did this. Not taking sides. But, in one phone call I was erased from his friendship. Not by my choice, but by his.

This issue of simply listening, even though you might disagree, is an important one that surfaces regularly within cross-race dialogues. The ability to set our personal belief system aside for a moment and open up to a completely different way of perceiving an issue or event is a skill.

But, as Spencer's story illustrates, we often do not know how important this really is until we have done it and experienced the results. Spencer spoke of his immediate reaction to the documentary and how it changed his life:

That film changed my life. Even though I'd been his friend all these years, it wasn't until I saw the film. It just changed the way I viewed my life . . .

I would still tell off-color jokes pre-film. I won't now. I would think that I wasn't a racist pre-film. Now I know I was 'cause there's no way I could not be with all the training and all the stuff. Yeah, it's just impossible for me not to have been a racist.

Although Lee Mun Wah's film had an impact on Spencer and helped him to better understand their conflict, this did not offset the pain Spencer felt. This is also a theme that runs throughout many difficult interactions across race. Just because we understand something from another's point of view does not mean that the pain we feel if we are misunderstood or injured automatically diminishes.

Spencer spoke of his experience that night at the premiere of the film saying, "I wanted to congratulate him and hug him and do all of those things, but I filed out of there and didn't talk to him for another two years." This is another issue we must face head-on. What do we do when we feel stepped on? Even if we come to see that our racial socialization helped create a problem, how able are we to confront the situation and work through the difficult feelings? Do we avoid the person and ignore the issues? If we can witness how white people very regularly distance ourselves from conflict and then choose instead to stay engaged with our friends and colleagues, we can help salvage many a relationship and collaboration.

Several years after the film premiere of *The Color of Fear,* with Spencer profoundly affected and Lee Mun Wah recognizing his loss, Lee Mun Wah contacted Spencer in an attempt to repair the friendship. At first, Lee Mun

Wah met with significant resistance and trepidation from Spencer. Spencer explained his reticence:

> Well, he called and said, "I really want to heal this. I realize that I have burned an enormous amount of bridges over these last few years and you guys are truly my closest friends that I got. Are you willing to meet with me?" and I said, "I'm scared to death to meet with you because I think you're going to do this all over again. I can't trust you. I don't know where you begin and where you end. You became an egomaniac monster around this film. You are not the person I worked with to help try and make the film, or supported you by helping raise the money, putting all the paperwork together, giving you the farm to record . . . a huge amount of support." This was not the person I knew. I said, "I don't want any part of that person. I don't trust you coming up here because I can see you blowing up and I definitely don't want to go to your house." So I picked a house in the middle, a mutual friend. I was willing to because I really valued this relationship. I wanted to heal it.

Once Spencer had the opportunity to fully express the pain he felt, and have it accepted, the friendship resumed. Spencer described the reconciliation and healing that resulted:

> So when he called and we met, he was very humble and very willing to listen. He'd been doing this for a few other people before he got to me . . . build up I guess [laughs]. I cried. I yelled. I was furious at him. And once I got rid of the anger, then what was left behind that was the pain and the sadness for being taken advantage of in our friendship. Once I said my piece, then he said his piece. And at that point, I felt like we could go to the next step because we had both said what we needed to say and where we had hurt each other.

Hearing from Spencer, I realized that although the pair had moved past this event and the resulting fallout, their interpretations of the core issues leading to the exchange had not been fully shared and resolved.

As my individual conversation with Spencer concluded, I had the sense that for Spencer, although he recognized that it would have been good for him to have listened to the musician tell of his experience, the key issue remained his trauma of being taken advantage of and abused by his friend. Yet Lee Mun Wah's description focused on his own anguish and Spencer's inability to self-identify with racism.

Sitting alone for a few moments, out in the garden, again with a surreal breeze and birds chirping, I prepared for a conversation with both men that was to immediately follow. I knew I needed to ask about this conflict. I felt my own anxiety rise, not sure how sensitive the wounds remained. It seemed clear that there was room for exploration, yet I questioned the degree to which the two men would go willingly into that conversation. Both men returned, sat down, and I asked my standard interview questions regarding the development of their friendships together. They did not speak of their fallout.

My own nervousness caused me to leave my questions about their conflict until the end. As it happened, just at the moment when I announced the issue as a final topic, we had to take a break for a few minutes due to an interruption. We all stood and disengaged awkwardly. I felt the mounting tension during that five-minute lag. Later, Lee Mun Wah and Spencer admitted feeling the same. We then resituated ourselves indoors to continue.

When we finally resumed the conversation, Lee Mun Wah began. What follows is only a small fraction of the dialogue spoken within that conversation. The text offers the most essential points so that you might notice the way the two men find resolution and understanding. It is likely that their current, more advanced understanding of racial identity partly facilitates this:

Lee Mun Wah: I can't speak for Spencer, but I didn't think it was ego for me. I think it was more what Spencer represented for me in the situation and also how much I had never really been able to express my own anguish . . . And also it was the time when I was becoming more able to put words to what I felt. The film gave me words to what I was really feeling that I had no words for . . . But it wasn't as much that I believed [the musician] as much as I wanted him to try and understand why a person of color would feel that . . .

Spencer: . . . I think in our case one thing that you stated later on the phone was that you wanted to hold myself and our relationship as this model for all these new things you were seeing and learning from doing the film. And as much as I felt honored by that, I had nothing to relate, to talk this way. I didn't know what it was to just witness what [the musician] had to say . . . I could not be the person you needed me to be. I think that's where I think you felt even more anger because you wanted to show me as an example . . .

Lee Mun Wah: . . . The reason why it was so important for me to have you meet him was because I thought, and I remembered when I told that I thought how easy it was for white people to choose not to have to deal with this . . . just to have the choice to just walk out of it . . . It was also around that period of time that I got ostracized because I was bringing up this issue.

Spencer: Yes, you were.

Lee Mun Wah: So I was watching how everyone could just avoid me and then how I got ostracized from the group.

Spencer:	First of all, I have to preface a lot of this with this is pre-film . . . I had no context for any of this. None. And I shared it openly post-film how much that I got out of this thing. This is all pre-film.
Lee Mun Wah:	Now the reason he doesn't have pre-film is because I sat in the room. So when I sat in the room and started hearing these things, it started putting words to my whole life experience. And I don't think he sat in the [filming].
Spencer:	No, I wasn't even there.
Lee Mun Wah:	He wasn't even there when we did the filming. So I left with all of these things that, some of these things that weren't even in the film. So it was like carrying this energy.
Spencer:	So, my point here is that this is pre-film. Post-film . . . I could totally see how I needed to witness for him, totally got that. That made perfect sense. Pre-this, there was no context. And there were several things that happened within this whole time, the first reason this really bothered me was, once again, no context of how to be hearing his point. We've got to keep that in mind. I'm coming from this innocent place in my mind, or so I thought.

At this point, Spencer described the various issues the man complained of, refuting their validity, and how Lee Mun Wah wanted him to accept that they were true without hearing his side:

Spencer:	And what I needed from my friend was to stand up for me walking into the room with him . . . Now my context, once again, was not about racial stuff. I didn't know I had anything to deal with . . . I wish I'd gone to the table with him and done it differently. But I wasn't aware enough to do that at the time. The thing that bothered me though was the amount of adamancy, mashed with rage, mashed with not willing to listen to anything . . . Whether I should have made the meeting or not, literally it was so fucked up. You were so hard on me that I got off the phone and I was hysterically crying. I just couldn't deal with it because you were so seething in those phone calls . . . And now I understand that whether it's real or not, I was the one guy you really needed to come to the table that day. Of all the people around in your life, I was your model for how maybe it could work . . . You really needed to go through this experience, to go through this thing you'd just learned. You had just learned it. But I didn't know that then. I wish I had. I would have gone open-heartedly. But I had no way of knowing.

Lee Mun Wah:	Yeah, you know. I think you're probably really accurate. I think the part that, I don't remember, the adamant, but the feeling that I had the truth. I think that's what it was when I look back on it . . . when I remember a little of the work I was doing at that time [it] was around, just hear him out.
Spencer:	Yeah, you wanted me to hear him out.
Lee Mun Wah:	Just hear him out. And I remember making that a real big point. And I remember that that was real hard for you. You were saying, "But it didn't happen. That's not true."
Spencer:	And the same aspect where you wanted me to hear him out, I needed you to hear me out.
Lee Mun Wah:	Exactly. And I didn't realize that what I was wanting, and what you represented for me was a white man . . .
Spencer:	. . . who could take this leap . . .
Lee Mun Wah:	. . . to not see himself as an individual, but to see himself as what he represented and to acknowledge himself as a [white] man. I wanted you to understand what he was talking about on the racial issue of here was a white man. But you insisted on staying on the level of just Spencer, and "This is just you and me, Mun Wah." . . . And I was trying to get you to understand what you represented for him.
Spencer:	And there was no way that I could've. What context could I have come to the table at that point in your, our, history? I was not in the film. You were barely talking about it. I had not seen the film or gone through a workshop. No context to hold it the way you wanted me to.
Lee Mun Wah:	You didn't. So that was part of the rising for me, was putting the words to "this is what I've gone through most of my life." And I realize now that that was such a huge disconnect. But I had no previous experience with it because it was coming out raw for me.
Spencer:	Right.
Lee Mun Wah:	And I had not begun my work around this. In other words, all my work prior had been with people of color. I had not begun my work with white people too with people of color. So I didn't have that experience of being in-between . . .
Spencer:	It was just incredibly raw, very caustic, very raw because it was something that you really believed in and you finally experienced it. And like I said, you were getting your words under your belt for the first time.

Years later, with both men able to negotiate the territory of white privilege and racism within the conversation, they worked through the old wounds in order to develop new understandings of the conflict. Lee Mun Wah took responsibility for the intensity of his anger and saw that his approach, his sense that he held the truth, posed part of the problem. Spencer, for his part, recognized that their prior experience did not equip either of them to maneuver through this difficult territory at the time of the conflict and that a great deal of the trauma lay in their mutual inexperience confronting issues of race.

A profound lesson we can learn from Spencer and Lee Mun Wah concerns our need to be witnesses even when the messages we receive do not come in calm, friendly tones. Both of these men had a lot to resolve internally during the height of their conflict. Had Spencer understood his need to witness and recognize what he represented in the situation, he might have been better able to withstand the fire that came from Lee Mun Wah's as-yet undigested experience of filming the documentary, an experience that left him raw and searching for the right language to express his new understandings.

Essential, however, is that we recognize this step as a true leap of faith. Choosing to stay within a heated, conflict-filled dialogue regarding race that at times might appear to be overly harsh or incorrectly managed is something that white people generally avoid. Our sense of ourselves as individuals, not marked by race, preempts our ability to really listen to someone who challenges us regarding issues of subtle racism, especially our own. Deciding that there is something hidden within the perhaps hurtful challenge that is of immense value to us must come at first through a sense of faithfulness.

Without prior experience, we have no evidence that staying through the dialogue will be productive. Yet if we can resist the urge to flee, if we can dedicate ourselves to listening deeply in order to find the kernel of wisdom contained within the argument, then we can become the kind of witnesses that continue to learn and are present for those who need to be heard. Understanding that this is often a challenge, we can ask ourselves:

- What does it take for someone to stay within a heated conflict?
- What would it take for you to set aside your sense of the truth to hear someone else's experience?

As difficult as it might be to do the type of listening suggested here and stay within heated conflict, these skills are essential in order to build the type of trust necessary to create sustainable cross-race friendships and collaborations that do not ignore the impacts of race. For far too long, we have allowed race to be the elephant in the room. For far too long, this pattern has come about when people of color make statements reflecting their experience, only to be questioned or dismissed by the white people around them.

If we are serious about witnessing our whiteness, then we will need to learn from Spencer and Lee Mun Wah that yes, sometimes the messages will come through in fiery, emotionally raw ways that can injure. And yes, we also must withstand that heat because we recognize that we represent something larger than ourselves. Finally, yes, the burning that we might feel may be a requisite part of building alliances with some people of color who continue to feel the effects of racism on a daily basis.

AFTER THE FIRE

When we see strong, mutually respectful relationships between people of color and Whites, we are usually looking at the tangible results of both people's identity processes.

—Beverly Daniel Tatum

Within each of the conflict situations illustrated we see that true resolution involves work on both sides. Although any individual can freely remove himself or herself from a conflict, white people have far too often walked away from conflict involving race. Further, when we refuse to humbly enter the crossroad and take the leap of faith to hear a person challenging us, we allow blind spots to remain. Our lack of self-understanding can then impinge on our ability to make and keep deep cross-race connections.

No doubt that sitting in the fire can burn. But let us remember that transformation comes from Hecate's brew. The cauldron containing our medicine boils, creating the needed energy for movement. Yes, the shadows and darkness surround, but the light from the fire might just liberate. I know it has for me. Sitting through the tough moments is what really helped me clarify my view of what whiteness is and how my racial self emerges, not abstractly, but personally.

Seeing how being white affects me not only helped me come to a more resolved relationship with issues of guilt, creating a healthier sense of myself, but I also began to notice that my relationships with people of color dramatically improved. The quality of my conversations began to change and our sharing flowed more easily and went deeper. This does not mean that I still do not occasionally find myself under fire. I do. In fact, Chapter 8 discusses strategies for how to move through this type of witnessing moment using one of my experiences as an illustrative example. Before we can do that, however, we need to take some time to talk about the ways that our country's legacy of racism conditions us and lingers within our psyche.

NOTES

1. Coll, C. G., R. Cook-Nobles, and J. L. Surrey, "Building Connection through Diversity," in *Women's Growth in Diversity: More Writings from the Stone Center,* ed. J. V. Jordan (New York: Guilford Press, 1997).

2. Ayvazian, A., and B. D. Tatum, "Women, Race, and Racism: A Dialogue in Black and White," *Work in Progress,* no. 68 (Wellesley, MA: Wellesley College, Center for Research on Women), 13.

3. Singley, B., 2002. *When Race Becomes Real,* Crazy Sometimes, by Leonard Pitts, Jr., p. 21 (Chicago, IL: Lawrence Hill Books, 2002).

4. Singley, B., 2002. *When Race Becomes Real,* Crazy Sometimes, by Leonard Pitts, Jr., p. 27 (Chicago, IL: Lawrence Hill Books, 2002).

Chapter 7

Interior Shadows

Lingering Racism

> Part of why I hate part of myself is simple: I can feel the lingering traces of racism in my own body . . . It's easy to test. Put my white body next to a black body. What do I feel? What reactions kick in, immediately, before I have a chance to think? What facts about race can I feel in my body in that moment? How honest can I be about that? The fact is, I feel something different—a certain kind of fear—next to a black body than I feel next to another white body. The difference matters, still, after years of actively trying to overcome that learned reaction.
>
> —Robert Jensen (2005)

Perhaps one of the greatest mistakes we make is underestimating the power and autonomy of our psyche. With our culture's elevation of an individual's "can-do spirit" and willpower, we wrongly imagine that we are more in control of our thoughts than is true. One of my friends and I came face to face with the way lingering racism affects us when we sat to interview each other.

We chose to do this because once I had begun to interview the cross-race friends highlighted in these middle chapters, it became apparent that I should also respond to the questions asked of them. So, one of my closest Black female friends and I sat one evening and talked our way through a range of subjects. Although we had spoken regularly regarding race for years, our conversation revealed areas of our continuing struggle of which neither of us had previously spoken.

For my part, I was prompted to admit for the first time how horrible it feels when ingrained images reflective of our racist history arise. Although there are many, the fiercest and most unshakable for me is the image of evolution. Seeing our collective development as moving from ape to human is not what hurts. It is that the pictures I saw as a child remain deeply embedded, and those images portrayed white people as the most highly evolved. My education, which considered Western civilization as the epitome of human development only served to reinforce that image. Sadly, my conscious rejection of this image does nothing to stop it from arising internally. It is a battle I wage whenever the topic of evolution surfaces in conversation.

It is an essential battle, one that we must consider, as its effects are far more reaching than we would like to admit. For example, the manipulative association of Black person and ape has been a centuries-old excuse for slavery, anti-Black violence, and discrimination, and its frequent and historic emergence in popular media and cartoons is easily traceable. What we fail to recognize, however, is that this image and others like it are so deeply ingrained that they are extremely hard to eradicate and they continue to affect our ideas and behavior.

For example, responding to the February 2009 New York Post cartoon depicting a chimp killed by two white police officers with a caption reading "I guess they'll have to find someone else to write the next stimulus bill," two researchers wrote an op-ed explaining why it historically makes sense that so many people inferred that the chimp was meant to represent President Obama. They then described one of their recent studies illustrating the degree to which this association is ingrained and dangerous.

In the article the researchers explained that participants in a study they conducted were exposed to words such as "chimp" or "gorilla" flashed on a screen so fast that it was beneath conscious awareness. The participants then watched a short video of police officers violently subduing a suspect whose race was unknown. They led some participants to believe the suspect was white and others to believe that the suspect was Black.

What they found was that although exposure to the words made no difference if participants thought the suspect was white, if the participants believed the suspect was Black then the participants were more likely to believe that the suspect was deserving of the violence. The researchers then went on to discuss what they found in regards to death penalty cases and how in at least one study they could predict a defendant's likelihood of receiving a death sentence based upon the number of ape-related metaphors used in the print media surrounding the case.[1]

My hope is that this horrifying information will prompt us to take seriously the degree to which we have all been affected, unconsciously, by the inescapably racist images we are exposed to within our society. If I believed my own lingering racism in regards to evolution were isolated and affected only myself as an individual, I would be more likely to rest silent. However, seeing my embedded racism as a reflection of our society's larger struggles pushes me to expand my understanding. I need to hear from others, like my friend, to hear how else we are struggling to eradicate the effects of racism.

My friend, for her part, told me about how as a little girl growing up in a largely white community, she was prompted to wish that she had white skin. Her own identity process has radically shifted since then and she is now an active advocate for her Black community and cherishes her African roots. Yet, this does not mean that she escapes the consequences of living within a society fundamentally structured around dominating whiteness.

We talked about how during some of our interactions she felt that the way I offered advice was due to me thinking less of her because she is Black. She recognized that she would then respond defensively, believing I felt superior. As we reflected, she also mentioned that she saw me interacting with everybody in that same way and that this helped her pull back and see that although my style may betray overconfidence due to a lifetime of privilege, she was also bringing some internalized feelings of inferiority to our conversation that grew out of living within a racist environment.

Although challenging to maneuver through the emotions that understandably arise while sharing such painful thoughts, my relationship with my friend benefited from this investigation and mutual understanding. There is less need to hide our shameful feelings and fears from each other, as we now use them to further note the pernicious way racism lives within our psyches without conscious consent. What my friend and I found is similar to my discussions with our fellow travelers. The work they have already done with one another allows each of them to courageously identify areas where they still struggle. Because of this, their messages are both inspirational and helpful.

My hope is that gaining clearer insight into the wide breadth of trauma and confusion bred from our history can help us stay connected to ourselves and those around us when racially loaded situations arise. To help us gather strength, I return again to the image of Hecate as a force to encourage our consideration of the themes that surfaced through my conversations with our guides. In addition to offering us her lighted torch, Hecate helps us to release the past, especially aspects that hinder our growth, and to accept necessary changes and transitions. In this way, as we move into a discussion of the lingering shadows of racism, we are asked to release our hold on what is familiar and secure and travel into the scary places of our psyche.

EMBEDDED SCRIPTS

Just as my mind has gotten images of evolution rather twisted, several of the people I spoke with talked about having internal "recordings" or "scripts" that arise. Whether acted on or not, these inner voices continue to plague many of us. And, sadly, all too often we are too embarrassed and ashamed to admit that the voices live deep within.

Karen (a white educator) has experienced enough to now expect the vestiges of racism to play a role in her daily life: "I've heard so many stories of African American men walking down the street and white women moving to the other side of the street . . . that I am very, very aware of that. And I am aware when I do it. You know, I so believe that I am racist that I expect it. I actually expect it." To be clear, Karen fights these internal messages whenever they are conscious. But, she knows that there are times when she is not as conscious as she should be.

Spencer (a white composer and musician) also spoke of how his upbringing has remained ingrained within his psyche long after deciding to challenge racism:

> Now, understand, I still had this underlying face that I was brought up to believe that Black people are scary and don't expect too much out of them . . . I never questioned it, until I started questioning it. I still couldn't get rid of the voices, the conversations that just came out immediately. Oh there's clouds outside, is it going to rain? There's a Black person, should I cross the street? It was just a gut instant reaction.

Spencer also spoke of the conscious work this struggle requires:

> As I got older and did a whole lot more work on myself, I started questioning all this stuff. Oh, . . . I'm having this reaction. I'm going to stay where I am on the sidewalk. I was challenging all these things that were coming up inside me constantly. This is bullshit. I don't believe this. Where is this coming from?

It was Bob (a white co-founder of Project Return), though, who was able to answer Spencer's question about where the internalized racism comes from most directly. Bob spoke extensively on what helps perpetuate the lingering racism within him. He spoke of "recordings": "We all get certain recordings when we're growing up. I believe this. Everybody has them doesn't matter where. From the ghetto there'll be different ones . . . It's there and I think we've all got it. If you don't acknowledge it, you're denying it." He told of his experience coming to see racism as wrong and yet still not being able to turn off the voices that emerge from deep within: "I've always been able to hear the racist voices from being raised as a Southern Baptist and going to where I am now."

In response to a comment I made that it is difficult to find people who speak so candidly, Bob revealed that he himself is only just beginning to talk openly about these issues:

Bob: In all my years, I've only talked to people about it for the last three or four months and now that I'm, after fifteen years of struggling with this, I'm realizing that it's not going to go away, and it's a discipline that I have to force upon myself and I think I'll always have to force it . . . Here's an example, and I've noticed this for years. If I'm watching the news, if a Black child has died, a Black teenager has been shot, there's a voice in me that tries to tell me that's not as important as if he were a white boy. And I have to say, "Oh, yes it is." I have to argue with that voice and say, "That mother loved her child just as much as if she were white." But I have to say that in order to . . . make it as important. It's not automatic.

Shelly: When did you realize that?

Bob: Years ago. Years ago when I first started this work I would realize how much I cared about the people I was meeting, Malcolm, Perry, prisoners, Black criminals, and so on when I began to see who was really there and was making all these tremendous changes in myself. And all these changes were occurring. And yet these voices were still there. And I kept thinking, well eventually they will go away. But they never have. And it's just in the last few months that I've said, "They're just not ever going to. They're just not going to."

Bob's admission reminds me of what might have occurred for whites while watching the fallout from Hurricane Katrina. How many white people unconsciously responded with less empathy because the trauma was happening to a large number of Black people? How many white people were aware enough of their internal racism to be conscious that fear of Black people was stopping them from getting into their vehicles and going to help some of those who were left stranded with no transportation or housing?

Bob went on to describe what happens when he is not conscious of the "recording" that is playing in his mind:

I sway from being oversensitive to, [during] times of stress, to being not sensitive at all, to reverting to my shadow, my worst side. So that's been my interracial struggle all along, to fight my way out of racism and turn off those voices and maybe, maybe it's going to help me to realize those voices are never gonna go away. They will always be my struggle. And that somebody else is just going to have a different kind of struggle.

Bob believes these recordings and voices affect everyone, regardless of race, but that the script varies depending upon a person's race and upbringing.

When Bob and I later sat down with his friend Perry (an African American colleague at Project Return), they talked about how these voices affect their work relationship. Bob began by attributing his sense of disconnection and mistrust between himself and Perry to these recordings:

Bob:	There seemed to be a barrier I couldn't break down. There seemed to be something that was still there about, that was racist that was because I was white. And now, I start thinking, have begun to think, that it's the very thing that I possess myself. It's these old tapes that we've learned and that are just there. It's in the mental banks . . . It's on our hard drive and they cannot be deleted. They are files that cannot be deleted.
Perry:	I said that yesterday, not in those same words, but I said that.
Bob:	And I've said before, I will never ever get Perry's complete trust. There were times when I would say things and he would say something back to me and I would think, that's just that stuff. I didn't know what it was then. But I felt excluded because of my race.
Shelly:	And the tapes that you're talking about, you have them, too? The tapes are that he's not trustworthy?
Perry:	Yeah. Right.
Shelly:	And he's got his own tapes that he was talking about?
Perry:	And you know, it's not something that I run around on a daily basis with it up front in my head. But it's there. I mean, it just needs to be triggered. I don't know what the trigger is. Maybe he could say the wrong thing and there it comes.
Bob:	Yeah, right, and I don't think it's ever going to go away.

Although Perry did not use a label like "recordings," he talked about how when he and Bob are in conflict, he is prone to imagine that Bob is thinking of him in racist terms:

So Bob calls me in and talks about [a moment of conflict]. And he starts to get loud and he starts to turn into the white man . . . And not 'cause he got loud, but I could see it coming that he's angry, that he's upset, and if I had to read his mind—'cause you can't hear what's on people's mind unless they say it—but if I had to read his mind, I would've said, "This Black motherfucker, this nigger, has done something I told him not to do." But that's what I would've said if I had to read his mind.

These inner scripts are so strong that even for two men who worked together for years and established deep care for one another, there are still moments when each of them recognizes that embedded racism and rewardings shows up within their interactions.

Just as with my friend and I, a solid friendship can form and years can go by without bringing these internal "scripts" out from the shadows. But, what if we did? What difference might it make? I had caught Bob and Perry at a time where they were just starting to deal with this question themselves and this led Perry to make a suggestion:

Perry: But you see what Bob has in the back [of his mind], he says those seeds that were planted by his parents, his relatives, and me, that's gonna be there. That's always gonna be there. But you know what? I think that becoming conscious, knowing that it's there, and knowing that it's poison . . .

Bob: And talking about it.

Perry: And talking about it.

Bob: Acknowledging it.

Perry: And when you get into a situation that consciousness will make you better able to deal with it and work it out. You see?

Bob, too, hoped that there might be a way to break through the "scripts" as he said: "And I'm just wondering if finally bringing it out, and not hiding it anymore, the problem was that I was constantly hiding it. I was just battling it . . . And I wonder if talking about it, like I have been for the last few months, is improving it, is having a possible effect."

This would be the hope. At the very least, even if we are not able to thoroughly eradicate these "scripts" and "recordings," perhaps our increased awareness will allow us to develop more open and honest cross-race relationships and a sense of humility so that we might be better able to receive critique and feedback as needed.

Some questions to consider:

- What racist "scripts" or "recordings" play out in your head?
- To what degree do you trust your cross-race friends and colleagues enough to share with them your struggles around your internal racial "scripts" or "recordings"?

EMBEDDED IMAGERY

A second, but related, theme that came up in conversations involved the way racist and stereotypical images have infected our psyche. These are the meanings of whiteness that are so present in our cultural surroundings that none of us escape them, like white people being portrayed as expert, powerful, the epitome of beauty, valuable, and innocent.

Michael (a white mythologist and storyteller) depends upon his multiracial network of friends and colleagues to help him avoid internalizing racist imagery. Yet he knows that when left without these resources of perspective for a significant period of time, he finds himself subject to influence from the media:

> TV is a great example. I need a break, but I'm always interested in stories. If I'm watching for a while I can start to think that the image of beauty is clean, thin, white, blonde. Then, if I suddenly see a woman who doesn't look like that I might not notice her distinct beauty. Or it could seem that the people in charge are white, that they should be because it looks that way. And there are assumed ideas. More of the people shown being arrested are nonwhite or all the rioting around the world looks to be Arabs or Africans or Mexicans. They don't show a bunch of white people doing some real damage as a group. They don't check in on the Ku Klux Klan. I don't think it's subtle really.

I asked Michael what he did in response to this awareness. He said:

> Oh, well, I usually start saying something to people and then I go, maybe I've been home too long. Aren't we supposed to go somewhere? Let's get an event going. Let's go get real people back together again. And it makes me realize that I've maybe isolated a bit. I haven't been on the phone talking with people or visiting with people. This stuff partially works on the basis of isolation.

Michael is not the only one who sees the inaccuracy of the messages our social surroundings feed us on a daily basis.

Cayce (a white photographer) also recognizes the need to consciously refute internalized images of whites as symbols of authority:

> Just the images of authority have white faces. Presidents, chairmen of the board, principals, teachers, they all have white faces . . . I was raised so that Jesus looked kind of like [my white husband], bearded and light-skinned, and God looked kind of like Willie Nelson. So I've tried to sort of rid myself of an anthropomorphic God thing anyway. But it's still, that's in my head as well, this notion that the biblical images and the biblical stories . . . Probably if we can really go back and look at . . . I'm sure there were no white people anywhere to be found.

It is partly this level of image and association that makes Barak Obama's presidency so powerful. Although only one of forty-three, this new image of what a president looks like can begin to disrupt the embedded images of authority that have dominated our country for centuries.

Assuredly, our culture is already breaking down these embedded images in many ways and forms. However, it will take generations of time and effort before the vestiges of racism can be excised from our unconscious minds. This is especially true because many associations and images touch extremely painful nerves and long-standing wounds within members of our community that are both passed down from one generation to the next as well as reinforced in our contemporary environments.

To illustrate, Lorraine (the African American CEO of YWCA-USA) offered a personal example of a time when the historic images of white women sitting on pedestals and Black women as Jezebel figures emerged for her so strongly that she left a meeting in tears. The experience occurred when Lorraine worked for a previous organization and a white, female board member publicly chided her instead of going through the usual channels of speaking privately with her boss and having him speak to her.

However, it was not the criticism that was paramount for Lorraine. What was paramount were the racial dynamics. The particular woman bringing the criticism was reputed as having highly questionable moral behavior. In stark contrast, Lorraine had grown up in a community and family in which the females strictly and consciously defied the negative stereotypes that have plagued Black women for centuries. Lorraine explained the trauma she experienced:

> To me . . . that was probably one of the most humiliating situations in life I can ever remember in life being in because, number one, I am sitting across the table from a tramp, a white tramp as far as I'm concerned, who is on the pedestal in the eyes of the world. Despite her reputation, she is the world's ideal. "Their ideal" is pointing her finger at me telling me that I'm flawed, telling me that I'm this and that and the other. She's putting me down. I just couldn't get past the dynamics to even deal with issues at hand that I considered all trumped up anyway. We volleyed back and forth and I felt that I refuted the issues. But that is not what bothered me about this scenario . . . And I left that meeting . . . I mean, I was incapacitated after this meeting. I had to leave. Just reliving that, it was just incredibly horrible and I can say that I was just totally, totally wiped out after that.

Years later, what continues to make the experience so painful is not recalling the criticism. The pain is the image of white women as pure innocents to be protected and Black women as promiscuous and readily critiqued. This is a poignant illustration of how deeply embedded the historic privileging of whiteness can be and how it can erupt without invitation, striking deeply regardless of one's consciousness of, or investment in, the ideas and images.

Lorraine's attentiveness to refuting these types of cultural stereotypes makes the eruptions of the images especially painful. Lorraine talked about her conscientious approach to work situations:

> Because Black women have had to endure negative stereotypes of being the Jezebels with low morals and all of that . . . that stereotype that only fast girls wore red fingernail polish. [I'm] constantly trying to refute those kinds of stereotypes about Black women, making sure that my dress isn't too short or anything like that. I just interviewed for a position not too long ago. I make sure that I have a long skirt when I interview so that when I sit down my skirt doesn't go up over my knees, wanting to make sure that I look even more than corporate. There are things you do with those stereotypes in mind.

An important thing to recall is that Lorraine's experience is an illustration of a collective, group trauma. None of these lingering, internalized, racist scripts are isolated. She is not the only one who experiences these dynamics playing out and she is hardly alone in feeling obligated to refute these harmful images on a regular basis.

The image of white women linked with goodness also affects Bob and Perry. One example included a time when Perry confronted a member of the management team at the nonprofit where they both participated in a community-building process. The conflict between the men arose as Bob later challenged Perry on the appropriateness of his confrontation of a white woman:

Perry: But when he confronted me, I didn't say it then, but it came about. He's doing that because this was this white girl.

Bob: And my image of that is that there would be times when y'all would confront [her], but [she] was a lightning rod. But still, she was management. And I didn't think management—just in general, Black, white, take all that out of it—that management confronted like that. And what I did, I would hold back and hold back from protecting [these two women] because they were white.

Here we can see how easily our attempts to subvert racism can remain troubled. Bob tried to consciously subvert the historical privileging of white women within the community-building process by *not* saying anything. Yet when Bob did raise the issue at a later time with Perry, Perry reacted to the situation as though Bob *was* privileging the white woman.

Lorraine, Perry, and Bob all spoke about how the emergence of the image of white women as holding a protected and honored place within the society has affected their interactions. This is hardly new. bell hooks notes how white women are deemed protected and pure, while African American women are considered all things opposite when she writes that "devaluation of black womanhood is central to the maintenance of white supremacist capitalistic society."[2] This also reminds us of the discussion around the creation of the white self in Chapter 3 where Toni Morrison links whiteness with the theme of innocence and newness within American literature.[3]

Important to acknowledge here is that for many people we have moved into more subtle territory. Much of our discussion now focuses on issues that many readers might find unfamiliar. This is likely due to many white people's interest in focusing on the future instead of looking back to see how our history of racism continues to damage our psyches. Unfortunately, the idea that avoiding our past will help us get over it is simply false. We continue to injure one another through our insensitivity regarding how lingering racism and their effects continue to shape our interactions.

Some questions to think about:

- In what ways might overexposure to media outlets affect your perception in racially prejudicial ways?
- How might images of historically-significant racial stereotypes emerge within conflicts in your social and work environments?

LACK OF SENSITIVITY

It goes without saying that what is subtle to one person might be plainly obvious to another. This perfectly characterizes what often occurs in racially-loaded situations. For white people who have not spent a lot of time questioning issues of privilege, subtle manifestations of discrimination, and internalized racism, we regularly either miss moments where they exist or simply do not speak about issues right in front of us.

When I met with Katie (the white founder of LEAP) she talked about a moment when she had an opportunity to witness Lorraine interviewing for a job position wherein race was felt to be a factor:

I saw [Lorraine] take total control of the situation, which at the time, I couldn't figure out what she was doing. Because, at the time, it seemed inappropriate for her to be doing that, and everybody, I could just feel the room reacting against how she was handling it. And I was surprised and didn't understand until later, after I read your proposal, that I said "Ah ha!" She was taking charge because she needed to. But if she had been a white woman who was taking charge . . . people wouldn't have made a judgment. It was the fact that this African American woman was taking charge of the situation even though they were very highly educated and saw themselves as very liberal. I saw them all reacting in fear of a Black woman taking charge.

What is important here is not Katie's belief that the rest of the group reacted against Lorraine taking control. Without their voices, that will always remain speculative.

But what we can see is that the basis for Katie's interpretation comes from *her experience* of the situation. Katie initially perceived Lorraine's approach as inappropriate. She felt the room reacting against Lorraine. She came to believe that it was the right approach and that Lorraine's race modified its acceptability only after more deeply considering whiteness and its unconscious effects while reading the proposal for my study. For Katie, this entire experience opened her eyes to how subtle lingering racism can be, even within highly-educated and socially liberal people, such as herself.

When speaking with both women together, I asked about the job interview to get Lorraine's perspective and to inquire further about Katie's initial response:

Shelly:	What was your experience of what [Katie] had to say about all this?
Katie:	It took me reading [the proposal] that I had this epiphany that this really was . . .
Lorraine:	It was about race.
Katie:	It was about race.
Lorraine:	And first of all, let me go back, it was my fear going in, knowing the organization. I articulated more than once, am I going to be wasting my time throwing my hat in the ring?
Katie:	Just to be a token.
Lorraine:	I said I don't really have time just so they can check off on their affirmative action list that they interviewed one. So I only want to do that [interview] if this organization, if you think given your involvement with this organization, it has changed substantially enough that they are ready to truly consider me for the wonderful talent and all the things that I can bring to this organization. And then going through the process, and we can fast-forward to the final outcome and look at what they were looking for. Look at the qualifications. Look at what they said they wanted. They wanted someone who could take them to the next level. I was overqualified in terms of the specific qualifications that were required. I certainly had everything they wanted, plus.
Katie:	Plus the imagination . . . and the fear factor was [there when] you took charge of the interview process.
Lorraine:	I don't think that was it. I could have interviewed any damned way.
Katie:	That's probably true.
Lorraine:	And the outcome would have been the same.

Katie:	They would have thought of a reason.
Lorraine:	I know that. They would have made up reasons.
Shelly:	Why did it take until my proposal to make you see what was going on?
Katie:	Well, because I kept saying, "No, these people can't be. These are chairmen of their departments and whatever."
Lorraine:	You know what other thing that was interesting was, that the concern later on that there was no white male interviewed. That says to me they were doing a little affirmative-action checklist for the interview process, but they ended up hiring a person who represented the largest racial demographic group in the profession, who met none of the qualifications in the original job description, which is supposedly what they were looking for even in terms of experiences and direct management of budget size. So, based on qualifications alone, it was obviously not the person that they had originally said they wanted.
Katie:	I wanted to talk about their unconscious fear.
Shelly:	Did you think it was an unconscious thing, Lorraine?
Katie:	That they weren't going to be able to control you?
Lorraine:	Oh yeah.
Katie:	I think some of it was unconscious at least.
Lorraine:	And part of it too is that I could have played the game. I know I could have played the game.

Lorraine later noted that "playing the game" in that situation would have meant being "conciliatory."

Important to highlight about this exchange is the way that Katie was at first unable to recognize the subtle race dynamics, but then later learned how her perception was not quite sensitive enough. Her process illustrates that part of what can keep us blind is refusing to admit that educated people whom we respect might also have unconscious, lingering racism within their psyches too. This is an essential point for those of us who are used to believing that we ourselves no longer carry any subtle racist tendencies.

Insensitivity does not always lead to high-level traumatic encounters, however. Sometimes it is the repetitive low-grade instances that build up and do damage. A common pattern is when white people are simply not attentive to race issues such that people of color end up feeling the need to consistently be vocal. For example, Michael and Luis (a Chicano author and poet) noted that within their conversations Luis is the one who usually brings up issues of oppression:

| Michael: | One day we were talking and . . . you brought up something because it was on your mind or on your heart or both, and I was going, I gave a response, just what was occurring to me which had to do |

with the symbolic nature of it or something like that. And you said something about, "We've got to level the playing field. It's not even a level playing field." And I remember saying, "That's not the point. I'm not talking about a playing field. I'm talking about what's under the field." That's where I was at. And you kind of stuck with it . . . and I was anticipating getting into the conversation of the poetics and how the poetic images and you must have been coming out of, and I forget what the issue was but it had something to do with justice and having to do with oppression.

Luis: Which tends to be my thing.

Michael: Yeah. And the image you were carrying was leveling the social playing field so that everybody has a fair chance. And I wasn't alert to it. I was actually anticipating getting into the poetic conversation where nothing is level. It's all about movement and depth and height. And I mentioned it because, yeah, that's right, I didn't check in with Luis, you know, where he's coming from. I was just thinking about where I was going. And I think that would be, in your terms, a difference based on race and experience, and even privilege . . . because I realized that I wasn't worried about the playing field.

Not feeling the need to continually raise the social and cultural issues to the foreground, Michael enters the mythic space freely. And, although Luis believes that the stories Michael presents capture the social and cultural, he still feels the need to speak about social justice issues directly so their participants do not to lose sight of them.

Luis' felt need to keep societal issues up front is in part because of how whiteness gets into his psyche:

Oh yeah. It drives you crazy. You want to know why Blacks and Mexicans go nuts on people? It can drive you crazy . . . Again, if it wasn't for the poetry, if it wasn't for the art, if it wasn't for the creative ritual space, it would be totally maddening. But those things help to address and alleviate things like this.

This craziness Luis refers to again calls to mind the essay by Leonard Pitts Jr., *Crazy Sometimes,* in which he speaks of how living with continuous racism while whites continually deny the experiences can cause one to begin to see it everywhere.[4]

Luis' need to constantly battle society's racist messages leaves him with intense anger. Luis used a metaphor linked to his earlier work as a welder to explain his process of coping, his attempt to find balance, and the important role writing and poetry play:

I have to temper my anger. I have to do two things with it. I have to temper it so it's not so fiery, burning everybody. But I also have to make it more precise . . . I think the issue of being sharper is good, too. I envision this like a welder. You mix the oxygen and the acetylene gas until you get what's called the blue flame. This is the little blue flame in the middle of the larger white flame. When you get the mixture just right, this makes for the best cutting flame. Then you can cut through steel. That is what I think the Mosaic [Multicultural Foundation's men's conferences] events help me get to—to the blue flame. I'm still hot, I'm still angry, but I become more precise about how I deal with it. With story, with poetry, you really get to that cutting point. You don't obliterate the anger or the grief behind it, but you get more precise about how you handle it, and about what you're really getting angry at . . . I hope maybe a guy like me can get to a place where we can't be angry like this. I don't think I'm going to get to that place. There is still a lot to be angry about. What I've learned, though, is to find a healing place for some of that. You know, the sweat lodge purifies and balances some of this. I'm learning more how to balance this anger . . . I know the more I write, the more poetry I do, the more I am able, with all of my traumas and pathologies, to handle them better, to balance myself better in relation to these issues.

There is no doubt Luis' pessimism inspires me to continually recommit to this work. In fact, it inspires additional resolve in me to prove that white people *can* come together to heal ourselves so that we might become more sensitive and match the dedication to healing Luis exemplifies.

Some questions for consideration:

• What are some ways that well-educated, white liberal people continue to act out racism and white privilege in your social and work environments?
• How often do you raise social/racial justice concerns in conversations?

PERCEIVED THREATS

From mild nervousness to intense fear, worry over how one is seen and accepted was a fourth theme that arose for many of our fellow travelers. For some, particularly the white people, the perceived threat was largely an internal battle waged against insecurities bred from becoming conscious of racial issues. On the other hand, for the people of color who spoke on this subject, the internal battles also carried a more pressing need to attend to personal, psychological safety.

Katie's story was a bit surprising to me, since she has worked directly with African Americans for over twenty years in the Cabrini Green housing projects in Chicago. Yet Katie recently struggled to feel accepted at a benefit for Lorraine's former nonprofit, an event attended primarily by African Americans:

When I was at [Lorraine's] benefit last year, I found myself going around thinking . . ."How was I perceived there?" Maybe I'm more conscious of my whiteness now. I was conscious of "How are people looking at me?" "How are people perceiving why I'm there?" You know? "Do I belong?" And I was finding myself doing it, but at the same time I was asking myself, "Why are you?" But I kept telling everybody, "I'm Lorraine's good friend" so that I would be okay to be there. I was justifying my presence, like I'm really on the in. I'm not one of those do-gooders over there. I'm here because I'm Lorraine's good friend.

This is a fairly common experience for white people who have experienced an increased awareness of their whiteness. Being a bit oversensitive as well as understanding the reasons for "do-gooders" to be rejected, we often try to distance ourselves from that image in order to be accepted.

Our worry over being accepted may appear nonsensical to some. But, when it strikes, we can find ways to protect our sense of self in many different ways. For example, Cayce spoke about a recent experience where she was called to admit that she rejects some people before they have a chance to reject her:

Cayce: I would have thought growing up that I didn't have a lot of prejudices. And then I still will occasionally, something will happen and I'll be like "Ah, wow, I didn't realize that I was still holding on to that."

Shelly: Could you name one?

Cayce: When we were just on our honeymoon, we were in Amsterdam and there was a young Black guy who was the concierge in the hotel and I found him irritating. I thought he was insolent and was irritated by him because we'd ask him about something and he was not very helpful. And [my husband] and I talked about it later and he said, "You know, sometimes you're really hard on young Black men." You know, I was like "Really?" He said, "Yeah." I said, "OK." That was just one of those things that I had to think about and I said, "I can't stand that sort of angry, insolent thing that I see." And he said, "But you aren't that way with young Brown men." And so, I don't know, I think there's always been a fear factor there, not a fear that somebody was going to hurt me, but a fear that I wasn't going to be liked. You know, that fear that I could not ever leap over that wedge.

When I asked her if her negative reactions to Black men feel like some type of self-protective leap at being the first to reject, Cayce explained her sense of it this way:

I'm just going to kind of be indifferent toward you before you can be indifferent toward me. So I think a lot of my issues around race come up in that way, in not putting myself out there . . . I give Amanda full credit for the fact that we've been able to maintain a relationship because I would never have assumed that she would have wanted to. So when she did, then I totally opened up.

In the same way as Katie worried over people at Lorraine's benefit rejecting her, Cayce imaged that her being white would limit Amanda's interest in forming a friendship with her.

But, for Cayce this goes one step deeper. Cayce not only worries about being rejected, she recognized in herself a tendency to preemptively reject people she thinks might reject her. When I recall Cayce's history I think it is likely no coincidence that those Cayce rejects, young Black men, represent a group with which she is least familiar. When we talked she had mentioned several important relationships she created with Chicano/as since moving to Los Angeles. However, she did not discuss any close working relationships with African American men. This could underlie her husband's observation that Cayce treats Black and Brown men differently.

For the people of color, worries concerning perceived threats to psychological safety were largely rooted in prior experience. For example, as Lee Mun Wah spoke of his childhood, he described two memorable experiences that brought him into awareness of his status as "other" within U.S. society. The first experience was when he was in grade school and his teacher did an ethnic count. The teacher told him that he was incorrect when he raised his hand as an American, informing him that he was Chinese, not American. The second experience occurred when he got into a fight with a young Black girl and they both used racial slurs against each other. After recounting these stories, Lee Mun Wah offered this statement:

> Just because we don't talk about racism, we internalize it unconsciously somewhere and it comes up when we are scared or angry or afraid. And so those were two very key moments. And then my father told me that he wanted to expand his restaurant, but that the woman next door who was white said that she would never sell it to a chink. And so I became more and more aware that as my father became more and more wealthy that it did not matter. Money did not change who he was. And that was a very profound lesson for me, because it probably makes me safer . . . I say safer so I won't hurt myself being in situations where I think I'm just like anyone else.

Even though Lee Mun Wah was born and raised in the U.S., he feels he must be continually aware of his place as "second-class" in whites' eyes to maintain safety and avoid emotional risk. Important to highlight is that safety involves remaining conscious of him being perceived as different even when he is in situations where he has been invited to speak or run a workshop.

Connecting Katie, Cayce, and Lee Mun Wah's stories, Jennifer's experience illustrates the self-protective walls that can build up over a lifetime spent battling the obvious and subtle racism of white people. Jennifer said that relating with someone who is consistently unaware of traces of racism takes its toll. In their book, Jennifer says that she feels she is battling "the ghost of racism" when she is with Karen.[5] This is perhaps why Jennifer does not often try to create close friendships with white people.

Jennifer shared how she sees potential friends: "When I enjoy people I don't care what race they are. That is what holds the potential . . . [But] I don't seek out white people. That's another thing. So any white person who wanted to be my friend had to seek me out first."

And yet, Jennifer also said that moving through this experience with Karen helps diminish the fears she once had when interacting with whites. In fact, when asked about her openness to having me, a white woman, come into her home for these interviews, she credited her relationship with Karen:

> That's one of the things I can see came out of our friendship. I'm not afraid of white people. Not that I ever consciously was, but I feel less threatened, like I've got to protect myself around them. And that's all credit to her.

As hopeful as Jennifer's process may sound, not everyone finds a way to release the fear developed over a lifetime.

Amanda spoke most extensively about the intimidation felt after having spent her childhood within a system where white people were the authority figures and she was made to feel less valuable. She also talked about spending time with her first husband's family, a white family:

Amanda: When you're raised with racism it leaves, I don't know how to define it, but you feel intimidated, you feel less than and even though you meet them on the same plateau you still feel less than because of the way you came up.

Shelly: So it wasn't even how they were acting toward you?

Amanda: No. It was my stuff. But I couldn't be around them. I was not myself. I remember them telling me, why are you always so quiet? Why can't you? . . . But I couldn't feel it. It was like "I shouldn't be here."

This sense of being intimidated around whites is not isolated to the family situation.

Amanda also discussed experiences passing through white spaces while traveling and how she coped with the feelings of insecurity:

> When I would leave town, even in the airport, and if you're like in Texas, in Houston, and you're catching a flight and it's all predominantly white, I would feel a little bit intimidated and I would have to talk to myself. "You know you

can get through this one. They are just like you. They are no different. Don't let them make you feel intimidated."

Although these experiences occurred in the past, Amanda recognizes that she still faces the same fear, intimidation, and self-critique when she goes on interviews today: "The only part I guess I struggle with when it comes to Caucasians is that when I try to get a job and it's a Caucasian person I have to fight that 'Oh, she's white so she's going to think she's better.'"

Years later, I spoke again with Amanda and shared with her some of the conclusions I came to out of our initial interviews. She then told me an additional story about one of her earlier jobs as an administrator at UCLA where she held a position equal to a group of white women. She recounted that her early experience watching her mother act as the maid for white people reemerged such that she began to act as a caretaker in her workplace and serve the other white women during meetings. We then discussed that as a white woman, had I been in those meetings, I might have interpreted Amanda's behavior as a culturally lovely way of being, as though she were simply being attentive to people's needs. I would have completely missed Amanda's discomfort and internal challenges existing within that space due our different life experiences.

The felt response in the face of whiteness that Amanda describes is not new. It relates to bell hooks' discussion of whiteness as terrorizing wherein she writes that "many of us pretend to be comfortable in the face of whiteness only to turn our backs and give expression to intense levels of discomfort."[6] For white people, this might be difficult to take. Yes, bell hooks can be understood as meaning that being around white people can invoke internal feelings of terror in people of color holding whatever level of status or rank. We might defensively suggest that this is a reversed, negative prejudice that is essentially unfair.

Yet bell hooks effectively counters this argument when she says that this representation "emerges as a response to the traumatic pain and anguish that remains a consequence of white racist domination, a psychic state that informs and shapes the way black folks 'see' whiteness."[7] Although bell hooks speaks particularly of whiteness as terrorizing in the Black imagination, Amanda's experience is perhaps not fundamentally different.

bell hooks' analysis can extend to the experience of any person of color still pained by living within a system dominated by whiteness. If so, this also describes the ingrained intimidation felt by Amanda any time she entered predominantly white spaces or when a white person appears in a powerful position and can make a decision that affects her livelihood.

Overall, regardless of the actuality of danger in any given moment, we can become more adept at navigating racially-loaded situations if we recognize that all of us might face internal fears or perceived threats. Even if this simply causes us to give pause and avoid responding defensively, that brief moment of reflection might make all the difference. That said, the only way we can know for sure what someone is feeling is to create deep enough relationships that we feel safe enough to share our own experience and ask about another's. Questions for reflection:

- To what degree do you avoid cross-race conversations and collaborations due to fears about racial issues?
- How comfortable are you in environments where you in are the minority?
- Do you ever want to distance yourself from liberal "do-gooders"? Why?

INTERNALIZED SUPERIORITY/INFERIORITY

White supremacy is not isolated to hate groups. As a main thread woven into the fabric of our culture for centuries, white supremacy infects our psyche. It causes many people of color to develop a sense of internalized inferiority and many white people to act out of a sense of internalized superiority. Here is perhaps a moment when Hecate's lighted torch is needed most, as admitting the truth of this message might be hardest to accept. Thankfully, a few of our guides are able to help us understand this process through their stories.

Similar to what Amanda said about how racism left her feeling "less than," Luis spoke about how living within a racist environment can breed feelings of inferiority. Yet Luis also discussed how he defensively flips the script in some ways with a sense of superiority:

> Sometimes I feel superior to white people in general because I understand Western culture, but they do not understand me. I understand me. I understand African American, and the otherness. But I also understand them. I know that doesn't put me in a superior place. Maybe it just puts me in a strategically better position. Who knows what it does? But it does change my perception on dealing with whites because in many ways I think part of the struggle with white people is that, on the one hand, if you make them a monolith and hate them then you are almost making them superior to you. But if you tear them down and make them less than "human," you might think you are better than them, which is also not right. People do this all the time. Maybe they do this for their own survival, for their own defense. "I'm better than even this most privileged, powerful white guy. I'm still better than him even though I ain't got nothing."

As destructive as Luis knows this response may be, his response is a rather understandable defensive move, given that we live in a society dominated by images of whites as valuable and powerful.

On the other side of the spectrum, Karen has encountered more than one instance where Jennifer questioned the way a sense of superiority pervaded Karen's actions and interactions. For example, recall that years ago Karen had invited Jennifer into her classroom in order for Karen to improve her teaching practice. Jennifer formalized this process as part of her dissertation with Karen's permission. At the end of the study, Jennifer approached Karen with her intention to publish the dissertation as a book. Karen then threatened a legal battle that she assumed she could win.

Karen described this experience as resulting in Jennifer making Karen see her internalized sense of superiority over African Americans:

> It must have been when we had the very emotional discussion about what had happened with the dissertation becoming a book. And [Jennifer] explained to me what I had done, did I understand what I had done? And I didn't think I'd done that. I just thought I was trying to protect what was mine. But the more she discussed that with me about how she felt, about what she saw me doing that she had seen so many white people doing in her life, and other friends' lives, that she just wanted to be sure that I understood what I was doing. And that's probably the first time that it occurred to me that I made a decision and acted on beliefs, taking action, based on some type of superiority complex.

Yet simply coming to see that this complex exists deep within does not immediately block continued eruptions or shed light on other past experiences where it emerges.

Jennifer told a second story about an experience when she and Karen were doctoral students at Berkeley and Jennifer asked Karen to read an article that Karen did not understand well. At that time, Karen confronted Jennifer in a copy room in front of a professor, asking her, "What the fuck is this?" Within our conversation, Jennifer, believing that Karen's behavior resulted from an unconscious aspect of white privilege, questioned Karen.

The dialogue that follows illustrates how resistant we can be to naming the feelings that arise when confronted with lingering racism. But the dialogue also shows the willingness Karen has to admit when she might be subject to their effects:

Karen: I don't know. I think I was joking around in some way because what she had me read was so esoteric and removed from my students' reality or my reality with them. And I was so shocked because of what I thought I knew about her and so on. And so I didn't like it. I really hate this esoteric, academic writing. I hate it, because a lot of it I don't understand. And I think, if I don't understand it, I mean, really, what are they trying to prove? What is the point of all of this? How is it going to improve education? So I think I was upset on that level. And then I really was incensed in a way, I guess. Also, I was probably nervous and conflicted because I didn't understand it very well and she was asking me to read it and get something out of it. And I wasn't getting anything out of it. But I also did respect her. So she must have gotten something out of it to ask me to read it.

Shelly: That is definitely not joking.

Karen: I guess not.

Shelly: So there was some actual serious anger in using that [language].

Karen: Yeah, and I really don't understand why I said it in front of [the professor] to her, because that was completely out of line.

Jennifer: And she knew how I felt about [the professor]. We had had months of conversations. I didn't like what he stood for and a lot of his work. So if you are you going to say this to me, it should be with me, you, and the copy machine. So it was a total disregard for my feelings.

Karen: Yeah. And so maybe it was kind of getting back at her for something.

Jennifer: Getting back at me for what? What did I do to you?

Karen: For having me read that and then I didn't understand it.

Shelly: You made her uncomfortable.

Karen: Yeah, you made me uncomfortable . . .

Jennifer: When somebody gives me something to read and I don't get it, the next time I see that person I say, "I don't get it." What would have been about that that you would feel uncomfortable enough that you needed to attack me unless you're like "Who the fuck does she think she is?" Then, why would I think I'm somebody? We were trying to get literature to support the presentation that we were preparing. So it was like an experiment. So what in that could be threatening? This isn't an "I'm your teacher, read this." This was like, "OK, I found this interesting. Read it." She could have easily said, "I don't think so." To me that's a big piece of white privilege right there. It's like, "How dare you make me feel uncomfortable?" Those are the times when I'm like, I don't need that.

Shelly: And that feels right to you that there might have been something in that, still beginning the relationship and made to feel uncomfortable preying on your insecurities of understanding by this African American woman?

Karen: Yep.

So how does Karen respond to the knowledge that this "superiority complex" exists internally and emerges without conscious intent? Karen takes her recognition of racism in stride, saying that she continues to work on it but expects to mess up. She says, "I just say there's another example. It's not over yet. It's still there, alive and well, and you need to keep working on it."

One of the challenges we face when actively attempting to battle lingering, internalized racism is the risk of over-intellectualizing. We can get preoccupied with the terminology and lose sight of the essential meaning. Allowing ourselves to walk humbly along this path with a willingness to hear that we have picked up hurtful psychic habits is the goal. This can help us as we negotiate the complex web of feelings we face, sometimes simultaneously, those that inspire guilt, shame, confidence, or fear.

Something to think about:

• What feelings arise as you consider that your speech and behavior might express an internalized sense of superiority or inferiority?

GUILT AND SHAME

Only one person I spoke with mentioned anything regarding guilt or shame. Because my original hope was to find people who could illustrate a life that appropriately manages these feelings, it makes sense that they are a small part of the stories shared. Yet this painful aspect needs to be acknowledged. Guilt and shame are too much a part of the lived experience of white people moving through an increase in racial identity to be left out.

Spencer spoke of the shame he feels for both the historic and contemporary forms of racism engaged in by white people, including himself. He recognizes that his behind-the-scenes advocacy on behalf of people of color is a part of his response to this inner feeling. Since Spencer's response to these feelings prompts him toward ally work as, this form of shame need not be seen as a negative, pernicious emergence that should be dismissed.

My feeling about this stems largely from my perspective that a fair amount of negative affect is a healthy response to a newfound recognition of one's complicity in the contemporary maintenance of racial domination. Yet it is also true that continued shame can lead to reactive violence or a sense of paralyzation.[8] Overwhelming guilt can also lead us to isolate ourselves from people of color because we do not want to face people who remind us of those painful feelings. For this reason, the guilt that whites carry needs to be managed and held in balance with a healthy sense of agency.

Yet there is an area where Spencer battles an unhelpful sense of shame ingrained deep within the psyche, a shame built upon loss and dissociation. In a book titled *Learning to Be White,* Thandeka writes of a systematic conditioning white people experience that results in feeling disconnected from others.[9] She suggests that a deep shame develops wherein whites feel personally flawed. She links this to an inner conflict that results in a simultaneous sense of being better than *and* less than others.

This theory perhaps sheds some light on the challenges Spencer faces regarding his relationship with Native American people:

> I always thought that you treated Native Americans with utmost respect. That is my spiritual or religious bent, so . . . I was always removed from it because I always felt that I was one down, you know, I'm not a person of the Earth like they are. I needed to untangle that . . . I wanted to look equal, but I didn't feel equal.

Spencer's experience highlights the conflicting and contradictory internal conditionings some white people fight to disentangle. On the one hand, the false messages of inherent goodness and the supremacy of whiteness remain embedded. On the other hand, a deep sense of shame and disconnection can reduce our sense of wholeness and intrinsic value.

Something to reflect on:

• In what ways do you experience guilt or shame regarding race issues?

SEEING IN THE DARK

We must admit to ourselves that no matter how hard we try, and however many years we struggle, racism lingers within us and bumps up against our sense of "progress" and the "can-do" spirit that many of us carry. We must guard against hopelessness, however. If we can face our deepest shadows, go willingly into the dark night of the new moon when Hecate rules most powerfully, we find that our power grows with increased consciousness.

As they say, knowledge is power, and we have much to offer when we harness our fears, honestly grapple with our internal psyche, and find ways to talk about these things. True, lingering racism might continue to emerge as recordings or unrecognized blind spots. But as we saw with our storytellers, speaking our concerns aloud, seeking out healing connections, acknowledging the continuing effects, and making use of their messages to inform our actions can help us stay in touch with ourselves and others as we locate the next steps on our path.

Before closing out this chapter, however, appreciation must be extended to those who took the personal risk to offer such an honest expression of their experiences. Collectively they offer self-critical and often painful testimony, allowing us to begin to understand the consistent effort necessary to liberate ourselves from lingering racism—in essence, to use bell hooks' phrase, "decolonizing our minds and our imaginations."[10] White people are purposefully placed within the category of the colonized here, not to equalize the positions, but to reflect how the domination and colonization essential to the development of whiteness depended not only upon lower-class Europeans seeing themselves in terms created by the wealthy elite in order to solidify and protect our capitalistic system but also the development of an inner sense of shame and disconnection.[11]

In this way, part of the movement toward witnessing includes the decolonization of our own sense of self. This might occur through an honest acknowledgment of the ways that racism remains embedded within our psyches, is unleashed without our conscious attention, and continues to terrorize and shame all of us. With this acknowledgment, we can work toward becoming challengers to the systems that perpetuate disconnections and dis-ease.

NOTES

1. Atiba, P., and J. Eberhardt, *A Hateful Link,* Los Angeles Times, Op-ed, A19, February 28, 2009.

2. hooks, b., *Killing Rage: Ending Racism* (New York: Henry Holt, 1995), 78.

3. Morrison, T., *Playing in the Dark: Whiteness and the Literary Imagination* (New York: Vintage Books, 1992), 52.

4. Pitts, Jr., Leonard, "Crazy Sometimes," In *When Race Becomes Real,* ed. B. Singley (Chicago, IL: Lawrence Hill Books, 2002).

5. Obidah, J. E., and K. M. Teel, *Because of the Kids: Facing Racial and Cultural Differences in Schools* (New York: Teachers College Press, 2001). This is a good text for examples of how a well-meaning white teacher can be party to the disengagement of students of color due to a lack of race consciousness

6. hooks, *Killing Rage,* 37.

7. hooks, *Killing Rage,* 37.

8. Gilligan, J., *Violence: Reflections on a National Epidemic* (New York: Vintage Books, 1996).

9. Thandeka, *Learning to Be White: Money, Race, and God in America* (New York: Continuum, 1999).

10. hooks, *Killing Rage,* 50.

11. Thandeka, *Learning to Be White.*

Part III

The Work of Witnessing Whiteness

Chapter 8

How Do We Witness?

Once we decide to include taking a stand against racial injustice as part of our practice, the question to ask is, how do we do that? What exactly can we do to effectively witness in our professional and social lives? One key is recognizing that witnessing is a verb, an action. We have to *do* something.

A second key is that we have to become responsible, or better yet, *response-able.* Moving from intellectually understanding racism and privilege toward developing a way of life that effectively deals with race requires us to have the *ability* to *respond* to what we see. This type of *response-ability* means engaging the journey toward becoming active in justice pursuits in both our social and work settings. This is required since developing knowledge without a shift in action simply reinforces our role as bystanders. Witnessing, therefore, requires movement, some action that brings us at least one step closer to ally work.

To be realistic, the primary work heading toward ally activities usually begins with personal investigation, learning, and practice among close relationships and peers. As we become increasingly competent, our circle of influence will expand. A level of humility is essential as we enter this dialogue, as is the recognition that most of us have a long way to go before we can confidently and consistently enact an effective antiracist practice. However, as we build our witnessing practice, over time we become more successful change agents at organizational and/or institutional levels.

To start off, developing the ability to respond to racially-loaded situations can be really challenging when newly coming to see the effects of race. If we are going to take a stand, we need to feel prepared to deal with our own sense of discomfort and potential resistance or rejection from others. For this reason, we need an action plan to guide our development. This chapter outlines four main categories of actions we can take in order to develop and support our efforts at witnessing.

To offer a brief introduction, we need to continue to *build knowledge* and make use of knowledge gained. We have to *build skills,* a set of tools we can use when witnessing either subtle or overt racism. Many of us also feel intense emotions when dealing with issues of race. We must *build capacity* to make use of our skills in the face of our emotions, a process that takes courage and practice. Finally, we need support to continue to practice these skills during moments when we feel confused, disappointed, or frustrated. For this reason, part of witnessing also includes *creating community,* consciously developing a community of people around us who understand our striving, re-inspire us when we fail, and celebrate our successful efforts.

This chapter suggests that we make use of each of these four elements— building knowledge, skills, capacity, and community. I imagine Hecate watching over her cauldron, her magical elixir offering transformative power, insight, and capability. Here, however, I see each of us taking up Hecate's position, creating a personal recipe from the list of essential ingredients.

Successfully taking up a witness position requires the addition of each ingredient into the mix of our individual brew. Although tempting to attend to each category in a defined sequence, one after the other, this can lead to difficulty. We could easily concentrate on building knowledge for an eternity, never feeling ready to take additional action. Therefore, my recommendation is to take up Hecate's position with creativity, working with each element simultaneously. In this way, each aspect supports the work of the other, creating a balanced recipe for the creation of a life that begins to subvert systemic white privilege and racism.

BUILDING KNOWLEDGE

If we do not know much about racism and its relationship to whiteness, then we cannot do much about racism or white-skin privilege. There are several ways to advance our vision regarding these issues, each of which deserves some attention. We can examine the whiteness of our own lives, continue our study, seek diverse informational outlets, and expand our base of experience.

Examining Our Lives

What do we need to examine? First, we need to notice how deeply our daily experience is shaped by whiteness, segregation, and privilege. This involves questioning where we go, what we encounter, what we fear, what we avoid, and so on. What follows is an initial series of questions that we can ask ourselves to get a sense of how evident racial segregation is in our lives. The questions in this section are best used as an activity (with emphasis on the *active* in activity). Take the time to write down the answers to each of the questions in exercise 8.1.

EXERCISE 8.1. HOW SEGREGATED IS MY LIFE?

- What is the racial makeup of my surroundings?
  - My family?
  - My housing community?
  - My place of employment or educational institution?
  - My place of worship?
  - My various social circles?
  - My favorite entertainment centers?
- Are any facets of my surroundings racially diverse?
  - What makes a place diverse?
    - What percentage of white folks are in these diverse places?
    - What is the percentage of different racial groups in these diverse places?
    - Which racial groups are absent?
  - How often do white people dominate my environment?
    - When do I experience places where 50 percent or more of the population is composed of people of color?
  - Am I ever one of only a few faces in a crowd of my racial background?
    - Where? How often? How do I feel in these situations?
- Are there areas of my city that I avoid?
  - If I do avoid certain areas . . .
    - Why do I avoid these areas?
    - What do I imagine it would be like to live in these areas?
    - Who are the people who live there?
    - Are people who look like me often negatively affected in these areas?
      - How do I know?
      - What sources of information do I rely upon?
    - What do I fear might happen if I go there?
    - Are my fears based on media reports?
    - Am I willing to believe that wonderful events take place in these areas that are worth attending?

- If I do not avoid certain areas . . .
  - Are there areas of my city that are predominantly populated by people of color?
  - What makes me feel welcomed in these areas?
  - Do I know people of color who live in these areas?
  - Does going into areas occupied primarily by people of color affect my perception of the world? If so, how? If not, why not?

Take a moment and review the answers to the questions in the exercise. Now consider the following questions:

- When do my surroundings inspire me to think about what it means to be part of my racial group?
- When does my environment challenge me about my race?
- Who or what raises questions about race for me?

At this point, we can remember the analogy regarding whether or not fish in a fishbowl notice the water in which they swim. For those of us who are white, if whiteness dominates the majority of our environments this indicates that we likely have difficulty seeing the whiteness around us. The answers to the previous questions then offer us clues as to the areas in which we may be so thoroughly entrenched within whiteness that we gain a relatively limited perspective.

When reviewing my own answers to the questions above, I noticed that my most segregated environment is my workplace. Although the student body where I teach is extremely diverse, the full-time faculty in my department is composed almost exclusively of white women. What this means is that even though there are explicitly-stated intentions to bring social justice into our program and to be conscious of ourselves as racial beings, I and my colleagues quite likely have blind spots regarding our curriculum and teaching styles.

For example, a workshop at a conference on white privilege alerted me to some problems with a particular text used in one of my courses. Even though I had already noticed enough problems to have carefully picked and chosen the elements used from the book, the conference prompted me to realize that the level of scrutiny needed was beyond my understanding at that time. Since then, I have decided to check in with some of my teacher-friends of color when developing new material. Their eyes bring a different sensibility that might help me increase my own vision regarding these things.

Of course, since segregation still marks many of our work and social spaces, many of us might not have someone to turn to for this kind of help.

Building relationships with people willing to serve in this capacity might take significant effort and time, and might not even be available at all. However, we must at least begin by recognizing the importance of making movements toward appreciating the helpful and important nature of feedback from people with different sensibilities.

Another way to examine our lives is by looking critically at ourselves to see how we relate to the various associated meanings of whiteness discussed in Chapters 3 and 5. To take but one example, whiteness is often associated with a segregated lifestyle that avoids the struggles faced by many people of color. How true is this for each of us?

EXERCISE 8.2. HOW COMFORTABLE ARE THE PEOPLE IN MY LIFE AND MYSELF?

Have I, or anyone I know socially, ever . . .

- Experienced fear-inducing harassment based on race at work or while walking on the street within the last several months?
- Lived in a place for over a year where the majority of people did not speak my or my friend's native language?
- Received an education primarily featuring people of a different race?
- Worked for minimum wage?
- Taken a job illegally paying less than the legal minimum wage?
- Had wages withheld illegally?
- Requested unemployment benefits?
- Applied for public assistance?
- Relied exclusively on public transportation to get around?
- Been unable to acquire health insurance?
- Relied on overcrowded health care facilities?
- Heard gunshots in the night on a regular basis?
- Had a family member impacted by street violence?
- Feared the police, health-care workers, or other public servants?
- Had to appear in court?
- Spent time in prison?

Impossible to miss is that many of the questions posed in exercise 8.2 might appear more associated with socioeconomic class than race. But please recall from Chapter 1 that whiteness is often associated with achieving middle-class economic status. Separating out the effects of race and class is a real challenge in a society that purposefully enacted racist systems, policies, and procedures in order to concentrate prosperity in the hands of white people. In other words, witnessing racial injustice also includes examining the effects of systems adversely impacting the working poor and economically impoverished, regardless of race.

Most activists emphasize that working to end one type of oppression requires the common work of challenging all dominating systems. For example, we should know that white people from lower socioeconomic strata suffer plenty of hardships and that the steps that lead to their advancement can also work to support people of color. However, we can simultaneously recall that this is a society in which a disproportionate number of those at the bottom rungs of prosperity are people of color. The 2005 annual report from the Census Bureau on national income data, for example, revealed that 24.9 percent of Blacks live below the poverty line, 21.8 percent of Hispanics, 11.1 percent of Asians, and 8.3 percent of non-Hispanic whites.[1] In essence, we cannot disregard the importance of the above questions simply because they are tied to socioeconomic class since race and class so often go hand in hand.

Yet the importance of linking race and class issues goes beyond simply identifying them as interconnected. Noticing the degree to which our lives shield us from certain difficult experiences is essential in recognizing where our gaps in knowledge may lie. Let me offer an example to illustrate. I once sat in a meeting with Gloria Killian, a woman who served over seventeen and a half years in prison for a crime she did not commit and whose story and work are featured in the documentary *After Innocence*. Gloria is not a one-sided speaker. She understands why many rules are necessary within institutions and she offers praise for those who treat people fairly. But the story she told detailing the inhumane treatment that often exists in prison, including the recent death of a friend occurring as a result of active neglect, both saddened and horrified me.

Why tell you about this woman upset about the death of another woman in prison? How does hearing her story relate to witnessing racial injustice? Simply, Gloria's story is important in improving our ability to witness racial injustice because she helps us understand the unfair, and sometimes ridiculously inane, treatment and policies encountered within a system that disproportionately impacts people of color. If we do not come into person-to-person contact with someone with her background, we likely would not think of such things. But if our lives include sitting with those who suffer under the weight of troubling systemic policies, we are more likely to feel inspired to support those who do the active work for reform in areas such as criminal justice, health care, education, public transportation, worker's rights, immigration, welfare, etc.

Coming into contact with Gloria did not occur because of my normal work or social routines. In order to look beyond my middle-class environment, I have to go out of my way to attend meetings and events that highlight experiences of people that do not normally enter my networks and social circles. Living in a fairly segregated city, making the time to enter intentional circles where people of different class and race backgrounds come together in dialogue requires effort.

Doing this leads me to listen intently to those who experience the world differently than I do and then to examine myself. This is invaluable in helping me understand the immediate need for large-scale policy change, changes that go hand in hand with racial justice efforts. With this broad understanding, I am also in a better position to recognize the issues faced by low-income students and their parents, predominantly people of color, who struggle under the weight of many of the policies currently in force.

Now, let me ask readers this question. As you read about Gloria and pictured her, what image came to your mind? What racial background would you assign to her? Would your reading of the last two paragraphs change if you learned that she is a white woman? Would it make a difference if you learned that her friend who died was also white? Would you be surprised? If so, why? The answers to those questions are extremely important. The answers tell us a lot about how we have been conditioned to see both prisoners and people of color.

One more question. Is it possible that, as bad as Gloria's experience was, it could have been worse had she been a person of color? What if she had *not* been a law-school student prior to her incarceration? What if she had *not* had the skills to know how to speak effectively with prison guards and wardens? What if those guards and wardens held racial prejudices? Considering these questions can highlight the ways that someone can sometimes experience disadvantage due to one social position, such as their gender or socioeconomic status, while simultaneously benefit from white privilege.

Yet, there is more. When Gloria offered feedback regarding my telling of her story, she asked me to include the fact that she was raised in an upper-middle-class family and received a solid education growing up. Important to her is that this book names that she, herself, experienced significant discrimination within the prison because she was seen as a privileged white woman, one who guards saw as needing to be controlled and put in her place. This is not to take away from the questions posed above. Gloria is absolutely clear that racism remains a serious problem. But what she wanted me to highlight is that this experience allowed her to feel "viscerally" what it was like to be abusively discriminated against because of her background. She indicated that most whites do not ever have that opportunity and she said that this experience helps her understand the battle against racism more deeply.

A third way we can examine how our racial position impacts our lives involves honestly reflecting on the ways that our white-dominated social world has played a role in our personal and collective achievements. Since our country tends to operate with an individualistic point of view, we tend to discount or overlook the variety of beneficial influences we receive in our own lives. We need to look at some aspects of privilege that can be so subtle that they commonly go unnoticed, the way our social networks have influenced our accomplishments. Again, slow down and take the time to write down the answers to the questions in exercise 8.3.

EXERCISE 8.3. WHO HELPED ME
GET TO WHERE I AM TODAY?

- Recall the elders, parent's friends, coworkers, coaches, mentors, teachers, and so on who made a difference in your life.
  - How did these individuals help you? Did anyone- . . .
    - Give you a tip regarding a job opportunity?
    - Facilitate you meeting someone in a position of power?
    - Encourage you to complete an application for something?
    - Put in a good word with a boss or advisor?
    - Write you a letter of recommendation?
    - Spend extra time or offer extra attention to help you learn something?
    - Let you know that your accomplishment is important to them?
    - Inspire confidence in your abilities?
    - Get you a good deal on a major purchase?
  - How often was that helpful, supportive person of the same racial background as you?
- Think of the various authority figures that made decisions related to you and your future. Recall the landlords, loan officers, hiring committees, admissions officers, government workers, counselors, and so on.
  - How did their choices affect your life? Were they a part of you- . . .
    - Being accepted into an educational program?
    - Contacting college or employment offices?
    - Getting a job?
    - Securing a place to live?
    - Knowing about funding or scholarship opportunities?
    - Moving quickly through a difficult bureaucratic moment?
    - Receiving a loan?
  - How often was that person making decisions of the same race as you?

An important point to highlight here is that our personal accomplishments are hard-fought and require much effort. Personally, I am very proud of my grade-point averages, degrees, awards, and job positions. My successes depended upon my own striving, dedication, and perseverance. However, also true is that I am not solely responsible for achieving these things.

Doors swung open for me. Beyond my parents, there were many individuals who helped me get to where I now stand. My coaches, teachers, mentors, and friends at various times, and in various ways, helped ensure that hard work did not go without reward. At times, benefits came from those who mentioned that I reminded them of themselves in their younger days. Other times, benefits came from open doors bred from social connections to which many would not have had access.

Further, benefits came from the fact that my entire racial/socioeconomic/ cultural background was similar to many of the decision makers in my life, such that I could easily inspire ease and a sense of camaraderie in an interview setting. Again, true, race and class cannot be completely separated. But I benefited from the fact that our white-dominated society often influences people of color, through *internalized racism,* to trust the abilities of white people over those of people of their own background.[2]

I inspired no subtle fear and was not perceived as potentially threatening or challenging by decision makers of any background. No one imagined that my presence might be disruptive or that my personality style might be too bold. To be sure, as our society increasingly sees people of color attaining positions of prominence and power, these disparities also see a shift. But benefits surely came to me due to the entire racist history that portrays whites as more likely holders of knowledge and power.

After all, when looking broadly at the power positions, such as in politics, corporations, organizations, educational institutions, and social support systems, white people continue to occupy high offices at disproportionate levels (exceptions and improvements notwithstanding). It should be no surprise that in a society based on historic inequality, the benefits white people derive from social contacts would tend to reinforce already existing power inequities. This social capital need not be transferred consciously.

In fact, quite likely, none of the teachers, mentors, or decision makers in my life consciously tried to reinforce a racially unequal power structure. The reinforcement occurs by default, with white young people far more likely to profit from social networks inhabited by socially powerful adults than young people of color. Recognizing this, we might begin to understand why those who make statements referring to a "level playing field" or asking someone to "pick yourself up by the bootstraps" can sound more like defensive denials of reality than constructive advice.

Let me reiterate that admitting that I received help in no way takes away from my accomplishments. Rather, examining the full story of how I came to occupy my social positions helps me recognize how racism and whiteness continue to affects people's lives and highlights that there are many who do not enjoy the same help. If this is a difficult thing to admit, we should ask ourselves, why? What does it mean for us if this is true?

Admittedly, examining the role of our racial placement in our lives can sometimes leave us with more questions than answers. What does it mean if the majority of our input comes from segregated experiences? What if our lives do not invite deep connection with people whose stories are significantly different from our own? What if we have developed a rudimentary knowledge of the impacts of race, but do not see how that might alter our own previously held understanding of politics, economics, and so forth? What if the angle of this analysis simply does not satisfy all of the questions inspired? One answer is to seek out additional sources of information.

Continuing Our Study

Books, compact disks, lectures, book talks, videos, documentaries, and periodicals are just some of the ways that we can continue learning about race, whiteness, and their impacts on our psyche and society. This book is meant to open us up to the idea, explain why we have a role to play, and get us started on the path toward witnessing. As a broad introductory text, there are a lot of important subjects that have been either treated rather superficially or skipped altogether. But if we wish to develop a truly comprehensive view, each of us needs to build knowledge on a variety of subtopics. These include:

- Our roots (ethnic, familial histories upon which we can ground our sense of self)
- History of the white supremacist system
- History of resistance against white supremacy
- People's history (multiple threads, many groups, stories white people generally ignore)
- White privilege (continued investigation into its meanings and manifestations)
- White racial identity
- Interconnections between race, class, gender, and so forth

Locating essential texts in each of the above areas is important in order to avoid a myopic view of how to notice racism and work to counter its effects.

Additionally, what follows is a short list of extremely helpful resources that you might choose in order to advance knowledge building beyond this book:

- *Why Are All the Black Kids Sitting Together in the Cafeteria?* by Beverly Daniel Tatum is a bestseller for a reason. Easy to understand, yet provocative, this book highlights the different paths toward racial understanding taken by various groups, including whites. Do not let the title fool you, however. This text can help white adults understand their own process as much as it informs us about what occurs with young people in schools today.
- *White Like Me: Reflections on Race from a Privileged Son,* by Tim Wise. This author stands as one of the most well-known and popular speakers on the issue of white privilege in the United States today. His style is easily accessible and he has a keen ability to link personal story with contemporary and historical examples of racism.
- *The Heart of Whiteness: Confronting Race, Racism, and White Privilege,* by Robert Jensen. This short, pocket-sized text offers a critical look at race and racism, using personal narrative to illustrate issues of white privilege and why white people can benefit from confronting this issue.
- *When Race Becomes Real: Black and White Writers Confront Their Personal Histories,* by Benestine Singley. This collection of short personal narratives by thirty of the best-known authors on race is powerful. Its structure makes it especially useful for those who want to hear from various viewpoints in short intervals.
- *Uprooting Racism: How White People Can Work toward Racial Justice,* by Paul Kivel. This volume is perfect for people who see the need for action and who want more tactics and information on a wide range of specific issues. For example, how can we take a stand on issues such as education, affirmative action, the police, religion, and public policy?

There are also taped lectures or public events where you might continue this aspect of the journey. Internet searches for any of the above authors or subjects quickly put you in touch with a wealth of information. There are also many websites devoted to uncovering racism and white privilege. Most include links and suggested authors and speakers.

Seeking Diverse Informational Outlets

The information received through text, lecture, and audio sources offer a foundational understanding. We then build upon that understanding when we make use of new knowledge to find linkages in our day-to-day world. How are issues of race reflected in our city, state, and country today in ways that might impact people of color? We can then listen to the events in the news with a more critical ear.

For example, witnessing would include taking notice of a story about a car insurance company considering shifting its policies so that the neighborhood in which a driver lives becomes less important than the individual's driving record when determining premium rates. For a long time, those living in poorer neighborhoods with high crime rates have paid higher premiums than those living in wealthier neighborhoods, regardless of driving record.

If we are paying attention to that news report about the car insurance rates, we might find out that what is prompting the considered change is pressure from groups claiming that the current policy discriminates against people of color. We might recall that a policy such as this would disproportionately impact people of color since more people of color are concentrated in poorer areas. Then, we might determine that an effort to dismantle one example of white privilege is underway.

We can choose to be a witness to this move and support the change, per-haps writing a letter or making a phone call to add our influence. If we pay close attention to various items in the news, we might start to see other areas in which policy decisions might have racially-discriminatory impacts. Yet, to do this, we might have to investigate further. Mainstream news coverage might not always offer an analysis that allows us to see the racial impacts.

Our regular news sources do not likely offer us a full accounting of how race plays a role in the events portrayed on the news. In fact, given that the vast majority of whites tend to believe that race is an issue of the past, our mainstream media tends not to link the current issues with their relationships to race. Seeking out diverse informational outlets can support our efforts to learn how current issues relate to race. Sources can include people, commu-nity leaders, radio news, websites, or news magazines that speak and write from either a social-justice or minority perspective. Some examples might include:

- *Multicultural Pavilion* (website)—www.edchange.org/multicultural—a website that offers links to social justice news and other educational related issues.
- *Democracy Now!* (radio program)—www.democracynow.org
- *Counter Spin* (radio program)—www.fair.org—a weekly half-hour show offering a critical look at the issues covered by mainstream media.
- *Global Voices for Justice*—www.globalvoicesonline.org—a news hub where they cover international issues by having reporters from various

countries writing about the issues. This is a good international resource to hear about struggles going on globally from people on the ground.

- *Color Lines*—www.colorlines.com—a magazine that covers progressive activists and organizing focused on people-of-color issues in the United States.

Certainly, we might not agree with all opinions that come from these programs or websites. That is to be expected. But, hopefully, we know that opening ourselves to see an issue from a different point of view can help us better understand how the policies we vote into law might affect those from whom we are isolated.

Once we expose ourselves to voices often pushed to the margins, we can look at the mainstream media with a slightly different eye. We can then begin to ask ourselves the following series of questions on a regular basis:

- Which racial groups would primarily benefit from a proposed policy, regardless of intention?
- Who are the promoters and decision makers on this issue?
- Are there any subtle allusions to race made using race-neutral speech but racialized images? For example, does the news story make reference to a social problem and link it with images of people of color at the same time?
- Is this issue one that affects primarily whites or people of color? If the issue affects primarily people of color, whose are the dominant voices explaining the situation?

Sitting alone to reflect on these questions might prove ineffective if our knowledge base remains thin. Reading and self-questioning only take us so far. Perhaps the surest way to build knowledge is to get out into the world in a new way and seek out new experiences.

Seeking New Experiences

The suggestion to seek out new experiences also comes with an acknowledgment that not all environments are equally instructive. We would do well to pick our entries into new spaces with some care and attention. To enter any new environment blindly, with assumptions of easy admission, acceptance, and potential learning, actually can be an enactment of privilege in itself. My suggestion, therefore, is to consider environments that offer an instructive, yet provocative, learning space. We might also need to openly ask about the potential for guidance and support. What follows are a set of environments that I have personally found to be most conducive to gaining new knowledge.

Individuals

Who are the people available in your life? Are there individuals in your life or social groups who might expose you to a new way of seeing that you have previously kept at arm's length? Would you be comfortable telling those persons what you are trying to do and asking for direct assistance? Although there is a definite risk of rejection, sometimes a person will offer the benefit of the doubt and the result can be beautiful.

Recalling my own experience, years ago I approached an African American female colleague at my school site and mentioned an issue that perplexed me. Why had I developed deep relationships with men of color, but had no women of color as friends? I shared with her my concern about this and my hope that she might be willing to talk with me. Over a decade later, she is now one of my best friends. But, in reviewing the manuscript for this book, she reminded me of how our friendship began and told me that she initially found the idea a bit strange but decided that it would not hurt to help out this sincere-appearing white girl.

Community Events

Where are groups coming together in your city that highlight issues with which you are unfamiliar? What programs are running? Where might there be community displays of art, dance, theater, film, or poetry? My attendance at Voices of Youth events, evenings of poetry put on by youth of color speaking about their experiences surviving inner-city life, opened up a whole new way of seeing young people. I walk away from those experiences both profoundly saddened by the violence and death that mark their young lives and also inspired by the resilience and courage they display.

Each event inspires more commitment to supporting programs offering young people opportunities and second chances. If you have never heard inner-city youth speak out about their experiences, you are missing something profound. Depending upon your location, there might also be social justice-oriented gatherings that intend to raise awareness for those in attendance. Do not be shy. Ask someone there to explain something you find confusing. More often than not, those who attend these events are more than willing to offer some information, especially if you share your interest.

Museums, Art Displays

Exhibits and programs that concentrate on evaluating or displaying the history of a particular group of people can also be an important vehicle for filling in our knowledge gaps. Our learning in these spaces largely depends on our approach. Do we take someone with us with whom we can discuss what we see? Or do we simply observe images and displays allowing us to see the history of other's experiences? If we choose this forum, we can challenge ourselves to keep this question at the forefront of our minds: how does this particular history inform the present?

Workshops/Retreats/Classes/Speakers

There are a number of groups offering workshops specifically oriented around raising awareness related to white-skin privilege and racism. Colleges might offer classes, and smaller bookstores often host guest speakers. The trick is keeping our eyes out for these opportunities. There are also retreats that bring together diverse groups in an effort to find essential connections as they simultaneously face social divisions and inequities. For men, Mosaic Multicultural Foundation's annual six-day retreat is a great example.

Conferences

Larger, more formal conference spaces also offer a great source of new learning. As more and more people recognize the need to confront issues of white privilege, more conferences related to social justice that specifically deal with race and whiteness have developed. A favorite is the White Privilege Conference, which is held in April each year. This conference brings together upwards of 900 people per year. The keynote speakers are generally some of the best-known thinkers and writers on the subject of race, and their insights can propel a year's worth of study and investigation.

What Makes a Good Learning Space?

To be honest, learning about racism can invite painful experiences. Our long history of ignorance and neglect on this topic rightly infuriates many. It is only fair to acknowledge that we are likely to run across people who are ready to share their pain and anger in ways that inspire discomfort for many people in the room. Although it can be healthy to confront feelings of guilt and emotional pain as we move into a deep recognition of our collective history, we might want to check that the environments we choose have an understanding that awareness and healing are some of the goals.

People of any background should be on the lookout for a stated purpose when choosing new learning spaces. What is the shared intention for people coming together? Are the people you speak with in tune with that purpose? If activists are planning the event, to what degree do they recognize that race is not the only lens worth utilizing?

What follows is an example of the types of explicitly-stated purposes that readers might look for when choosing a class, workshop, or conference. This list comes directly from the advertisement material related to the White Privilege Conference, and demonstrates the clear thinking and acknowledgments that help to bring together a collection of people who are invested in challenging the status quo, learning, and healing:

1. It is not a conference designed to attack, degrade, or beat up on white folks.
2. It is not a conference designed to rally white supremacist groups.
3. It is not a conference just for white folks; WPC is open to everyone.
4. WPC is grounded in the historical premise that since America was founded for and by white people, white privilege is a historical and current reality.
5. WPC is a conference designed to examine issues of privilege beyond skin color. WPC includes diverse voices and perspectives to provide a comprehensive look at issues of privilege, including race, gender, class, sexuality, disability, and so on—the ways we all experience some form of privilege, and how we're all affected by that privilege.
6. WPC is an exciting conference that examines the challenging concepts of privilege and oppression and offers solutions and team-building strategies to work toward a more equitable world.
7. WPC attracts students, professionals, activists, parents, and community leaders/members from diverse perspectives. WPC welcomes folks with varying levels of experience addressing issues of diversity, cultural competency, and multiculturalism.
8. WPC is committed to a philosophy of "understanding, respecting, and connecting."

Building our knowledge base requires us to *look within* to examine how often white spaces dominate our lives and *look without* in order to seek out new sources of information and experiences. If the thought of attending a class, lecture, workshop, or conference on this topic inspires reticence, we should ask ourselves why. What do we have to lose? Book learning alone, with no action, simply does not move us any closer to healing ourselves and deepening our relationships across race. True, we might feel nervous because we do not yet have the skills to engage in dialogue. Knowledge without skills does not do us much good. So building skills is another ingredient we must add to our mix.

BUILDING SKILLS

Once we see the issues surrounding racially-loaded situations more clearly, what do we do? How do we put our learning into action? How do we speak to people who do not recognize that our racial placement is meaningful, racism continues, white-skin privilege exists, and racist jokes are problematic? How do we conduct ourselves with people with whom we would like to talk about race? In essence, what tools can we use in anxiety-provoking moments? This section focuses on two main areas of concern. One, we need to have some practiced options. Two, white people need to find ways to learn from people of color without reenacting white privilege.

Speak Up—Naming the Problem

There is just no way around the fact that witnessing requires us to use our voices. If we see racism, we have to name racism. There is also no doubt that for most of us this is easier said than done. They are bystander moments, times when we get caught off guard by some comment that we cannot believe we just heard. At the same moment, we might be trying to sort through: (1) What are the issues surrounding what this person is saying? (2) Do I feel safe enough to say or do something? And if so, (3) how should I respond?

All of these questions are important, but they can also immobilize us within the conversation or situation. We can get caught like a deer in the headlights. We sometimes become still, mouth agape, so confused that we often end up simply smiling strangely, perhaps muttering some type of disagreement under our breath, but otherwise just trying to get past that uncomfortable moment. These moments can also occur very rapidly, which only adds to the difficulty.

One of my most remarkable bystander moments occurred while I was in Washington, D.C., to conduct interviews with Katie and Lorraine. The diversity of the city impressed me. For the first time in my life, I ate at a fancy restaurant that catered to a relatively affluent, African American clientele. One evening during the trip, on my way down to meet Katie in the hotel lobby, I entered the elevator, scooted around a few people and positioned myself near the back. An Asian American man was at one side and five or six white people were in the center.

Apparently I entered in the middle of an ongoing conversation because one of the men said to another couple, "Well, it is just nice to be with white people again. I mean it's like you can't get away from them here. They're everywhere." He went on to say a few more rather objectionable things that I cannot recall. But, by the time I got my head wrapped around what he was really saying, the "ding" sounded, the elevator stopped, and the man and his group walked out. The couple the man had addressed said something about how he must have been drinking and just as soon as they made their comment, they walked out of the elevator. The Asian American man had slipped by me quickly as well. I then stood there, alone, not quite sure what to do. Katie stood before the open elevator doors, and I just slowly walked out and said, "I can't believe what just happened."

The entire event surely took less than thirty seconds. Easy consolation comes by saying that there had not been enough time to say anything. And true, the situation did happen rapidly. But it is also true that a practiced repertoire of responses would have allowed me to be less immobilized and more able to say something to bear witness to the racism before me. Even though the man might not have dialogued with me further, the racism present in that moment could have been named.

The next section offers a set of approaches we can practice to develop responses to moments such as these. Moments where something really ought to be said can occur anywhere: at home, school, work, with friends, at parties, at church, out for coffee, in a restaurant, on the bus, in airports. Really, anywhere can be a place to let someone know that something said or done is mired in some level of racism or privilege. We might struggle with how to do this at first. But as my father always says, practice makes perfect. Besides, the more we practice in our day-to-day lives, the easier it becomes to take action with supervisors or administrators in our companies or institutions where the personal stakes might be higher.

Practiced Responses to Racism

Here, we concentrate on person-to-person contact. Some might consider this a more basic form of witnessing than writing a letter or calling to complain about discriminatory practices. However, witnessing racism in front of another individual can be far more daunting for many people. For that reason, we really do have to ask, how do we respond when faced with racially-loaded comments or jokes that we recognize as objectionable? What follows are a series of effective strategies that we can practice.

Questioning

This approach asks us to speak in a way that gives people the benefit of the doubt, acting as though they could not possibly mean what they appear to be saying. For example, when a person offers an analysis that appears either subtly or overtly racist, we might respond with a question such as, "When you say _____, it sounds like you are saying that _____, but I am not sure if this is what you mean?" This offers the person an opportunity to reflect and perhaps alter his or her speech.

If the person truly believes in prejudiced ideas, this approach surely will not change his or her point of view—but at least it might disrupt the conversation enough for the speaker to find out that prejudice is not welcomed or acceptable in your presence. This pattern can continue as needed, with the questions becoming more explicitly challenging. We might actually have to say, "I'm sorry, but that sounds rather prejudiced. Are you comfortable with sounding that way?" The essential idea is simply that we act a bit dense, as though we simply cannot believe that an intelligent person would ever say something with such obvious racial overtones.

Educating

This approach asks us to make use of the knowledge that we gain and try to inform the people around us why their statements are troubling for us. Note that this approach is not called lecturing. Instead, we can make short statements, such as, "You know, when I hear what you are saying, it reminds of when I thought something similar. But then I read something that made me realize that _____." Or, we might say something like, "Hey, I know sometimes the media makes it seem like that, but I found out recently that _____." In both of these sample statements, we avoid directly naming either the person or his or her speech as involving racist elements.

Depending upon the need and our own comfort, we can go farther. We can say, "Hey, I am sure you don't mean it this way, but it sounds like that idea comes from a perspective that can be seen as pretty racist." With this approach, the words we say may or may not be heard. The person may or may not continue with the subject, stick around to continue the dialogue, or feel comfortable with us. But, whatever the result, we have let that person know that we are not someone with whom he or she can safely speak using racially derogatory speech.

Express Personal Emotional Reaction

This approach asks us to tell a person making racist comments or jokes what it is like for us to hear those things. By letting the person know how we feel, we are avoiding directly challenging the content of what is being said, but instead asking the person to respect who we are and notice that his or her speech is not OK with us. We might say something like, "When you say that, I feel _____ and that makes it hard for me to be here with you." This approach can be especially effective with people close to us because we are not directly challenging the content of what the person is saying as much as the level of respect existing within the relationship. If these people care about us, won't they want to make sure that we feel good about spending time with them? At least, that is the question we can ask to try and get the person to shift his or her use of language.

Empathetic Relating

This approach asks us to invite the person speaking to imagine how he or she would feel if a similar negative statement were applied to him or her. We might respond to a racist comment or joke by saying, "Wow, when you say that, I can't help but imagine what those people would feel if they heard that. Can you imagine what it would feel like if people were sitting around talking about us like that? What if they were teasing about the way we . . . ? (Here, we might include something that we sense might be a meaningful stereotype that is used to injure). We can then ask, "Wow, how would that make you feel?"

Repeated Opportunities

Even with these strategies, we might not always respond perfectly. Sometimes we still might get confounded. Other times we might feel unsafe. Still other times, we might realize that we are up against a losing battle. There may be some serious power issues at play. Are we willing to challenge those who are in charge in our schools and workplaces? Of course, if we are serious about this, we would like to find some way to do this. However, the degree to which we respond always depends on the context, who is there, the relationship we have with the person, and how much time we have at that moment. However, when we do see an opening, having some options to draw upon can help.

Lastly, we also can give ourselves permission to return to a person once the situation has shifted and deal with the issue at a later time. For example, we might return and say, "You know, yesterday (or last week) you said _____, and I just want to ask you what you meant. I felt _____ hearing it and wanted to check in with you about it." We can choose to question, empathize, educate, or express our own feeling. But this way, even if we miss a moment, we still see that there might be a chance to respond once we have developed more clarity about the issue and a plan of approach.

Important to acknowledge is that these approaches are not necessarily designed to change the mind of the person with whom we are interacting. A person we challenge might develop a new awareness depending on our ability to explain ourselves, the openness of the person, and a myriad of other factors. But this is not a how-to-change-people's-hearts-and-minds guide.

The effort here is about naming what we see out loud in front of people so that we at least offer everyone the *opportunity* to see things in a different way.

Going Deep in Conversation

Speaking up in front of our family and close friends can often be the most challenging situation. If we enjoy dialogues full of debate, confrontation, and open acknowledgments of feelings, we likely struggle less. However, many of us have been trained to be rather reticent to express the types of difficult emotions and pains that disrupt the status quo. As painful as it is to admit, I know this is true not only within my own family but within the majority of my white friends' families as well. Also, recall that some of those interviewed spoke of their white families needing everything to stay "tidy," "neat," and "sanitized." To the degree that we feel this to be true of our own relationships, we might struggle more to witness in front of the white people in our lives. To get a sense of this, we might want to ask ourselves these questions:

- Do you fear that confronting and/or discussing racism and white privilege within your family or circle of friends will cause you to be treated differently?
- Will your family shut you down if you start talking about race at a family dinner?
- Can you already imagine the kind of negative responses you might face?
- Do you fear that you will lose your standing with some of your friends if you challenge their racism or unrecognized white privilege?

Our intuition and fears might tell us a lot about our potential to deal honestly with this subject. On the other hand, they might not. If we have never engaged in this type of conversation, armed with our newly-acquired knowledge and skills, how do we really know that we will not be heard? Perhaps we can invite the dialogue in a way that reveals more possibility than we currently imagine. This is perhaps the most essentially personal area. No one knows our relationships better than we do. Each of us needs to evaluate the possibilities for ourselves and follow the path that feels right. Yet we should not rest too comfortably before at least attempting to push the margins a little bit to investigate areas where there might be an opening. Here are a few ideas to consider when witnessing within our closest family, friendship, and workplace relationships:

- *Begin slowly.* No need to speak out on every new piece of knowledge all at one time if our friends or family are not asking for more. These are our closest relationships. We have plenty of time to initiate people into this way of seeing the world. Besides, jumping in too quickly might very likely only push them away.

- *Speak from the heart.* Refer to recently-acquired information and how it has been personally affecting. Ask only for them to listen and to try and understand why you feel as you do.
- *Demonstrate excitement.* If we offer some of our new realizations with excitement and interest, we stand a better chance of getting people on board. A sudden shift into anger alienates and makes our journey less appealing.
- *Challenge sensitively.* Using the previously-described strategy of expressing our personal emotional reaction to statements can be extremely helpful when we need to challenge something said within a dialogue.
- *Be humble.* Becoming angry with our families, friends, and colleagues for not seeing issues of race as we do is a sure way to get shut down and turn them off.
- *Pick battles carefully.* Some people just are not ready to hear what we have to say. Reserve energy for moments when our efforts can make a difference. Retreat and come back a different day, or a different year, depending upon the individual.
- *Plant seeds.* Know that we plant seeds every time we witness actively. We might not see immediate results, but some new epiphany might be growing in someone that will someday emerge, even if we never see the tangible results.
- *Extend the invitation.* Invite family, friends, and colleagues to join this journey with you. Give this book as a present to someone. Ask someone to watch a movie that features a racially provocative theme with you. Invite someone to attend a culturally or racially diverse art show, musical performance, or other event with you. Ask questions and prompt conversation to see what people are thinking.

My hope is that these strategies for engaging people in dialogue and ideas for how to witness within our most sensitive relationships empower each reader to make this book come alive. Even if we begin with fits and starts, as we continue to practice standing up against racism, we internalize these skills and make them our own. Once this occurs, our ability to explain how being part of our racial group makes a difference in our lives improves and, simultaneously, so does the effectiveness of our explanations.

I remember back when I had just decided to make whiteness the focus of my dissertation. One night I sat at a family dinner absolutely petrified that either my parents or our family friends would ask about my topic. They did, and I blushed and blundered, saying as little as possible to keep from having to say more. Since no one knew anything about whiteness anyway, they all let it drop, probably glad that they were not mixed up in any kind of academic pursuit. That was about six years ago. Things are markedly different today. Speaking about issues of race and white privilege now feel natural. My parents even offered feedback on the original draft of this book, and my father now brings up examples of white privilege he notices. And now when our family friends question me about my work, they get a more confident and extensive explanation.

This practice with my closest family and friends has now expanded so that I no longer suffer any discomfort when race becomes a topic of conversation. This level of ease with the subject is directly related to the amount of effort made over the months and years. But at the same time that my ability to talk with white people has improved over time, there has also been a long road traveled to improve my ability to interact successfully across race.

Listen Up—Inviting Dialogue in Diversity

Some of us enjoy a diverse set of relationships. Perhaps we discuss race on a regular basis, but perhaps we do not. Others of us have never had real, honest relationships with anyone but other white people. For those of us in this position, we might be more nervous about trying to start a conversation about race with someone we only know on a professional or surface level. Wherever each of us lies on this vast spectrum of experience, hopefully at least some of what follows will prove helpful.

This book generalizes what it means to be white in order to create a picture of a certain reality to which many of us are generally oblivious. My hope is that those reading this are now able to at least see the outline of how being white offers benefits and are motivated to spend additional time seeing through this racial lens. For white people, this is usually a departure from the norm and we can readily return to our vision of ourselves as individuals without a stake in racial identity.

On the other hand, society regularly pushes people of color to see life through a racial lens. If white people take up our efforts at witnessing in ways that reinforce that push, we further the problem rather than act as part of the solution. In other words, we will do a better job witnessing whiteness if we examine ourselves in terms of some generalized patterns of behavior common to many white people. Here are a few things we should know about how our group is experienced:

White People can be Incredibly Rude

How would you feel if a stranger walked up to you, began to touch your hair, and asked you how it got that way? Most people I know would be outraged at the audacity of someone disrespecting their personal space and asking personal questions without permission. Unfortunately, white people regularly offend with these sorts of approaches. One day one of my Black female friends called me to ask, "What would make this white woman feel she had the right to touch me like that?" She had been in a campus bookstore waiting to pay for an item when a white woman approached her from behind and began touching her hair. My friend was perplexed, outraged, and a bit hurt, and hoped I could help her understand the behavior of this white woman.

The sad part is that this white woman probably thought that she was demonstrating her acceptance and interest. Unfortunately, what we really reveal in these moments is our ignorance, disrespect, and privilege. We have to really question ourselves about how we approach people. Can we see how our approach might unwittingly dehumanize? Are we conscious of the degree to which we ask people we hardly know to trust and accept us? Do we ask permission before we attempt to enter a personal, racially-loaded dialogue?

White People Can Be Too Self-Focused

Many of us have so much hidden anxiety and emotion over race that we sometimes try to push relationships too quickly. When my collegial relationship with three Black teachers at my school initially formed, I was thrilled. I enjoyed their company and was honored that they invited me to join their monthly gatherings. However, at our monthly dinners, one of the women hardly looked at me when she spoke. During those moments, I felt invisible and wondered if she did this consciously. I took it rather personally and almost decided to end my participation until one of the women prompted me to just relax and let the trust build slowly. As it turned out, as my sincerity and interest were demonstrated over time, the relationship became stronger.

White people can all too often get stuck in our own heads and forget that the people we are building relationships with might also be moving through difficult territory. We have to be ready for someone to say "No thanks" to our outreach efforts without feeling personally insulted. History has given a lot of people good reason to be wary of white people, especially as it relates to social and racial-justice work. If we can get out of our own head for a while and see that we are not the only ones taking risks, we stand a better chance of getting through the rough spots.

White People Can Treat People of Color Like Objects

When we become oversensitive to race issues, we run the risk of treating people more like racial beings than human beings. There are two aspects to this difficulty to which we need to pay attention. First, we must be careful not to turn people into representatives for their race. If we are curious about an issue, we can consciously ask the question, "How do you feel about this issue?" or "Would you be willing to share how this issue has affected you?" instead of "How do people of color feel about this issue?" Although seemingly simple, this is the type of thing we can forget about when our own anxiety gets the better of us.

There is also nothing wrong with telling a person that we are a bit embarrassed or feel nervous about admitting our lack of knowledge or experience on certain topics and are looking for a different viewpoint. The essential thing is to remember that at the same time that we recognize living in the United States offers different experiences for people of color and white people, each of us also has a unique experience that must be honored.

A second aspect to which white people ought to be attentive is that we should assume nothing about another person's experience. At times, my group of white friends, in our attempts at subverting racism, can sometimes drift into assuming how people of color will feel in a certain situation and alter our behavior in an attempt to solve a problem that we do not even really know exists! My suggestion is that we need to use our sensitivity to raise questions that we then check out with people, instead of imagining that we already know how another person feels. Basically, we should check in with individual people to find out if what we imagine is true for that particular person. Doing this can help us avoid a tendency to enact a type of caretaking for others in a patronizing way that disrespects people's personal power and decision making.

White People Can Be Both Vulnerable and Strong

Sometimes white people have to extend our hand and keep it humbly extended in the face of refusal. After first meeting Jennifer Obidah, the African American professor who co-authored *Because of the Kids,* years before inviting her to be interviewed, she chose not to participate in a dialogue series I produced. She said that it did not fit with her interests at that time. I accepted her refusal without question. However, that did not stop me from recognizing what an amazing source of feedback she might be.

Although Jennifer thought that her critiques would frighten me off, I returned and asked her to speak with me at a later time, admitted my sense of inadequacy, and stated out loud both my hopes and my fears. I asked her for her guidance and named my interest in hearing the truth, even if it would be challenging. Over time, a relationship grew so that she is now not only a mentor but also a friend. When we meet, our conversations around issues of racial work are part of our personal sharing, incidental to our relationship, no longer primary. Showing my vulnerability to her while demonstrating my resolve to stay with the issue helped build the trust we share.

The above set of suggestions can hopefully help those of us without much experience move into respectful dialogues with diverse groups. But being actively engaged with the people in our lives sometimes requires additional skills. The most essential skill is listening. We have to listen deeply. There are two key aspects that might make our listening more effective. However, developing our capacity to really enact these suggestions follows in the next section. Briefly, if we choose to engage people in dialogue regarding their experience with race and white privilege, we can do the following:

First, we need to *dismiss the devil's advocate.* I still fight this one. One evening, when going out to dinner with one of my friends, she took offense to the behavior of our waitress, interpreting her actions as racist. I did not. As my friend described her interpretation of the situation, I found myself trying to poke holes in her theory and challenging her view. In truth, there is no reason to believe that her explanation is not accurate. There are no facts that can offer conclusive evidence. My only honest argument against her interpretation is that if I were that waitress, I might have mistakenly done the same thing out of a misinterpretation of the situation.

In other words, my questioning of my friend stemmed from my identification with the white waitress. In defending her, I defended my imagination of myself acting in her place. Thankfully, I am now at least semi-attuned to this process and stopped myself before doing damage to our relationship and was able to shift my approach to ask my friend to elaborate on her felt sense of the situation. From my experience thus far, arguing facts and possible misinterpretations gets us nowhere. Listening to the felt experience of the people in our lives is far more important.

Second, we need to *value new information.* Hearing critical feedback is not easy for any of us. When I first got challenged about the ways my lingering racism emerged in my conversations and behaviors, my frustration emerged on a regular basis. Sometimes it felt as though I was walking on eggshells because everything I said or did seemed like a problem. Looking back at that time period, I am really happy that I stayed in those difficult conversations and tried to find the truth in the critique. Even when I wanted desperately to dismiss opinions that did not resonate for me, I could not escape the fact that people were telling me I was acting similarly to the majority of whites they encountered. I can now see how that information is priceless. If we can sit with new information about ourselves and soak it up even when personally offended, we can learn so much more.

Developing these skills is essential. And yet, there may well be times when our own capacity to sit in the moment to absorb the information offered will be challenged. It is during those times that we will rely on the various ways we can build our internal capacity.

BUILDING CAPACITY

Take a moment to imagine a time when someone verbally challenged you. Sit for a minute and reflect on how the scene played out. Did you feel anxious, stressed, confused, or angry? What did you do with your feelings? Did you express them in the moment? Did you start to concentrate on the feelings more than what the person was saying? How did you overtly respond? Did you argue back, seek the nearest escape route, or complain to a confidant? Did you instead simply dismiss the criticism in favor of labeling the person crazy? Or, were you able to stand in that moment and calmly hear what was being said? Did you have the capacity to listen attentively, offer some type of apology as needed, and dialogue about how you both could resolve the situation?

Now imagine a conflict that involves a high level of intensity (if the previously imagined situation did not). How would you respond if the person displayed a lot of emotion and raised his or her voice? Have you ever been in a situation where the criticism became generalized so that the person suggested that you *always* make this mistake, and not only that, but *everyone* like you does the same thing? Has critique ever started to feel not only uncomfortable but also unfair?

Personally, my immediate tendency is to want to escape and then dismiss the critique. In my better moments, I can approach the person later and admit where I see the truth in what he or she said. But my defensiveness arises rather easily. Managing my inclination toward avoidance takes a lot of effort. On the other hand, one of my friends is spectacular at standing in front of angry colleagues, remaining calm, searching for a common goal, and moving things forward in a way that acknowledges everyone's emotions and reactions. She is a sight to behold, her emotional maturity offering me a valuable model.

Please take note that none of this necessarily involves race. Emotional maturity is a hard-fought commodity for anyone, regardless of race, class, age, or culture. We should reflect on the answers to the above questions in order to locate the areas in which we need growth. This internal work is essential if we are going to be successful standing up for injustice. Here is why.

If we already know that we have difficulty handling conflict, how much more difficult might it be for us when we add to the above scenario the simultaneous pushing of all of our emotional hot buttons regarding race? Since white people have overwhelmingly been able to avoid facing race issues in the past, there are a lot of emotionally-charged, unreleased, unheard, unwitnessed emotions just waiting for us when we invite dialogue with people regularly brutalized by racism in this country.

Our ability to move toward better cross-race relationships depends on our capacity to witness the angst, really pay attention to it, even if it appears personally undeserved at times. Ultimately, as a group, white people have been protected for so long from certain types of critiques that our skin can be rather thin. In this respect, witnessing asks us to develop some coping strategies so that we can handle tough situations.

The essential question dealt with in this section on capacity building is, *how can we develop the ability to stay receptive during moments of challenge?* None of us is perfect, and inevitably, we will make missteps that call for critique. To the extent that we develop relationships with people of color highly perceptive and sensitive about race issues, we will find ourselves taking some heat. Depending upon the level of pain or anger and personality style of the person with whom we share relationship, we might receive more direct and fiery heat than we are comfortable handling.

We need to be able to withstand these difficult moments in order to (1) respect the relationship, (2) put our skills to good use, (3) learn something new about ourselves, and (4) become witnesses to the anger, frustration, and pain that eats at many people of color in this country. Let me restate, in case this point is not clear: Building our capacity to witness is as much about our own education and growth as it is about being helpful contributors to larger, collaborative reform efforts. My deepest hope is that when white people increasingly witness the expression of people of color's rage and grief, something positive can result for each side. What follows is a personal story illustrating my increasing capacity to withstand the heat of challenge.

Creating a Strong, Healthy, and Permeable Sense of Self

A particularly challenging experience helped me clarify areas of additional internal work. This is a story about a dinner among colleagues. The hostess, Ms. Moussa, is an African American elementary school teacher who lives in Los Angeles. She is maternal, strong, savvy, and a veteran teacher who carries an authority about her that people respect. One winter evening Ms. Moussa invited a group of three younger African American teachers over for dinner, former colleagues from the elementary school where she teaches. Among them were Keisha and two of my best teacher-friends. Since I had also taught alongside all four women years earlier and got along with each of them, my friends invited me along, with Ms. Moussa's permission.

Conversation flowed easily throughout dinner, as we each spoke of our current projects, school, life changes, and future collaborative ideas. To some degree, there was a feeling of homecoming for me, not having been with some of the women for several years. The mood was jovial and warm. After dinner, we settled in on Ms. Moussa's long black leather couch to watch a previously tape recorded *Oprah* episode featuring members from the cast of the movie *Crash*. After the show ended, dialogue began and my friends and former colleagues offered commentary on pieces that they found either interesting or troubling, and how they related it to their experience of the world. I participated, and then went one step further.

I began to offer criticism regarding the show featuring only the African American and white cast members, noting that race issues in the United States often wrongly become dichotomized in this way. One of my friends gently reminded me that Oprah is not a political figure and that she simply featured the most well-known celebrities. Instead of letting the point drop, I continued to speak on an area I considered problematic about the movie itself. In a city where approximately 40 percent of the population is Latino/a, to have only one rather thinly developed character representing that population seemed an area worthy of critique.

Without awareness or intention, I had stepped all over some deeply-felt opinions and feelings within my former colleagues. Ms. Moussa began to instruct me rather strongly about how African American issues are, in her opinion, the most important ones upon which we ought to focus due to the intensity of the history between African Americans and whites and its long-standing and continuing ramifications. She sat forward in her seat, obviously upset by my statements. For a while, I tried to explain myself, offering reasons for why I said what I did. I spoke about the need for each group to work together for the benefit of the whole. As I continued, Ms. Moussa's responses became more personally revealing, at times angry and frustrated. Finally, Ms. Moussa made it clear that she is primarily interested in working with her African American community. That is her focus because that is where she perceives the most intense need.

In this situation, my critique demonstrated my ignorance of the intensity of this need. Simultaneously, my critique of the show's guests had unwittingly stepped all over Ms. Moussa's sense of purpose in the world. Realizing this, I tried to explain *my* intentions in the world, my hope to raise awareness within white people to battle racism and that in order to do that my orientation was best served by having a broader focus. As we continued talking, my sense was that we seemed to reach a mutual understanding, hard-fought, but respected.

Keisha also took issue with what I said and spoke on a more deeply personal level of the suffering she sees around her on a daily basis, the pain she experiences firsthand, and the inescapable tragedy continually swirling around her. Her expression was heated and I was under fire. For what seemed like a very long time, Keisha spoke through angry tears of experiences that I knew nothing about, pressures and pains that cut her to the core, and how my perspective reminded her of the inequity and injustice that surrounded it all. There was nothing for me to say. I sat, listened, and nodded in agreement.

Throughout it all, my two best friends sat silent. Throughout it all, I wanted desperately to escape the fiery tones that came at me. Throughout it all, however, I also knew that something really important was happening. I had to sit there and listen as best as I could even if I did not feel good about everything in the moment. Time would give me the chance to evaluate things, but in that moment, my job was to stick it out and soak up whatever was offered. The evening came to a close with hugs all around and the extension of another invitation to return the following month.

I went home with my head spinning, both kicking myself for starting what to me had felt like an argument, and yet pleased that I had not let my emotions get the better of me. The following day one of my friends called to offer me praise for sitting through it, offering her opinion that I had not necessarily deserved all of the force that came at me. A few days later, my other friend also talked with me about the evening and said something rather similar. We then talked about what I learned from that experience.

There are a number of important lessons that can be learned from that evening's dialogue. Hovering around each element is the global recognition that we need to develop a strong, healthy, and permeable sense of self if we are going to be effective witnesses. Included underneath that wide umbrella are the following associated capacities. We should be able to:

Take Responsibility

Great importance lies in me admitting that I began the dialogue that brought tears to Keisha's eyes. Although I am not directly related to the source of her pain, my comments steered the conversational flow. Had my presence and my commentary not been present, the group's post-Oprah dialogue surely would not have ended with Keisha wiped out and exhausted. My lack of awareness due to my privilege led to the pain she experienced that night. I have to take responsibility for the role I played in moving our conversation in that direction.

What can we all take from this? First, we do a better job witnessing if we accept responsibility for triggering emotional upset. Exactly what pulled the trigger is not as important as how we respond. Perhaps we enacted our privilege or displayed our ignorance. Perhaps a person feeds off of the response of another. Ultimately, the fact that we did not intend to create emotional upset means little. Even if the emotion that comes up stems from an entire history of experience, if we help stir up the emotion in someone, we should have to sit and deal with the emotion alongside him or her.

Second, my two friends sat quietly because their job in that moment was to bear witness to the situation at hand, not to rescue me. In essence, we should take up our responsibility, the *ability* to *respond*, by sitting in the fires we set for ourselves without either (1) judging the person reacting as "overly emotional," which white people tend to do, or (2) expecting to be rescued from the fiery heat.

Accept Multiple Truths

Also important for me to recognize is that my critique of the television episode appeared as a statement of fact. This manner of speaking is related to my upbringing within white society. Whites regularly learn to speak as though our thoughts contain absolute truth, even when we are novices within a subject area. "The problem with the show is that . . ." I sat on Ms. Moussa's couch and offered my best, professional analysis of race issues facing the United States with no qualifier, no sense of humility, and no questioning stance. No wonder our conversation took on the tone of a debate.

There are several things we can take from this. First, we would do well to consider to what degree we believe that we are holders of the truth. Part of privilege involves many of us being trained to assume that our opinions should be accepted or, at least, politely received and debated. Life outside of white circles often does not work this way. Second, purposefully qualifying our statements about loaded topics with openers such as, "From what I know so far . . ." or "It seems to me that . . ." might help. While a subtle shift, this language conveys the message that we recognize the difference between our *personal truth* and *absolute truth*. Finally, the more we remember to do this, the easier it becomes to remain conscious that we also should accept that other people's experiences have led them to different truths about the world.

Demonstrate Dedication

With Ms. Moussa, there was no need for me to abandon my perspective. Nor was she going to abandon hers. Although starting from very different points of view, we found a place of mutual understanding. How? First, being able to describe why my approach makes sense when talking with white people helped. Even as I went back and forth with Ms. Moussa, the thought came to me that even six months previously, I would not have had the clarity of understanding to stand so strongly in my position. Nor would my dedication to my position have been warranted. My continuing efforts to learn as much as possible about these issues supported me.

Second, my expression was not detached from emotion. Ours was not an intellectual debate. The honest truth—that I am wholly committed to, passionate about, and invested in advancing racial justice—was evident. For those of us who end up sitting within uncomfortable conversations, the ability to choose wisely which positions to hold with strength becomes paramount. My strength in this setting was not out of defensiveness; the position held had been deeply considered. When we have put in the work to truly understand something deeply, we do not have to abandon our position. However, we will be more successful if we hold our position tenderly and simultaneously work to understand why others feel differently.

Stick with It

The desire to flee the scene enveloped me for a good portion of the time that I sat in witness to Keisha's outpouring. Yet leaving was not an option. Staying required me to rely on some personal coping strategies. Yes, I actually counted to ten at one point. Yes, I actually concentrated on my breathing. Yes, I actually used some visual imagery. From what my friends told me later, this helped me to remain visibly calm and hide the fact that internally my heart was beating at twice its normal rate, my stomach was in knots, and I was sweating profusely.

What learning can we take from this? I know that I am not the only one who experiences this type of anxious reaction. For those of us who (1) have not spent a lot of time talking about issues of race, (2) avoid conflict as a general rule, and (3) realize that our privilege makes our staying in the fire a choice, sticking with it requires a great amount of courage. But if we can develop some coping strategies to calm ourselves so that we can really be present in the experience, great learning can result.

Draw upon Our Knowledge Base

As Ms. Moussa began to more pointedly express the reasons why she disagreed with my position, I began to recall the different statuses of racial identity development outlined within Dr. Beverly Daniel Tatum's book, *Why Are All the Black Kids Sitting Together in the Cafeteria?* I took note that Ms. Moussa and I were speaking out of different statuses. Neither status is to be seen as higher or lower, but simply different orientations. I then recalled an article I once read regarding conversation patterns among people utilizing different status positions. Yes, these things did actually flash into my mind during the most heated moments of the conversation. Was my mind drifting? No. Rather, I was trying desperately to find the best way through the experience and to understand the situation fully.

Drawing on what I had gained from my knowledge-building work helped me see that any attempt by either of us to alter each other's positions was going to be futile, not because anyone was more stubborn than the other but because we were both operating out of radically different racial identity statuses. What can we learn from this? Knowledge is power, and the more we know, the more effective we can be at judging the situation and moving forward.

Depersonalize Appropriately

In the room that evening, I started out sitting as a white woman at ease with four Black women, talking about race, acting knowledgeable, assuming my opinions would do no harm. I then sparked a furious condemnation of how ignorant white people are regarding the pain of Black America. I witnessed the depth of Keisha's anger at white America. That evening I *became* white America: past, present, and future.

I represented the entire history of my race, its blindness in the face of injustice, and its refusals to face the enduring legacy of trauma. Keisha let me have it, verbally. However, Keisha also knew that the fullness of her verbal expression, though directed at me, was not all about me. She even said so at one point. I knew it, too, and that made it tremendously difficult for me to sit and take it in. And that is exactly what I learned from this. If we take it *into* ourselves, take it personally, and hold it, we are more likely to either explode or run away.

On the other hand, if we know that the rage, although directed at us, is not for us alone, we can see it as a wind that can blow *through* us. I literally sat and visualized the emotion moving through my body, letting it freely move past me. This allowed me to really listen to Keisha, really witness her describe the deep pain held by her community, appear calm, and refrain from cutting her off. Had I shut her down, white America would simply have injured her all over again. If we are to witness, we have to be permeable.

Appreciate the Intimacy of Conflict

One of the thoughts that crossed my mind as I tried to survive my own anxiety that evening was that I was sure I would never be invited back to the house again. My assumption was that I had ruined their evening. Not only that, but I was sure whatever closeness our mutual past offered was also dissolving. To my great surprise, these women did not seem to hold anything against me and I have since been invited back for dinners, lunches, and gatherings.

Upon reflection, I see how much I relate to Karen and Bob's stories about relationships always needing to be polite and without difficulty. Clearly, my own whiteness emerged in this moment. I could not see that their dedication to staying in the conflict was actually a testament to their investment in the relationship. They were taking the time and effort to teach me. Instead, I feared the conflict signaled the end.

Recognizing this, I can understand why an experience such as this can be absolutely overwhelming to a white person like myself but hardly memorable for someone else more comfortable managing conflict. Perhaps this is why one of my Black friends now can hardly recall the evening's events. The point for us, however, is that knowing how our racial position has shaped us can help us refrain from overreacting to conflict, and prematurely and unwittingly ending a relationship that might not only be life-enhancing but also rich with collaborative potential.

Recognize the Value of Releasing Rage

Finally, were it not for moments like those with Ms. Moussa and Keisha, I might not be as aware as I am regarding the extent of the trauma suffered by people of color in this country. One thing I also realized is that rage does not have to be destructive. Psychologists know the value of having a witness after a traumatic injury. For someone who feels injured in some way, having someone there who can *honestly* say, "Yes, I hear you, I can see what you mean" can make a difference. Our nation as a whole requires healing. Our shared history is rife with violence done to all of our spirits. People of color have had to turn to each other with their pain long enough. Growth and healing cannot be complete until white people learn how to witness the constructive rage that awaits us—if only we can stay open.

Surely, we should *not* try to elicit rage and difficult emotion. But if we are going to attempt to develop meaningful relationships, it is likely that we might unwittingly do so anyway. Essential is that we recognize that our capacity to bear witness to the pain residing in our friends and colleagues is instrumental in developing trust and demonstrating our dedication and commitment to our internal work. This is one of the keys that can help solidify cross-race relationships, thereby enhancing what we can accomplish and furthering the reform and diversity work we intend to do together.

Developing a sense of self that is strong and healthy enough to withstand rage yet permeable enough to let the fire pass through us takes a lot of work. Yet this capacity is not uniquely applicable to racially-loaded situations. Our practice can begin any time conflict emerges in our lives. The more we can develop our emotional maturity, the better we can witness. However, for those like me who avoid conflict like the plague, we might not create many opportunities for this type of practice. We also might be overwhelmed at the thought of even entering the room when we sense deep anger present, much less sitting through the type of conversation described in this book. This is where our final ingredient requires addition. We need to build a community that can help us sort through our feelings, propel us forward, and support us as we figure out our next step.

CREATING COMMUNITY

Race is on the tip of my tongue just about all of the time. No surprise, then, that my college courses often involve conversations on race issues. One semester one of my students, an assistant principal at a Catholic high school who also has a legal background, spoke up and mentioned his early training's emphasis in critical race theory. He later talked with me on our way out of class and told me that he knew what I was trying to do, respected my efforts, had already gone through it, and was a bit uncomfortable being dragged back into race issues. After a lengthy discussion, I asked him to consider that perhaps his discomfort with the subject indicated that there might be some room for additional personal work.

During one of the many conversations we had that semester, this student asked me, "So, how long will you be into this?" Essentially, he saw working on race issues as a phase that would ultimately lead to burn out. I responded that this feels like lifelong work. What makes my experience different from his? Our academic programs had led us to very similar perspectives on systems of inequity and privilege. But why did he experience a focus on race as an intellectual pursuit that translated into being a "phase," while I see it more as a lifelong commitment?

After class later in the semester, standing in the parking lot near our cars, this student spoke about the pressure he received from others to "stop making everything about race." His colleagues, mainly people of color, were tired of being reminded about race. But this left him without anywhere to share his continuing thoughts and feelings regarding how he relates to being white and how to battle against the white privilege and racism he sees around him. In response, he shut down and went on with his day-to-day work.

I then told him about a community of white antiracists of which I am a part, why we meet, and how it is helping me to form an explicitly antiracist, Radical White Identity. Upon hearing my explanation, my student asked me to repeat something I had said, excitedly telling me that he needed a self-validating affirmation, something that he could tell himself on a daily basis to reinforce what he truly believed deep down.

This is what I said that struck him. "It is okay to still concentrate on race. There is a lot of work still to be done, and our work to end racism is a life-long journey." Although simple, this kind of validation does not generally come from our white community. And, communities of color have carried the weight of supporting white people for a long, long time. No wonder that my student's colleagues wanted him to stop analyzing race around them. They needed a break themselves.

The important question for this section is, *in the face of pressures to stop concentrating on race, how can we make witnessing a lifelong commitment?*

The AWARE-LA Community: Who, What, and Why

For the past six years, my participation in a group called AWARE-LA, an Alliance of White Anti-Racists Everywhere-Los Angeles, has offered me validation, inspiration, comfort, support, challenge, knowledge, skills, a space for reflection, and, above all, a sense of belonging. Knowing that I am not alone keeps me hopeful and motivated. I attended the first AWARE meeting. There were about six of us. One of the founders of the group came to tears that day as he reflected on the multiple efforts he had made previously to get a group like this going. This time a continuing group began, successfully creating a community from which many of us benefit. The group list now includes over 300 individuals, about 60 of whom attend meetings fairly regularly. Who are the people who come? What do we do? And why is a group like this beneficial and necessary?

A main part of AWARE is its Saturday Dialogues. These are monthly meetings for white people who are interested in challenging and supporting each other to see our privilege more clearly, and learning skills to act against racism. Some people who come are just starting to hear phrases like *white privilege,* while others are practicing social-justice activists who want to investigate how their work relates to their whiteness.

The entire Saturday Dialogue project is built upon AWARE's model of Radical White Identity.[3] This model essentially involves recognizing that white antiracists need a healthy, explicit white identity that involves investigating our (1) roots, (2) history, (3) privilege, and (4) organizing potential. Yes, we work on building knowledge, skills, capacity, and community. But, first and foremost, we recognize that we need to have a healthy sense of racial identity for any of our knowledge, skills, and capacities to be enacted well.

For me, this is the space where white people work together without requiring people of color to be our teachers. We work to heal ourselves. We admit our resistances, question our actions, support each other's growth, and challenge each other to desegregate our lives. We see our work on Saturdays as instrumental in supporting our ability to do the real work of witnessing, which is to be in continued relationship with people of color, working together toward increased racial and social justice, and combating the continuation of white privilege. (Please see www.awarela.org, Saturday Dialogues, for an expanded rationale of why we meet as a racially-caucused space.)

What do we do during our dialogues? A facilitation team develops an agenda for each monthly meeting. Each dialogue begins with a check-in. We discuss our "homework" and the ways race has played a role in our lives the previous month. Meetings also include an orientation for new people, a thematic topic for the day, exercises to help us relate to the idea, small and large group dialogues, and role-playing activities.

Some topics we explore include the interaction between race and various other social positions, such as gender, class, sexual orientation, religion, age, and education. We also discuss issues such as immigration, cultural appropriation, gentrification, and interracial relationships. Some of the questions we might ask in relationship to any of these issues include the following:

- Where do racism and/or white privilege play out within this issue?
- How do we feel about this issue and our role as white people in it?
- How can we challenge the racism and/or white privilege?
- What capacities do we need to develop to effectively challenge the racism and/or white privilege?

We brainstorm together, each of us adding our knowledge, and each of us contributing to each other's toolkit for how to respond to racially-loaded situations.

Why is a white antiracist community so helpful and necessary? As essentially social creatures, humans benefit from validating experiences. Whether that validation comes from parents, teachers, friends, colleagues, or supervisors, we all want to know that our contributions are valued. When we take up witnessing, we need people around us who understand our striving and can support us.

Given our history, the more white people can become supportive witnesses for other white people, the less we need to seek validation from people of color. For me, I know that being a part of a white antiracist community has helped me become less needy in my cross-race interactions. Not so terribly long ago, I needed my colleagues of color to tell me I was doing a good job in order to feel like I was one of the "good white people." But now I confer with people of color on a more equal footing, checking in to remain accountable and gain additional insight, but without the psychological need to be validated.

Also, recall from Chapter 2 that when we move into community work without working through issues of guilt, we can often act out of a savior complex. There is nothing wrong with wanting to make a difference in a person's life. However, quite often, we go about this work in order to fill a hole within ourselves. We *need* to make a difference because of the guilt that eats away at us from within. My approach to people at my school shifted as a result of feeling connected to a group of white people who support and challenge me.

For example, there was a time when I felt that my dedicated efforts to teach inner-city students of color were my way of redeeming myself in the world. Being the vehicle for a student to extend beyond the boundaries in view made me feel good in the world and gave my life meaning. I needed the students to need me. Since deepening my relationships with AWARE, my approach has changed in a very subtle but meaningful way.

I noticed the change upon my return to my former middle-school site to visit a friend. While waiting for her, I happened upon a former student, Jesse, a stocky kid with a shaved head and an infectious grin. We sat to talk and he shared his most recent experiences with me, including the ones that had removed him from my classroom just a few months prior. He showed me his bullet wounds, talked about the reach of the Mexican Mafia, and how he saw little hope of escape. We talked about his future and mine, his continuation in school, and my outline for this book. We talked about his fears and my hopes. I talked about groups who have effectively gotten youth out of the reach of gangs to ensure their safety.

By the end of a lengthy conversation, Jesse had my phone number with explicit instructions to call me if he ever needed someone to come get him out of the area. I reinforced my belief that his life is important and that I would do whatever was in my power to see that he stayed alive. He then left for home, indicating his need to walk with his friends so as not to be alone on the streets. I have not seen or heard from him since.

Later, I thought about my role in that situation. Was I responding to an internal savior complex? We both recognized and spoke about the fact that I was quite literally trying to save his life. That is absolutely true. But reflecting inward, I noticed a subtle yet important difference. I did not need Jesse that day to make me feel better about myself. Offering him support did not make me feel like a better person than anybody else.

Sure, the connection and ability to be of potential aid offered a good feeling. And perhaps there is still more of the savior complex deep down for me to explore, more work to be done. However, my internal sense shifted. No longer did I need Jesse to validate me in the world. The skills and validation gained through my work with the other antiracist whites helped me approach Jesse with more awareness, less superiority, less pride, and an increased ability to hear his concerns. Being less full of myself, I was more available to just *be* with Jesse.

Although the AWARE meeting space has helped me tremendously, there are many people who understandably distrust any group of white people meeting without any people of color present. Many believe that whites cannot be trusted without being either monitored or guided by people of color when it comes to dealing with racism. Simply, many believe that white people alone together always indicate racism in action.

White people do need to be in consistent and meaningful relationships with people of color in ways that allow us to see ourselves more clearly, especially when we are trying to do ally work. It is also certainly true that for as much internal work as AWARE members have accomplished, we likely regularly miss things, essentially taking one step back for every few steps forward. On the other hand, we do not deny this reality, and experience with this group has convinced me that we do end up farther ahead in the end.

Additionally, AWARE's work is largely concentrated on investigating ourselves as white people and developing the kinds of skills that are commonly referred to as part of an "accountability" practice. We learn to listen, recognize the emergence of our privilege, and confront our defensiveness on many subjects. To be even clearer, this means that AWARE Saturday Dialogues are *not* used to plan advocacy or activist work in the service of communities of color. Instead, the AWARE meetings are about investigating ourselves so that we can be more (1) just within our day-to-day diverse settings and (2) useful to multiracial collaborations working for educational, social, racial, economic, and environmental justice.

What it boils down to is that, just as sometimes men and women need separate spaces in which to do their own particular gendered work, so white people need a space in which we can move through our own learning process. In this way, we see our group of antiracist white people as a *community of necessity,* an essential and temporary creation, as we work toward the abolition of all remnants of white supremacy and its historic privileges.

Of course, this work cannot be conducted wholly in isolation. The movement is a breathing process. We move in and then out. We come together and we go into our multiracial spaces. Back and forth, together and apart, learning and sharing each step of the way. With this frame, a sense of community among whites working at witnessing offers validation for efforts made without draining people of color's energy. To be sure, the goal is to recover from this social construction called race so that we exist primarily in integrated spaces. However, creating witnessing communities may be a necessary intermediary step.

Building a Community of Witnesses

Although AWARE works as a racially-caucused group, that does not mean that witnessing groups cannot be multiracial. In fact, AWARE also works in alignment with a multiracial group of racial-justice advocates called the Racial Justice Alliance (RJA).[4] Important to name is that the concept of witnessing can be used by anyone of any background. The essential idea, though, is that developing a witnessing practice requires creating a community that helps retain focus on learning how to notice racism and white privilege, develop practical skills, and the internal work of capacity building. Anyone motivated to be part of that conversation should be welcomed.

If we develop a core group of people around ourselves to help with this process, we can avoid the isolation that many people feel when they begin to speak out regarding racism and white privilege. Then, as we combat loneliness through the development of a supportive community, our witnessing is more likely to become a lifelong dedication. Keep in mind that AWARE began with a small circle of people. Even if we have no intention of developing a large group, what can we do for ourselves to stay motivated?

- *Start small.* Speak to people you already know who might be open to a conversation on race. Perhaps you begin with two or three people. Expand as your ability to initiate the dialogue increases.
- *Create a book club.* If you find this book helpful, move through it with others using the free downloadable discussion guide found at www.witnessingwhiteness.com. Invite trusted colleagues and friends to be part of your process. Talk about each chapter, what feelings you have about it, what is meaningful, and how it motivates you to take action.
- *Create an intentional community.* Determine the purpose of why you meet and what you would like to accomplish in general.
- *Set goals.* Look at each of the four aspects of how to witness: building knowledge, skills, capacities, and community. Decide which actions you plan to take and hold each other accountable.
- *Create shared agreements.* Talk about how you can support each other. What are the avenues for challenge? How are you responsible to each other for following through with the goals that you set?
- *Move outside of yourselves.* Talk about your experiences within the diverse spaces you inhabit. Explore how racism or white privilege exists there. If

there are no multiracial spaces in your lives, brainstorm how to expand your lives to experience more diversity.

- *Extend your learning.* Once your group has read the book, conduct a series of workshops for a second round of dialogues using pre-planned workshops available at www.witnessingwhiteness.org that delve more deeply into selected book themes. Allowing yourselves to practice facilitating each other through the exercises is a great way to practice skills and build leadership capacity.

Sharing this work can help make the suggestions in this book come alive. Also, putting these ideas into action can help avoid overintellectualizing the journey. Even if the idea of convincing others to take up this work sounds daunting, you might be surprised. If you have found the ideas and suggestions motivating, others might as well. It is worth a try. Not only that, but for the sake of our larger effort at reducing racism, we have to make this effort.

The most helpful approach I have found involves inviting a friend, family member, or colleague to read this book alongside. Let him or her know that you have been working through some ideas and you could really use some support. In this way, the invitation is about becoming more connected to you and joining your process rather than suggesting the individual needs some work. This can help reduce defensiveness.

MOVING FORWARD—IMAGINING POSSIBILITIES FOR ALLY WORK

The more we put understanding and skills into action, the more we might find ourselves invested in becoming part of a larger network. If we become so inspired, we can seek out other social-justice-oriented organizations and we might come into contact with many wonderful people with plenty of good advice about how we can increasingly take on ally work. The possibilities are endless, and the need is great.

During my third year with the AWARE group, I found myself increasingly invested in attending political events, leadership meetings, and development opportunities (including the creation of the RJA). What drives this higher level of commitment and activity? Is it my increased knowledge? Yes. Is it the increased confidence in my ability to enact skills learned? Sure. But, in addition to that, I like spending time with these new friends. They are there when I am confused. They support and challenge me when I make mistakes. They push me to take another step forward. They accept that we might disagree on some political issues. However, we are on the same page regarding our efforts to work toward personal and collective understanding and transforming our society into one that is more equitable and humane.

Ultimately, I feel good when I am around AWARE and RJA members. My journey into witnessing is not a lonely one. Following Hecate's torch into the shadowy places of my soul has led me not to isolation and darkness. Instead, I am connected to a larger body, a collective, multiracial movement of people who are willing to respond to the call to witness, who are similarly invested in creating both personal and collective recipes for advancement. This collective movement comes with tremendous possibility, a power that feels boundless. Ultimately, when enough of us make this shift and begin to influence others in our environments, I believe the culture will transform as well.

NOTES

1. Havemann, Joel, and Ricardo Alonso-Zaldivar, "Middle-Class Workers Ailing in Census Checkup," *Los Angeles Times,* August 30, 2006. Also see: Income, Poverty, and Health Insurance Coverage in the US: 2005 (external link, pdf), available at www.radicalmath.org/browse_category.php?cat=data.

2. This abbreviated definition for *internalized racism* is taken from Donna Bivens, "Internalized Racism: A Definition," Women's Theological Center, 1995. A more complete explanation can be found at www.evaluationtoolsforracialequity .org/termRacial.htm.

Internalized racism is the situation that occurs in a racist system when a racial group oppressed by racism supports the supremacy and dominance of the dominating group by maintaining or participating in the set of attitudes, behaviors, social structures, and ideologies that undergird the dominating group's power.

It involves four essential and interconnected elements: decision making, resources, standards, and naming the problem.

3. Goldberg, S., and C. Levin, AWARE-LA, *Toward a Radical White Identity,* http://awarela.wordpress.com/toolbox/.

4. For more information about the Racial Justice Alliance, please visit http:// awarela.wordpress.com/alliance/.

Chapter 9

How Can We Create a Witnessing Culture?

Did you ever have a teacher or mentor who dared you to dream bigger than you might have on your own? Was there ever a figure in your life who challenged you to make a grand leap and fulfill a vision you held dear? This chapter is dedicated to the people in our lives who have asked us to see beyond ourselves, follow our numinous dreams, and live them as if they were already reality. In other words, this chapter is dedicated to those who modeled for us what it truly means to live out of our freedom. For me, this includes two fierce women professors who bridge the soul and the world, linking deep psychology with social justice.

Whereas the previous chapter is a call to individual reflection and action, this final chapter asks readers to join in a collective dreamlike pursuit to dig deep down into our cultural soul and imagine our way through to a different way of being in community. It asks us to see ourselves as the creators of culture. Bringing this dream to manifestation requires all of us to expand ourselves and the scope and reach of our work. What follows is intended to invite a broad, deep, and uplifting reflection. Ultimately, the vision offered reflects my grandest hope for our country.

The goal: Transform the current, dominant form of white culture into an antiracist white culture that regularly names and dismantles racism and white privilege. This work may be started at home, extended into our social lives, and infused into our work settings. This is long-range work. Transforming culture understandably requires much time and collective effort. But, in the midst of our individual struggle, we must simultaneously hold a larger view of our collective role. Yes, we may start this work with a small circle of friends, family, and colleagues. However, our ultimate goal must remain the transformation of white culture overall.

Since the existence of "white culture" is in itself contested, let me be really specific. What we need to transform is the white culture people speak of that is associated with segregated social lives, isolation, disconnection, individualism, sanitization, arrogance, obliviousness, entitlement, unrecognized privileges, the avoidance of social concerns faced by disproportionate numbers of people of color, the sense of self as normal, innocent, and unaffected by race, and the acceptance of Western ideals as universal and the only valid way of seeing the world.

The caveats: First, each of us has a different relationship to the features of whiteness listed above, and therefore the amount of personal change required necessarily differs. However, for those of us who are working toward cultural transformation, we need to recognize the broad parameters so that we can locate ourselves within the shifting terrain.

Second, the beginning of anything is often the hardest part. We face a fairly steep learning curve so that our first attempts may be clumsy. Thankfully, there is a history of antiracism on which to build. Foundations have been laid demonstrating how to do the work of witnessing. There are also groups of antiracist people already living out witnessing practices for us to relate to and with whom we can build community.

Third, cultural shifts generally take place within a complete alteration of worldview. Is reading this one book sufficiently provocative to alter a person's entire view of the world? Perhaps the answer is no. However, continued increases in our knowledge base, social connections, and experiences can support movement in that direction.

Finally, choosing to dedicate our time to a new effort in addition to our regular, daily responsibilities can be extremely difficult. For white people, we have the privilege to choose whether or not to take up a witnessing role. No one will force us. We have to be intrinsically motivated to make this shift.

The motivation: In the face of our constraints and resistances, what can prompt us to give energy to a witnessing practice on a regular basis? We must have a vision, some imagination of how our life will improve. This idea of creating a witnessing culture has just such a vision. At its core, this is a vision of our own healing, the creation of a healthier sense of self so that we can then guide others beyond the dis-ease most of us feel regarding race issues.

This imagined reality includes forming enough communities of witnesses that perceiving racism and privilege becomes the norm for us and our colleagues, families, and social networks. In this vision, attending to the effects of race is such a regular part of life that white people in general become skilled at giving voice to race realities. This is one way we can earn a positive sense of our racial selves, standing proud in our antiracism practice, knowing that we are truly working toward developing a culture around challenging the dominating whiteness that has injured our collective spirit for too long.

How to effectively make this cultural shift happen on a wide scale understandably raises many questions. This last chapter imagines the answers to the following: What will it take for us to transform white culture? What values are essential within a witnessing culture? And is it really possible for a witnessing culture to exist in the United States?

A HOPEFUL, EXPANDING, STRATEGIC COMMUNITY

The truth is that the problems we face regarding race are huge. In the face of the overwhelming challenges, we need both a sense of hope and a strategic approach. The fact that many already feel overwhelmed by just the *thought* of speaking up and taking action in regards to race issues is a serious problem. Although true that many feel hopeless in the face of our history and its effects, another truth is that many feel powerless in general when it comes to our social, economic, and educational institutions. This lack of perceived power runs so deep that we see it in our responses to movies and advertising.

The reactions I heard to the film *Minority Report* can serve as an example. There is a scene within the film in which the main character, played by Tom Cruise, moves through a high-tech mall. Cameras recognize each customer by name, calling out to each with a welcome and an invitation to purchase. Just imagining that as a possible future horrified me. However, a deeper distress emerged as several acquaintances proclaimed that the scene displayed our future as though it were an already-foregone conclusion. Did they like that future? They all agreed that the vision offered within the film was bothersome to say the least, and some called it frightening. However, they all appeared to submit to the eventuality of its impending reality. Why?

These reactions speak to a pervasive problem. Many of us believe that we lack personal power within our collective world, regardless of whether or not the subject is race-related. Hopelessness emerges when we take in other people's visions for our future as though we have no say. With this as a starting point, the reader might rightly ask, from whence can come a sense of hope? How can we hope for widespread change in the face of this lack of social agency?

My relentless hope comes, in part, from my own recognition of the limitless creative potential within each of us. We hold enormous possibility within ourselves, and this expands exponentially when we come together in community. Our future is ours to create together, and when we create shared

agreements about how we wish to live and how we intend to be in relationships, the strength of those social contracts creates unseen movement.

This internal sense receives external support in the book *The Cultural
Creatives: How 50 Million People Are Changing the World,* by Paul Ray and
Sherry Ruth Anderson. This text draws upon thirteen years of survey research
conducted with over 100,000 U.S. Americans. So, what do the authors mean
when they speak of the Cultural Creatives? They write,

> Since the 1960s, 26 percent of the adults in the United States—fifty million
> people—have made a comprehensive shift in their worldview, values, and way
> of life—their culture, in short. These creative, optimistic millions are at the lead-
> ing edge of several kinds of cultural change, deeply affecting not only their own
> lives but our larger society as well. We call them the Cultural Creatives because,
> innovation by innovation, they are shaping a new kind of American culture for
> the twenty-first century.[1]

The call to transform our culture into a witnessing culture aligns with this
movement. In this way, those of us responding to the call to witness racism
and white privilege are engaged in a similarly directed track with those who
push for social and ecological change in other ways.

According to the authors of *The Cultural Creatives,* this movement is
largely unnoticed by many people. Yet they also offer impressive evidence
that a cultural wave is already taking shape that can alter the economic realities and political dialogue of this country. Some of our friends and associ-
ates may already be influenced by the cultural shifts in play. As our voices
strengthen and our economic choices and demands follow, businesses and
institutions are increasingly forced to pay attention.

Recognizing that we are a part of a larger wave of movement offers hope
because although *The Cultural Creatives* focuses on people involved with
movements oriented around ecological sustainability, healthy living, and
psychological/spiritual development, part of this emerging group also works
toward a more equitable and cross-cultural world. Of those defined as "core"
Cultural Creatives, approximately half, twenty-four million, are said to be
concerned simultaneously with both social justice *and* personal growth,
rejecting the notion that they are mutually exclusive.[2]

This core of the Cultural Creatives is the group with whom I feel myself
most aligned. (Although there is no breakdown to suggest how many of
these twenty-four million people are white, we can at least conservatively
imagine that the number is substantial.) This group recognizes that there
is a large matrix of issues, interconnected and mutually reinforcing,
each of which requires its own efforts. Working on each can simultaneously work to support the others. Coalition building between educational

reform, social justice, and ecological groups naturally emerges with this understanding.

True, not all of the twenty-four million are currently concerned with race issues at this time. But their current interests are likely to make them more open to the concerns raised within this book, more likely to fold the ideas into their awareness of other issues, perhaps then witnessing injustice and the effects of whiteness on multiple levels. In this way, we can take up responsibility to share with others how to witness whiteness, thereby expanding our communities of witnesses.

If these Cultural Creatives are already creating new forms of culture, what is it about contemporary American culture that they reject? Among other things, they reject "materialism, greed, me-firstism, status display, glaring social inequalities of race and class, society's failure to care adequately for elders, women, and children, . . . and intolerance and narrowness of social conservatives and the Religious Right."[3] True enough, this list hardly mirrors the above list regarding what a witnessing culture might work against. However, some linkages are there. The Cultural Creatives have the potential to become a wave of cultural transformers that expand a community of witnesses. In this field of potential witnessing agents there is a place of beginning and a wellspring of hope.

Ray and Anderson's conclusion offers an explicit vision for what Cultural Creatives seek and it deserves a full reading:

> There is nothing inevitable about the kind of life we have now in modern society, and nothing inevitable about the kind of future that lies before us. Cultural Creatives are quite clear that they do not want to live in an alienated, disconnected world. Their guiding images refer again and again to a sense of wholeness. They say that each of us is a living system within a greater living system, connected to each other in more ways than we can fathom. If we focus on that wholeness, we can begin to imagine a culture that can heal the fragmentation and destructiveness of our time.
>
> The appearance of the Cultural Creatives, we suggest, represents a promise that a creative vision of the future is growing. It is a resurgence of hope, of imagination, of willingness to act for the sake of a better civilization. The work toward a reintegration of, and design for, a new culture can have great power in our collective imagination. What we want and what we choose can shape our future.[4]

True, not all Cultural Creatives are witnesses for racial justice . . . yet. But they might become witnesses if we let them know how essentially linked racial justice and identity issues are with environmental equity, healing, and psychological-development efforts. We can start there.

Another reason that a hopeful stance makes realistic sense comes from the analysis offered within *The Tipping Point: How Little Things Can Make a Big Difference,* by Malcolm Gladwell.[5] We can learn a lot from his book, taking its suggestions and using them to propel real movement. A main premise is that big changes come from small events. This energizes when we see how the wave of Cultural Creatives might become the critical mass necessary to allow our message to take off and inspire both local and multinational businesses and politicians to respond.

The Tipping Point also offers strategies that can help make our efforts more successful. For example, the book explains three types of people we can target with our messages regarding witnessing. We need to locate the connectors, those who walk in many worlds, know many people, and link communities. Second, we can bring our message to the knowers, those who act as the voices of expertise in particular areas. These are the people who others seek out to find out if a product or message is valid and valuable. The knowers act as our consumer controls. They are socially invested and want people to know the truth about things. If we can get them on board, others will follow. Finally, we know the persuaders when we see them. They are the people who can sell us anything. Their charisma precedes them. If we can convince them of the importance of witnessing, they will convince others.

Taking a strategic approach to our witnessing work, both personally and as communities, might help us reach the point where our message sticks. Also important is that *The Tipping Point* describes what is called the *Rule of 150.*[6] Apparently, the best-functioning groups within organizations are those that do not grow past this crucial number. The key element for success over time appears to be community, the sense of knowing the various people in various roles and feeling a sense of personal accountability to the individuals that make up the team.

If we construct witnessing groups to keep us accountable to each other as regards the development of our antiracist practice, the potential for growth and expansion increases. Our self-identity becomes involved and we experience increased motivation and dedication. In sum, the messages within *The Cultural Creatives* and *The Tipping Point* offer us a realistic and well-researched vision of a group of people likely to be open to the development of a witnessing culture and some strategies to help us develop the necessary communities. The beauty here is that there is no reason to feel alone and powerless. We have concrete steps to take that can connect us with a movement of people. We can capitalize on the massive wave of change already underway, albeit seemingly hidden from view.

CULTURAL VALUES OF WITNESSING

In truth, a good number of us are part of the wave of cultural transformation taking place and already promote many of the values that run counter to the dominant forms of white culture listed above. It would make sense that many readers might already be aligned with the twenty-four million core Cultural Creatives mentioned in the previous section. Still, we cannot simply reject the dominant form of white culture without defining specific alternatives. If we are to turn away from some attributes of white culture, what alternatives do we seek? What are the values that a witnessing culture might display?

To start this imaginative process, I returned to Kelly Oliver's, *Witnessing: Beyond Recognition*[7] as well as countless conversations with other people about what helps frame their perspective regarding race issues. Surely this chapter does not offer a complete list of what is possible or desired. But for the sake of beginning, a culture of witnessing would value multiplicity, interconnection, passion, obligation, vigilance, accountability, historical memory, and reconciliation. Let us look at each one to see how it supports a cultural practice of witnessing whiteness.

Multiplicity

When we look at ancient myths across cultures we find that their power lies in their portrayal of essentially human themes. Regardless of the culture of origin, within myth we meet characters, both human and divine, that struggle as we struggle. We find that our ancestors grappled with the same troubles and joys we meet today. We confront conflict, greed, generosity, envy, pride, love, heroism, sacrifice, fear, arrogance, friendship, death, and initiation, to name just a few. Within mythological realms, all of these energetic forces, these characters or gods that personify human characteristics, have a respected and honored place.

In depth psychological terms, these energies are the multitude of archetypes that exist as part of the foundation of our consciousness. We understand what it means to be a hero because that archetype already exists within our psyche. In the same way, we have the capacity for greed, spite, and maliciousness as much as we do for love, sacrifice, and devotion. We recognize the wise mother and the lover just as we recognize death and the thief.

The innumerable qualities that live within the depths of our psyches, taken together, are what are referred to as the *multiplicity of the psyche*. Essentially, we are fragmented to the core and we have the capacity to act out of any of the various archetypes imaginable. Bits and pieces often emerge without our control, which can leave us feeling confused, lost, and in pain. However, our inner aspects in combination, fully accepted, also offer us a sense of wholeness. Nothing is left out. All energetic forces have a place within our deepest selves.

If taken seriously, the recognition that even the most obscene action has its roots in an energetic, archetypal force that lies hidden within each of us asks us to begin to approach the world differently. True, our upbringing often stops us from acting in certain ways. True, our own personality styles affect us. True, our cultural framework and environmental influences have shaped our tendencies and conscious restraints. And yet, if we are really honest with ourselves, we should be able to imagine that if our social conditionings were completely stripped away, if crisis befell us and our stable sense of self, place, and safety fell away, none of us really knows what we might draw on to survive.

Important shifts in thinking occur when we see the truth of our inner multiplicity. First, we can more readily move beyond the *either/or* dichotomy of the modern worldview and, instead, increasingly take the position of *both/and.* "Can two things be true at the same time?" we begin to ask. Might something be both horrible and profoundly educational? This shift is essential as white people reconsider our sense of identity and what characteristics we hope to exemplify.

Recall that part of the historic development of white identity included demonizing certain ways of being and excluding them from our sense of self. From a mythic perspective, this is tantamount to banishing a divine energy from the pantheon of the gods. Part of healing from dissociated white culture involves white people reimagining ourselves so that we make room for what, historically, has been split off from the white self. For example, white people traditionally claimed the energy of Productivity while demonizing what the modern world sees as the opposite, Laziness.

The use of capitalization asks us to imagine Productivity and Laziness as archetypal deities. Just for a moment, let us note that each attribute, or mythic deity, might associate or conspire with others. For example, we can see that Laziness in our culture is generally doomed to existence as the jailor of Ambition. Spending hours sitting under a tree watching the birds and feeling the caress of the wind or filming the twists and turns of a plastic bag dancing in the breeze are things that would generally be seen as nonproductive.

Yet, in this judgment we also dismiss the importance of Laziness' possible co-conspirators, the Calm, Receptive, and Subtle, the moments that touch our Soul. From this point of view, is it possible that what we might sometimes call Laziness can be a partner to that which invites Soul into our world? Is it possible that our white culture's loss of meaning, in part, stems from our inability to stop and wait patiently for the world to tell us something essential about life?

Valuing our multiplicity can help us reclaim the soulfulness that many of us feel is missing in our lives. Following this logic, we might also find the benefits that come from sitting in extended, diverse dialogues and deepening our sense of self in the world. This means that we would value taking time to truly connect with others in ways that satisfy our soul, but appear less productive to a largely isolated, segregated white culture.

Further, we can examine the contemporary cultural myths and stories prevalent in the United States. We might consider how stories pertaining to cowboys, explorers of all sorts, and heroes, to mention just a few, reinforce a particular set of values. We can ask how the cultural stories and myths we grew up with reflect and reinforce problematic aspects of white culture. How do we continue to condition ourselves to see people as either all good or all bad through our storytelling and interpretations of events? Then we might imagine, what might be the new stories that would promote the values of a witnessing culture? The collective answer will emerge as we each make choices regarding how we interpret events, which stories we decide are worth repeating, and how we tell the tales.

Another shift that comes with valuing multiplicity is that this perspective helps us tap into our deep sense that we are neither more nor less human than anyone else. People's actions spring from a well of possibility that exists simultaneously within each of us. No longer can we point to a few bad apples or name someone a monster in order to disconnect from the uncomfortable reality that our own humanity, our own culture, requires serious work.

Instead of looking at *those racists over there*, an appreciation of multiplicity prompts us to self-identify in an effort to locate where that disturbing conditioning exists in us and the systems we inhabit. In so doing, we see the blood on our own hands as humans struggling to better deal with the same old themes that our ancestors faced, the disconnections between peoples and the efforts to move beyond blindness to self and prejudice toward others.

Ultimately, truly recognizing our multiplicity helps us see our personal responsibility for the development and evolution of our culture and our humanity. As such, we can consider the following:

- In what ways is the value of multiplicity already expressed in your interactions with colleagues, family, and friends?

Interconnection

Important to recall from Chapter 3 is that the individualistic perspective depends upon the conception of the self as autonomous, independent, self-determining, unique, separate, and free. Remember that this orientation matches the modern worldview, which is also associated with being Western and white for many people.[8] Witnessing ourselves asks us to take a hard look at the degree to which we value this type of *individualism* and imagine moving in a different direction.

In general, white culture teaches us that we exist as separate bodies, islands without obvious and imperative connections to others. We often link this sense of individualism with the glory of independence and freedom. In many ways, these have become gods in the mythological sense. Yet there is a price paid for this stance. Mythological gods are constantly entwined in complex relationships. Independence and Freedom do not travel alone. With them can come Separation, Isolation, Alienation, and Loneliness.

Bowling Alone, by Robert Putnam, offers a complex view of the increased lack of social engagement evident in our society over the past several decades.[9] That millions of Americans feel this alienation is indisputable in a gated-community culture with an epidemic rate of depression and self-medication. While this connection oversimplifies the torment of depression and addiction, there is something real about how our individualistic, independent self frequently feels misunderstood, fearful, and alone in the world.

As mirror images and complements, some type of Imprisonment arrives with the heralding of unrestrained personal Freedom. We somehow become trapped within ourselves, our desires, and our individual destinies. Our isolated achievements become objects of envy, inspiring the need for better personal protection and security. We build more gates. Our Independence can thus invite the sorrow of someone free to feel . . . alone.

With all of the beauties and benefits that Independence does bring, the image of ourselves as islands in a vast sea not only ignores the deep, underlying connectedness of our common ground beneath the water; it also fails to value equally the shared ocean and our mutual dependence upon the sun, the salt, the water, and the wind. Advancing a witnessing culture means challenging the way individualism leads to isolation and segregation, naming its associations and problems.

Unfortunately, the suggestion that we need to challenge individualism can be easily misunderstood and resisted. This occurs because many confuse individualism with the job of becoming an individual. These are two completely different ways of relating to the world. The modern self who subscribes to *rugged individualism* risks becoming isolated, disconnected, and competitive. On the other hand, Carl Jung, one of the fathers of depth psychology, offers us a different way of seeing the self as an individual. He describes *individuated* people as those who are conscious of the way that familial, societal, and cultural factors shape them.

The *individuation process* includes becoming aware of our groups' influences and evaluating ourselves against them.[10] As part of this process, we would ask, do the white social norms listed above reflect how we wish to be in the world? We can then make our own choices regarding how we want to relate to society's value system. The degree to which we are able to consciously choose is the degree to which we are actually free. If we do not even know how social conditioning affects our day-to-day lives, how can we consider our choices freely made?

Important to note is that the individuation process cannot be completed within one workshop, retreat, year, or even one life stage. This is a lifelong effort. Even the most sophisticated people still have blind spots regarding the ways culture impacts their decisionmaking. Most white people have hardly even begun considering how being white shapes perceptions, attitudes, and behaviors. For us to create a witnessing culture, we need to open our minds to the possibility that what we see as simply our individual personality is also reflective of white culture.

In my opinion, one of the most beautiful ideas within Jung's vision is that the individuation process is one that ties us back to the social collective. Interconnection is not forgotten. The price we pay for separating ourselves out of the group for a time through our self-reflection process is that we must return with our newly-acquired wisdom.[11] In this way, becoming a true individual requires us to find the divine within our deep self, discover our intrinsic relationship with the collective, and offer something beneficial back to society. In this way, our sense of self develops along with our sense of connection with others.[12]

Particularly important is that this approach helps us see that we can give up *individualism* without sacrificing our sense of *individuality*. We can develop our internal sense of value and personal destiny while simultaneously recognizing our essential interconnection. Witnessing ourselves then becomes both personally liberating *and* socially transforming.

Given that white people are generally extremely unconscious regarding how our racial placement affects us, we really need a majority of whites to start delving into this question and then return to share with others. We can then serve as illustrative models of this individuation process in order for it to become widely understood and engaged as part of the development of a witnessing culture. We also should consider:

- In what ways is the value of interconnection already expressed in your interactions with colleagues, family, and friends?

Passion

Passion penetrates, persuades, and inspires. Each of us can likely reflect on moments where our passion has helped spark interest in someone. Similarly, we know when we fall flat, when the emotion evaporates and a cold, dry feeling pervades. We become dry and unpersuasive. If we are going to successfully initiate a shift in our cultural frame, it will come because of our passion.

Part of approaching race work with passion, though, involves healing from our cultural splits wherein our history has encouraged us to value the head, mind, and rational over the heart, body, and emotional. To be sure, men have suffered under the pressure not to display emotion, and women have suffered by being portrayed as overly emotional. Thankfully, the past several decades have involved significant shifts in these historic patterns. Yet, unfortunately, these patterns do continue and our witnessing practice benefits if we confront their effects in a few different ways.

First, we might need to become more sensitive in order to (1) notice the emotions that arise within us and (2) pay attention to that feeling-knowledge. In uncomfortable situations, when race issues come to the foreground, we need to attend to the sensations flowing from our heart and stomach. If we can notice the aches and pains that come with witnessing something challenging, we can use that information to name our own resistance, defensiveness, and discomfort. This is essential because dominant white culture's love of rationality supports our tendency to act as distanced spectators. It is much easier to watch, analyze, and judge. But when we invite our hearts to be part of our process we can stop acting like experts all of the time, engage in a way that admits when we are unclear or unsure, and acknowledge our vulnerabilities.

A second way that we might need to alter our relationship to passion involves breaking through the sanitized and controlled way many of us deal with difficulty. To truly be passionate, we have to reconcile our need to be neat and tidy all of the time. When we go back to the etymological roots of passion, we find it linked with being pathetic. Are we ready to be pathetic for racial justice? Will we risk standing up, speaking out and being perceived as the fool? Can we allow ourselves to break down in order to build ourselves back up anew? This may require small, initial steps, but we will all benefit profoundly if this level of honest expression becomes a cultural norm.

A third way that our relationship to emotion and passion needs to shift involves accepting the importance of feeling-oriented knowledge that comes from others. We may trust what our gut or heart is telling us, but there often remains a strong tendency to discount this kind of knowing from someone else. The repeating pattern I have observed is that we may become passionate about issues close to our hearts, but we can become cold in the face of others' concerns. We might listen, but we often intellectualize the issues.

From a symbolic point of view, this might have to do with the way our socialization into individualism has allowed us to see our cardiac system as a closed circuit of energy. If our heart remains closed, passion cannot fill us. Compassion then becomes impossible. My suggestion is that a necessary cultural shift involves letting our hearts become more than simple pumps. Instead of seeing the heart as an empty vessel used to move energy around within ourselves, we can recognize the heart as an organ of perception.[13] When our hearts see and hear concerns raised, our *response-ability* then can kick in.

If we combine an open-hearted and passionate perception with a sense of interconnection, then we can move a long way toward reducing the percepticide we may have fallen into over the course of our lives. When we see how the myriad social justice issues actually make a real difference in people's lives, we are more likely to express our witnessing with the kind of infectious passion that can influence others to join us in taking a stand to make necessary systemic changes. We can also think about the following:

- In what ways is passion already expressed in your interactions with colleagues, family, and friends?
- How might you need to open your heart further in order to better hear concerns raised by others in your social and work life?

Obligation

A sense of obligation is not a foreign value to most of us. We regularly obligate ourselves to our families, friends, and so on. In this way, there is already something essential we understand and value about obligation as part of our culture. Yet a witnessing culture would require us to extend our sense of obligation. Instead of only having an obligation to do our best for a select few in our lives, we also need to feel an *obligation to the social collective.*

When we truly recognize the interconnections between us all, we see that we truly are all one people and that our obligation to one another must increase. This suggestion also mirrors what Robert Putnam calls for in *Bowling Alone,* as he imagines what is required for our society to remake the social glue that keeps us together.[14] Without an increase in the type of civic engagement that both binds us and creates bridges between groups, our country will move toward increased divisions.

For white people, being obligated to the social collective means three things, several of which have been discussed in previous chapters. First, we must choose to regularly and purposefully face the privilege we benefit from in this white-dominated society. Second, we have to challenge ourselves to act against racism and white privilege in spite of our freedom *not* to act.

Third, for a witnessing culture to emerge, we have to support each other's work to end systematic racism and white dominance.

Racism is far more entrenched within our systems and institutions than we generally like to admit. Although essential to take up our task of thoroughly looking at ourselves to find remnants of racism and how we benefit from whiteness, we also are obligated to recognize that large-scale, systemic change only occurs when large numbers of people begin to support an issue. In this way, to have a witnessing culture, we would need to be ready to extend the messages of social-justice activists and support their efforts with our votes and donations.

When we feel obligated to witness for social justice, we might find that the conversations between Cultural Creatives can also expand. For example, efforts toward environmental sustainability are tremendously important. A witnessing culture would ensure that corresponding issues of environmental racism also make it onto the discussion table. Linking our work with spiritual and psychological healing movements is also essential. A witnessing culture will ask these movements to see how taking issues of race into account can actually increase self-awareness and add a grounded, soulful element to spiritual growth.

For me, it also comes down to a basic premise that we cannot simply ignore the struggles of those around us and enjoy psychological health. The trend toward healthy living, then, is a dedicated effort toward increasing the health and well-being of our collective. Surely becoming aware of how race impacts our lives should be part of that healing effort. In the end, the degree to which we feel inclined to take up a witnessing stance with a sense of obligation will be the deciding factor in whether or not we reach enough people to inspire a real movement of change. We have to ask ourselves:

- Where do you see openings to link race issues with other social justice concerns within your life?
- To what degree do you feel obligated to work on racial/social justice concerns?

Vigilance

Given that the predominant cultural norm for white people is to turn away from race, the decision to witness involves a dramatic reversal of perspective. Developing a sufficient number of people dedicated to witnessing requires a cultural shift that supports vigilance in several areas. We need to (1) break through percepticide, (2) commit to the long-term nature of the effort, (3) build a collective process, and (4) continually seek out feedback.

First, valuing vigilance means that we confront our long history of collective *percepticide*.[15] What are all of the various ways we have killed off our own perceptions? For a long time, percepticide has been one way that white people have denied evidence that we are unintentionally complicit in systemic injustice. Valuing vigilance means stripping ourselves of this defensive pattern on a day-to-day basis. The benefit for white people is that this vigilance offers us a viable path away from our reliance on a false sense of innocence. Instead of depending upon a sense of inherent goodness for a positive sense of self, we can start to feel proud of our efforts to face our history and dismantle white-skin privilege.

Second, valuing vigilance means that we thoroughly understand the long-term nature of the commitment to witnessing. We have to guard against the belief that our internal journey to excise racism from our psyches will ever be completed. At precisely the moments when we become comfortable, we are really ready for our next breakthrough. That is when the next layer of our psyche can be peeled back. In this way, our relationship to witnessing racism and the ways it embeds itself in our psyches is like peeling an onion. There are layers upon layers upon layers.

For us to have a witnessing culture, we have to be consistently on guard. Yes, we need to appreciate our progress. At the same time, we also need to appreciate the depth of challenge we face. It will be important to avoid beating ourselves up mercilessly when we encounter our blind spots. Continued self-flagellation only makes us want to give up and retreat into a privileged disconnection. That is why our vigilance is so important. Dedicating ourselves to a lifelong effort of uncovering blind spots, although painful at times, also can bring feelings of pride that keep us moving forward.

Third, valuing vigilance as part of a witnessing culture requires building a collective effort. To do this, we have to interrogate the way that the vestiges of our individualism can influence what we imagine it means to be vigilant. When we think of someone on guard, we might imagine that person alone, the only one up late at night. This is a really hard position. If we imagine that we are going to be the only one on watch for an extended period of time, we are likely not to want to sign up for the job.

Part of our ability to stay vigilant depends on creating communities where members keep each other awake. We need the rejuvenation that comes with camaraderie. In the darkest hours, we need people around us who are equally committed to keeping watch with us. A witnessing culture's vigilance, then, goes hand in hand with a rejection of the ideal of the lone hero who shoulders the weight of the world in isolation.

Finally, part of valuing vigilance involves continually searching for feedback. True, we are generally correct in believing that we know ourselves better than anyone else. However, when it comes to the way that our behavior betrays our socialization into white culture, white people are generally hopelessly inept. After years of inquiry, we are still likely to miss subtle areas. If we are really going to remain vigilant, we need to open ourselves to taking in information from those who have spent their lives trying to move effectively within white spaces. In other words, we are likely never to be as sensitive to issues of white privilege as a person of color, and therefore part of our vigilance involves us seeking feedback from willing contributors.

To the degree that we value vigilance, we continue to do the work of increasing the skills, knowledge, and capacities that enable us to respond to all that we see within our work and social lives. We can then begin to inspire vigilance in others. Some things we ought to consider include:

- What are the challenges that can get in the way of our intended vigilance?
- In the face of our challenges, what supportive structures can we create to help keep us engaged?

Accountability

When we increasingly notice racism and white privilege and employ active responses, our witnessing can quite organically lead us toward what many consider "ally" work. The possibility that our witnessing might be confused with ally work is a good thing. That would mean that we are really making great strides. One thing we would have to prepare for, however, is that discussions involving the word "ally" usually include the word "accountability."

Since accountability is a concept that a witnessing culture must value, there are several questions we ought to at least briefly discuss. What does being accountable mean? Why should we value this concept? And how does this term relate to some difficulties we may run into when developing witnessing communities?

A primary requirement of accountability is that white people do not create collective actions against racism without collaboration with people of color. This is essential because too many white activists have rallied together and set out to battle racism without listening to the people of color impacted by such racism. Given our relative ignorance of the subtleties of the issues, white people acting against racism are highly susceptible to error. Therefore, it is a *requirement* that when we act, we do so in solidarity with people of color.

Additionally, a witnessing culture valuing accountability recognizes that although we do this work for our own humanity, we are not the only ones invested in the outcome. We must ask questions and listen. For example, there is no way I would have written this book without checking in with people of color. Problematic issues both of content and style emerged that I would never have noticed on my own. The contributions of people of color have been essential in making this book what it is.

The idea of being accountable can raise complicated questions, however. What exactly might accountability look like? Does it mean that white people need to take a backseat to people of color and be told what to do? Does it mean that we cannot use our own voices to offer opinions? The honest answer is that it depends on the context: the situation, the people involved, our knowledge base, and our experience. Sometimes we will need to simply take directions. Other times we might be asked to be in the lead. Still other times we will be full, equitable partners. These are questions that can only be answered within our cross-race relationships.

As we move more fully into the work of witnessing and become increasingly seen as allies, the development of accountability guidelines becomes essential. These guidelines can be really valuable. For example, being accountable can help us troubleshoot so we save ourselves the pain of messing up badly on a larger stage. Second, setting up accountability measures for our witnessing work also helps us develop nonoppressive communication skills that can help us create multiracial dialogue spaces where relationships can deepen.

As discussed in Chapter 8, white people will likely run into critical questions if creating witnessing communities that include only white people. We may find ourselves in a bit of a catch-22. On one hand, we know white people need to talk to other whites about these issues, work together to advance our own understanding, and take up some of the burden that has fallen upon the shoulders of people of color for far too long. In this way, we know racially-caucused groups of white people may be seen as *communities of necessity* and, ultimately, we have been asked to do this work by people of color. On the other hand, our lack of experience and collective history of making inappropriate decisions when operating on our own makes us understandably untrustworthy in regards to this work. Where does that leave us?

My answer is that we can, and should, do both. We can struggle together as white people to understand our own identity process, our pains, guilt, and fears. A witnessing space filled with white people doing this work together is where we can share our successes, failures, and emotions in a community that encourages us to keep moving forward. When we realize that we are doing this for our own humanity, we have an invested interest in this, regardless of whether there are many people of color in our immediate environments.

However, we also have to ensure that we do not reinforce our own isolation. We must be part of communities that include people of color who are invited to comment on what they see as either beneficial or problematic about our process. We can use that feedback to improve our own internal process with white people. In the end, the white space should exist solely for the purpose of helping us (1) learn about ourselves, (2) better sustain and participate in multiracial spaces, and (3) develop our witnessing practice. Healthy, sustainable integration in a just society is the larger goal! Some questions to keep in mind:

- Are there any people in your life who might be willing to offer you feedback regarding your witnessing efforts?
- What type of witnessing community are you most likely to form: racially-caucused, multiracial, or both? Why?
- How will you make sure that your work with white people does not unintentionally reinforce problematic aspects of racism or white privilege?

Historical Memory

We have all sat in history or social-studies classes where teachers have argued that we can avoid tragic errors by attending to past events and applying the lessons learned in our present. This is true. However, *historical memory* refers to something different. Historical memory refers to the way the past is in evidence in the present and requires attention for the sake of our future.

If we appreciate the strength of historical memory as part of our witnessing, we need to develop our vision from at least three different angles. These include recognizing (1) the way our socio/political/economic history influences what we see in society today, (2) how historical memory is passed down through generations of families and communities, and (3) from a decidedly non-Western point of view, we need to imagine how our unhealed ancestors continue to require attention in order for personal and community healing to occur.

First, we can ask, how does our country's history play out in the present? The last section of Chapter 3 offers some examples of how the historical development of whiteness has shaped some contemporary issues. However, when we expand our view we can begin to recognize how our history of racism contributes to each of our sociological patterns and institutions.

To take but one example to illustrate a much more expansive reality, how do we explain the great concentrations of African Americans living within inner cities and the preponderance of whites living in predominantly segregated small towns and suburbs across our nation? I recall wondering about this myself years back. My ignorance led me to draw upon stereotypes to surmise that African Americans either simply chose to coalesce together out of a felt sense of familiarity, did not have enough money to move, or perhaps, since I live in Los Angeles, did not want to go somewhere with a cold climate. These explanations are rather common among white people. I knew nothing about Sundown Towns. Most white people have not heard of them either.

James Loewen's book, *Sundown Towns: A Hidden Dimension of American Racism,* details how at least 1,000 towns and/or suburbs went "sundown" between 1890 and 1968.[16] A sundown town is defined as "any organized jurisdiction that for decades kept out African Americans (or others)."[17] Many of these towns are still exclusively white today. An initial reaction might be to assume that this simply meant not selling property to prospective African American homeowners. This would be wrong.

Loewen offers, in painstaking detail, the various ways that communities of Black and other minority families were removed from towns, sometimes within one night! He discusses middle-of-the-night violence, threats, the rise of the KKK *after* 1915, ordinances, and official government action. These towns often posted signs that read, literally, *N——. Don't let the sun set on you in _____*. Until you have read this book, you have no idea how close this might hit to your own hometown. I was personally affected as I read that Long Beach, California, the city where both of my parents grew up, had been one of the more vicious sundown towns in my state.

The issue here, beyond our need to learn about this history, is that white people generally have a lot of opinions about why things are the way they are. We do this within a society that encourages us *not* to see how our history of racism is a key factor. Educators then teach from this perspective. The new mantra is that class and personal choice are largely to blame for our contemporary segregation. But Loewen offers evidence to support the conclusion that "racial and religious exclusion came first, not class"[18] and he treats the various explanations whites usually offer to excuse ourselves from our role as the protectors of this pattern.

If, as we build our knowledge base, we look for books on just about any of our social systems and institutions, we find that racism set patterns in place that continue today. Unless active work is engaged to disrupt these cycles, they will not stop. A witnessing culture has to be knowledgeable enough to (1) see through conversations that continue to ignore the effects of unjust social structures that white people put in place and (2) demand an education that does not sidestep the impacts of our racial history. We then also have to do something about the unjust social structures.

A second way to appreciate the strength of historical memory is to see how earlier generations' experiences are passed down to subsequent generations. Elders regularly teach their children and grandchildren coping mechanisms and strategies to deal with social stressors present in earlier years. If the external influences change markedly, the young ones might cast off those increasingly unnecessary skills and strategies. However, if the environment appears to stay the same, we should not be surprised that new generations carry their elders' messages of how they should expect to be perceived and treated and how to navigate their way through a society marked by racism.

This pattern extends far beyond familial relationships. Generational transmission of a person's sense of possibility and place occur wherever a young person walks in society. Youth learn from authority figures, other community members, and media sources. We have a duty to look really carefully at the messages young people receive from society these days both about themselves and their opportunities. This transmission of historical memory is a little-discussed but gigantic issue within our schools. The more we can understand the messages students receive and why, the more we can appreciate the issues we face and the work we must do to facilitate a different experience of the world.

A third way we can understand the idea of historical memory involves the spiritual viewpoint that our ancestors remain connected to our world in ways that continue to affect us. If we can extend ourselves out of Western, modernist thought, we can see this as a metaphysical reality wherein the unhealed ancestors of our traumatic history continue to require healing. Most white people I know pretty much shut down at this concept. Our Western conceptions often cannot imagine that the anguish of someone killed years ago would haunt our present reality.

However, there are also many who understand that the blood spilt on this country's ground reflects deep, unhealed wounds and that the spirits of those who participated and died require healing gestures before any of us can move on. If you have ever sat with someone who appears to actually tap into this ancestral pain, you might understand what I am saying. Figuring out how to honor that pain and anguish so that we might build a better future together requires us to recognize the reality of this historical memory and value reconciliation gestures. We need to ask:

- In what ways do you take historical memory into account when judging situations?

Reconciliation

In refusing to attend to the wounds of the past, the majority of the white population generally pushes forward believing in the old adage that time heals all wounds. Although possible that time does heal, an important factor is what we do during that time. Do we turn a blind eye to what caused the wounds in the first place? Or do we seek a deeper understanding and a way through to a different life? Overall, the United States has not set a good example of how to recover from crimes against humanity.

When Dr. Roberto Cabrera spoke of reconciliation processes and peace building in a lecture in Belfast in 1998, he posed the question, "Should we remember?" Even though he was speaking of reconciliation processes in Guatemala after the thirty-six-year internal war, his fundamental question seems equally applicable to issues surrounding race relations in the United States. In response to that first question he then asked, "Has any victim forgotten?"

Dr. Cabrera suggests that we consider the following: Who benefits if the atrocities of the past are forgotten? He goes on to say, "Most of the excuses not to remember say that it must not reopen the wounds of the past. I can certainly say, that denying the past will never lead to the closing of wounds. They are there, fresh and painful, unless the society as a whole [does] something to heal them."[19]

What might efforts at reconciliation look like in our communities? There are more possibilities than can even be imagined. They might involve small-group dialogues, art projects, or written expressions. They may be truth and reconciliation panels. Or, they could involve community gatherings and dialogues, public apologies, affirmative-action policies, reparations, political activity, and so forth. The point is not to suggest any particular form. More important is conveying the idea that each person might be inspired to offer something back in his or her own way. When that happens, and if the effort is sincere, we can be supportive of that effort.

For example, Andrew Hawkins, a descendant of Sir John Hawkins, and a group of his friends recently traveled to The Gambia, knelt in chains in front of 25,000 Africans and asked for forgiveness for the sins of his direct forefathers. Perhaps not surprisingly, the group's "reconciliation walk" did not impress some of the village elders they passed. However, the elders' attitudes reportedly changed after they engaged in dialogue with the British group. Andrew Hawkins stated that, "I think they wanted to see an emotional connection from us, and to see that we had gone there in humility. All I could say was that we have got to do more listening and learning."[20]

Regardless of whether or not you would ever imagine being part of a gesture of that sort, the question is, how would you respond to Andrew Hawkins? At this point, the dominant white culture holds disdain for his actions, wondering how someone can apologize for a past action in which he did not directly take part. A culture that witnesses whiteness does two things. First, a witnessing culture supports those who have the courage to step out of our collective denial and irresponsibility in order to stand up for the sake of healing old wounds, for the sake of healing our historical, ancestral memory. Thankfully, there are some U.S. states that very recently officially apologized for their role in our collective history of slavery. This is a start.

Second, a witnessing culture ensures that if and when we ever decide to participate in a healing ritual of any kind that we first check our level of sincerity. As a spiritual move, that would surely make all the difference in the world. Here, it also bears repeating that any move in that direction would surely warrant a check-in with those who would hold us accountable so that we can ensure that our efforts are as effective as possible.

Lastly, Michael Meade spoke rather eloquently on the topic of trauma, healing, and ancestral memory during our interview. As a mythologist who incorporates healing rituals into his work, Michael combines his love of symbolism and ancient wisdom to capture some ideas that offer an image to work toward without glossing over the horrors of our past. His thoughts deserve a full reading.

> I think America is an experiment in trauma as much as an experiment in freedom. I think America is a traumatic collision of people pitched into, dragged into, escaping into a place which becomes an aggregation of historical trauma. And if there's an American dream, and I think there is, it's that a nightmare could become a dream, not in some naïve way, but in the sense of an awakening to a healing ground where historical and even ancestral trauma could be worked on.
>
> That view comes out of a little vision born of working with diverse groups of people in ways that allow distinct medicines to come out. Just as there are literal medicines that come from roots in the Amazon, there are certain medicines that can come out of old Europe, medicines from Africa, medicines from each land.
>
> Like if you were above the Earth looking at all the trauma and all the wounds in all the peoples, you might also see the medicines in all the different places as well. Then, if all the people meeting in a given place brought the medicines from their backgrounds and their root forms of knowledge, the trading of these medicines might induce a mutual healing. That's the best image of America I've ever had.
>
> Ultimately, people have to learn to trust in people unlike themselves because the difference, the Otherness, is also the medicine for the illness one inherits. That's how I see it. People unlike oneself turn out to be carrying the medicines one's own tribe doesn't have or else has lost . . . some of the best healing I've found for those wounds have been with people from other cultures dealing with similar damages. Mutual healing is the hope that I have for America; but it depends upon cracking the white shell, the shell of "white thinking."
>
> If you go into African cosmology, white is associated with bones, shells, stones, ash, and salt . . . Some of the essential symbolic associations include

deep memory, ancestral connection, language, stories, poems, metaphorical shapes for rich communication. So what I think has to happen . . . is that the deeper memory that is ancestral to humans has to awaken. Not, the Balkanized level of tribal memory, that's the traumatic layer that requires great healing, but below that the deep medicine of the Old Mind, the ancestral mind and soul that is the inheritance of all humanity.

Take special notice that the ability for us to get to this level of healing, where the various medicines residing within each cultural group can be offered and accepted, depends on our ability to break through whiteness. We need to take time to reflect on how this deep message might find translation into our social and work lives:

- Is there room in your life to promote the value of reconciliation efforts?
- What type of conversation might be required to create a sense of appreciation for the reconciliation efforts you might support?

To conclude, each of the eight values discussed—multiplicity, interconnection, obligation, passion, vigilance, accountability, historical memory, and reconciliation—all combine to invite us to move away from the dominant forms of white culture so prevalent at the beginning of this twenty-first century. If we (1) choose to collectively express the values described above and (2) entice others who are invested in creating a new culture to attend to the effects of race, we can create a witnessing culture that might make a real difference in our society.

JOINING THE HIDDEN AMERICA

The final question for us to consider is whether or not a witnessing culture can exist within the United States. The answer is that yes, assuredly it can. The truth is that a witnessing culture has always been here, hidden under the surface, just waiting for enough of us to notice and grab hold. The culture of witnessing has a long history. It is a culture with well-worn paths, albeit not ones that are well publicized. For those who are most active, the path can be rocky and appear treacherous at its beginning. Following it to its end, one enters the world of the allies. For those who speak of this way of being, they often include the recognition that it is a different world. In a letter to antiracist activist Anne Braden, William Patterson, an African American activist, offers that:

> You don't have to be part of the world of the lynchers. You do have a choice.
> You can join the other America. The other America has always been here. From

the time the first slave ship arrived. It is the people who fought against slavery. Against injustice. The people who fought for humanity. It was Black and it was white.[21]

This "other America" is home for those who witness actively, those who might someday be considered allies.

This is the hidden America, an America that strengthens and supports all of her residents, an America that includes rather than excludes, and an America that fulfills its deepest purpose. This America has so far existed in the shadows. If white people en masse join this other America in the spirit of witnessing, we can heal the dis-ease we feel about race. In our healing, we can help make America what it has yet to be for so many, the America of our ideals. This is the American dream many of us hold in our hearts. So, really, the question is, will enough of us stand up and witness so that America's dream can come true?

NOTES

1. Ray, P. H., and S. R. Anderson, *The Cultural Creatives: How 50 Million People Are Changing the World* (New York: Harmony Books, 2000), 4.

2. Ray and Anderson, *The Cultural Creatives,* 15.

3. Ray and Anderson, *The Cultural Creatives,* 17

4. Ray and Anderson, *The Cultural Creatives,* 341.

5. Gladwell, M., *The Tipping Point: How Little Things Can Make a Big Difference* (New York: Back Bay Books, 2000).

6. Gladwell, *The Tipping Point,* 179.

7. Oliver, *Witnessing: Beyond Recognition.*

8. Tarnas, *The Passion of the Western Mind.*

9. Putnam, *Bowling Alone.*

10. Jung, C. G., "Conscious, Unconscious, and Individuation," in *The Collected Works of C. G. Jung,* vol. 9, trans. R. F. C. Hull (Princeton, NJ: Princeton University Press, 1969), 275; original work published in 1939.

11. Jung, C. G., "Adaptation, Individuation, Collectivity," in *The Collected Works of C. G. Jung,* vol. 18, trans. R. F. C. Hull (Princeton, NJ: Princeton University Press, 1969), 451; original work published in 1970.

12. Jung, C. G., "On the Nature of the Psyche," in *The Collected Works of C. G. Jung,* vol. 8, trans. R. F. C. Hull (Princeton, NJ: Princeton University Press, 1969), 226; original work published in 1947.

13. Romanyshyn, *Ways of the Heart.*

14. Putnam, *Bowling Alone,* 400, 404, and 411.

15. Lorenz and Watkins, "Silenced Knowings, Forgotten Springs," 3. The concept of "percepticide" is taken from Taylor, *Disappearing Acts.*

16. Loewen, J., *Sundown Towns: A Hidden Dimension of American Racism* (New York: New Press, 2005), 80.

17. Loewen, *Sundown Towns,* 213.

18. Loewen, *Sundown Towns,* 145.

19. Cabrera, R., "Should We Remember? Recovering Historical Memory in Guatemala," in *Past Imperfect: Dealing with the Past in Northern Ireland and Societies in Transition,* ed. by B. Hamber, 1998 (Incore/Derry/Londonderry, North Ireland).

20. Hamilton, Alan, "Slaver's Descendant Begs Forgiveness," *The Times Online,* June 22, 2006, http://www.timesonline.co.uk/tol/news/world/article677647.ece.

21. Thompson, *A Promise and a Way of Life ,* 52.

Bibliography

Allen, T. W. 1997. *The Invention of the White Race.* New York: Verso.

———. n.d. Summary of the Argument of *The Invention of the White Race.* Part Two. Available at http://clogic.eserver.org/1–2/allen2.html.

Alonso-Zaldivar, R., and J. Merl. 2004. Booklet That Upset Mrs. Cheney Is History. *Los Angeles Times,* October 8, A1.

American Anthropological Association. 1998. *Statement on "Race."* May 17, 1998. Available at http://www.aaanet.org/stmts/racepp.htm.

Association for Supervision and Curriculum Development. 2003. *Closing the Achievement Gap: A Vision for Changing Beliefs and Practices,* edited by B. Williams. Alexandria, VA: ASCD.

Atiba, P., and J. Eberhardt. *A Hateful Link,* Los Angeles Times, Op-ed, A19, February 28, 2009.

AWARE-LA. "Doubletake 08: Taking a Second Look at Race and Racism in the 2008 Presidential Elections." http://doubletakeblog.wordpress.com/

Ayvazian, A., and B. D. Tatum. 1994. Women, Race, and Racism: A Dialogue in Black and White. *Work in Progress,* No. 68. Wellesley, MA: Wellesley College, Center for Research on Women.

Better, S. 2002. *Institutional Racism: A Primer on Theory and Strategies for Social Change.* Chicago, IL: Burnham.

Bigelow, B., B. Harvey, S. Karp, and L. Miller, eds. 2001. *Rethinking Our Classrooms: Teaching for Equity and Justice.* Vol. 2. Milwaukee, WI: Rethinking Schools.

Bivens, D. "Internalized Racism: A Definition." Women's Theological Center. A more complete explanation can be located at www.evaluationtoolsforracialequity.org/termRacial.htm.

Brown, M. 1991. *Race, Money, and the American Welfare State.* Ithaca, NY: Cornell University Press.

Bruce, P. A. 1902. *Social Life in Virginia in the Seventeenth Century: An Inquiry into the Origins of the Higher Planting Class, Together with an Account of the Habits, Customs, and Diversions of the People.* Richmond, VA: Whittet & Shepperson.

Cabrera, R., "Should We Remember? Recovering Historical Memory in Guatemala," in *Past Imperfect: Dealing with the Past in Northern Ireland and Societies in Transition,* ed. by B. Hamber, 1998 (Incore/Derry/Londonderry, North Ireland).

Coll, C. G., R. Cook-Nobles, and J. L. Surrey. 1997. Building Connection through Diversity. In *Women's Growth in Diversity: More Writings from the Stone Center,* edited by J. V. Jordan, 176–98. New York: Guilford Press.

Crass, C. 2004. *Beyond Welfare Queens: Developing a Race, Class and Gender Analysis of Welfare and Welfare Reform.* Available at: http://colours.mahost.org/articles/crass6.html

Cushman, P. 1995. *Constructing the Self, Constructing America: A Cultural History of Psychotherapy.* New York: Addison-Wesley.

DeGruy Leary, J. 2005. *PostTraumatic Slave Syndrome.* Milwaukie, OR: Uptone Press.

Festinger, L., S. Schacter, and K. Black. 1950. *Social Pressures in Informal Groups: A Study of Human Factors in Housing.* Oxford: Harper.

Frankenberg, R. 1993. *The Social Construction of Whiteness: White Women, Race Matters.* Minneapolis: University of Minnesota Press.

———. 1997. Introduction. Local Whitenesses, Localizing Whiteness. In *Displacing Whiteness: Essays in Social and Cultural Criticism,* edited by R. Frankenberg, 1–34. Durham, NC: Duke University Press.

Gilligan, J. 1996. *Violence: Reflections on a National Epidemic.* New York: Vintage Books.

Giroux, H. A. 1992. Postcolonial Ruptures/Democratic Possibilities. In *Border Crossings: Cultural Workers and the Politics of Education,* edited by H. Giroux, 19–38. New York: Routledge.

Gladwell, M. 2000. *The Tipping Point: How Little Things Can Make a Big Difference.* New York: Back Bay Books.

Goldberg, S. and C. Levin, AWARE-LA. *Toward a Radical White Identity,* http://awarela.wordpress.com/toolbox/.

Hamilton, A. 2006. Slaver's Descendant Begs Forgiveness. *The Times Online,* June 22. Available at http://www.timesonline.co.uk/article/0,,3-2236871,00.html.

Haney Lopez, I. F. 1995. White by Law. In *Critical Race Theory: The Cutting Edge,* edited by R. Delgado, 542–50. Philadelphia: Temple University Press.

———. 1996. *White by Law: The Legal Construction of Race.* New York: New York University Press.

Hartigan, J., Jr. 1997. Locating White Detroit. In *Displacing Whiteness: Essays in Social and Cultural Criticism,* edited by R. Frankenberg, 180–213. Durham, NC: Duke University Press.

Havemann, J., and R. Alonso-Zaldivar. 2006. Middle-Class Workers Ailing in Census Checkup. *Los Angeles Times,* August 30.

Helms, J. E. 1992. *A Race Is a Nice Thing to Have: A Guide to Being a White Person or Understanding the White Persons in Your Life.* Topeka, KS: Content Communications.

————. 1995. An Update of Helms's White and People of Color Racial Identity Models. In *Handbook of Multicultural Counseling,* edited by J. Ponterotto, J. Casas, L. Suzuki, and C. Alexander, 181–98. Thousand Oaks, CA: Sage.

Hillman, J. 1983. *Healing Fiction.* Woodstock, CT: Spring.

————. 1986. Notes on White Supremacy: Essaying an Archetypal Account of Historical Events. *Spring* 46:29–58.

HistoricalDocuments.com. n.d. The Immigration Act of 1924. Available at http://www.historicaldocuments.com/ImmigrationActof1924.htm.

hooks, b. 1995. *Killing Rage: Ending Racism.* New York: Henry Holt.

Howard, G. 2006. *We Can't Teach What We Don't Know.* New York: Teachers College.

Hughes, L. 1994. Let America Be America Again. In *The Collected Poems of Langston Hughes,* edited by A. Rampersad and D. Roessel. New York: Alfred A. Knopf.

Ignatiev, N. 1995. *How the Irish Became White.* New York: Routledge.

Jackman, M. R., and M. C. Crane. 1986. "Some of My Best Friends Are Black . . .": Interracial Friendship and Whites' Racial Attitudes. *Public Opinion Quarterly* 50:459–86.

Jay, G. 1998. Who Invented White People? A Talk on the Occasion of Martin Luther King, Jr. Day, 1998. Available at http://www.uwm.edu/~gjay/.

Jensen, R. 2005. *The Heart of Whiteness: Confronting Race, Racism, and White Privilege.* San Francisco: City Lights.

Jordan, W. D. 1969. *White over Black.* Baltimore, MD: Penguin Books.

Jung, C. G. 1969a. Conscious, Unconscious, and Individuation. In *The Collected Works of C. G. Jung,* vol. 9, translated by R. F. C. Hull. Princeton, NJ: Princeton University Press. (Original work published 1939)

————. 1969b. On the Nature of the Psyche. In *The Collected Works of C. G. Jung,* vol. 8, translated by R. F. C. Hull. Princeton, NJ: Princeton University Press. (Original work published 1947)

————. 1970. Adaptation, Individuation, Collectivity. In *The Collected Works of C. G. Jung,* vol. 18, translated by R. F. C. Hull. Princeton, NJ: Princeton University Press. (Original work published 1970)

Kendall, F. 2006. *Understanding White Privilege.* New York: Routledge.

Kivel, P. 1996 *Uprooting Racism: How White People Can Work toward Racial Justice.* Gabriola Island, BC: New Society.

Lipsitz, G. 1998. *The Possessive Investment in Whiteness: How White People Profit from Identity Politics.* Philadelphia: Temple University Press.

Loewen, J. 1996. *Lies My Teacher Told Me: Everything Your History Textbook Got Wrong.* New York: New Press.

————. 2005. *Sundown Towns: A Hidden Dimension of American Racism.* New York: New Press.

Lorenz, H. S., and M. Watkins. 2001. Silenced Knowings, Forgotten Springs: Paths to Healing in the Wake of Colonialism. *Radical Psychology* 2, no. 2. Available at www.radpsynet.org/journal/vol2–2/lorenz-watkins.html.

————. 2003. Depth Psychology and Colonialism: Individuation, Seeing Through, and Liberation. *Quadrant* 33, no. 1:11–32.

Mahoney, M. R. 1997. Segregation, Whiteness, and Transformation. In *Critical White Studies,* edited by R. Delgado and J. Stefancic, 654–57. Philadelphia: Temple University Press.

McIntosh, P. 1989. White Privilege: Unpacking the Invisible Knapsack. *Peace and Freedom.* Philadelphia, PA: Women's International League for Peace and Freedom.

Meade, M. 1993. *Men and the Water of Life.* New York: HarperCollins.

Mennott, M. 2005. Spotlight Skips Cases of Missing Minorities. *USA Today,* June 12.

Moore, S., and R. Fields. 2002. The Great "White" Influx. *LA Times Online,* July 31, 2002. Available at www.uwm.edu/%7Egjay/Whiteness/latimesarticle.htm.

Morales, A. L. 1998. *Medicine Stories: History, Culture and the Politics of Integrity.* Cambridge, MA: South End Press.

Morgan, E. S. 1975. *American Slavery, American Freedom: The Ordeal of Colonial Virginia.* New York: Norton.

Morrison, T. 1992. *Playing in the Dark: Whiteness and the Literary Imagination.* New York: Vintage Books.

Obidah, J. E., and K. M. Teel. 2001. *Because of the Kids: Facing Racial and Cultural Differences in Schools.* New York: Teachers College Press.

O'Connor, A. M. 2006. Diverse Realities of Mysteries. *Los Angeles Times,* July 5.

Oliver, K. 2001. *Witnessing: Beyond Recognition.* Minneapolis: University of Minnesota Press.

Olson, R. A., 1998. White Privilege in Schools. In *Beyond Heroes and Holidays: A Practical Guide to Anti-Racist, Multicultural Education and Staff Development,* edited by E. Lee, D. Menkart, and M. Okazawa-Rey, 83–84. Washington, DC: Network of Educators on the Americas.

Omi, M., and H. Winant. 1994. *Racial Formation in the United States.* New York: Routledge.

Parvez, Z. F. 2002. Women, Poverty, and Welfare Reform. *Sociologists for Women in Society.* Available at www.socwomen.org/socactivism/factwelfare.pdf.

Pitts, L., Jr. 2002. Crazy Sometimes. In *When Race Becomes Real,* edited by B. Singley. Chicago, IL: Lawrence Hill Books.

Putnam, R. 2000. *Bowling Alone: The Collapse and Revival of American Community.* New York: Simon & Schuster.

Race, Place, and Segregation: Redrawing the Color Line in Our Nation's Metros. 2002. *The Civil Rights Project,* Harvard University. Available at www.civilrightsproject .harvard.edu/research/metro/three_metros.php.

Ray, P. H., and S. R. Anderson. 2000. *The Cultural Creatives: How 50 Million People Are Changing the World.* New York: Harmony Books.

Roberts, R. 2003. *My Soul Said to Me.* Deerfield Beach, FL: Health Communications.

Robinson, E. 2005. (White) Women We Love. *Washington Post,* June 10, A23.

Rodriguez, L. 1993. *Always Running: Gang Days in L.A.* Willimantic, CT: Curbstone Press.

Roediger, D. R. 1991. *Wages of Whiteness: Race and the Making of the American Working Class.* New York: Verso.

———. 2002. *Colored White: Transcending the Racial Past.* Los Angeles: University of California Press.

Romanyshyn, R. 2002. *Ways of the Heart: Essays toward an Imaginal Psychology.* Pittsburgh, PA: Trivium.

Sentilles, S. 2005. *Taught by America: A Struggle of Struggle and Hope in Compton.* Boston: Beacon Press.

Singley, B. 2002. *When Race Becomes Real.* Chicago, IL: Lawrence Hill Books.

Tarnas, R. 1991. *The Passion of the Western Mind: Understanding the Ideas That Have Shaped Our World View.* New York: Ballantine Books.

Tatum, B. D. 1994. Teaching White Students about Racism: The Search for White Allies and the Restoration of Hope. *Teachers College Record* 95, no. 4:462–77.

———. 1997. Racial Identity Development and Relational Theory: The Case of a Black Woman in White Communities. In *Women's Growth in Diversity: More Writings from the Stone Center,* edited by J. V. Jordan, 91–106. New York: Guilford Press.

———. 1999. *Why Are All the Black Kids Sitting Together in the Cafeteria?* New York: Basic Books.

———.n.d. 1992. Talking about Race, Learning about Racism: An Application of Racial Identity Development Theory in the Classroom. *Harvard Educational Review* 62, no. 1:1–24.

Taylor, D. 1997. *Disappearing Acts.* Durham, NC: Duke University Press.

Thandeka. 1999. *Learning to Be White: Money, Race, and God in America.* New York: Continuum.

Thompson, B. 2001. *A Promise and a Way of Life: White Antiracist Activism.* Minneapolis: University of Minnesota Press.

Twine, F. W. 1997. Brown-skinned White Girls: Class, Culture, and the Construction of White Identity in Suburban Communities. In *Displacing Whiteness: Essays in Social and Cultural Criticism,* edited by R. Frankenberg, 214–43. Durham, NC: Duke University Press.

Vanderryn, J. H. M. 1993. *A Qualitative Analysis of the Meaning of Being White American.* PhD dissertation, University of Colorado, Boulder, 1994.

Wertenbaker, T. J. 1959. *Patrician and Plebeian in Virginia.* New York: Russell & Russell.

Wise, T. "This Is Your Nation On White Privilege." Red Room: Where the Writers Are, http://www.redroom.com/blog/tim-wise/this-your-nation-white-privilege -updated

Zinn, H. 1980. *A People's History of the United States.* New York: Harper & Row.

———. n.d. *History Is a Weapon: Drawing the Color Line.* Available at http://www .historyisaweapon.com/defcon1/zinncolorline.html.

Index

abolitionist, 46–49, 61

accountability, 237, 246–47, 256–57, 263

Allen, Theodore, 56, 59–61, 78–80, 267

ally: activities, 48–49, 199, 237, 256; model of white, 47–48

American: as a new identity, 61–68, 79n42; use of term, 80n44; values, 65–66

ancestors, 22, 56, 64–65, 130, 137, 247, 249, 258–60

Anderson, Sherry Ruth, 244–45, 264, 270

anecdotes by author: conflict with a mentor/friend, 141–42; doing community work without neediness, 235–37; growing up with ethnocentric education, 53; liberal approach to student discipline, 45; racist treatment of parents in schools, 42–43, 76

antiracist practice, xvi, 199, 246; elements of, 200, 215, 225, 233; techniques, 215–225

antiracist white culture, 241

appropriation, cultural, 25–26, 235

assimilation, 21–23, 26, 48, 61, 65–66

AWARE-LA, xvi, xviii, 16, 33, 47–48, 151, 234, 267

becoming white. *See* American: as a new identity

Better, Shirley, 8, 17, 33n7, 119–20, 124–25, 267

Bowling Alone, 129, 139, 250

Brewer, Spencer, 93–95, 120 22, 125, 128, 144, 159–68, 174, 193–94

Brown, Michael, 15, 33n20

capitalization of Black and white, vi

Cabrera, Roberto, 261

Calloway, Cayce, 106–11, 119, 125, 130, 134–35, 178, 186–87

Cole, Lorraine, 102, 104–6, 179–83

colorblindness, 3, 12, 26–28, 36, 107

Color of Fear, 93, 112, 160, 162

comfort, role of in our lives, 203

communities of necessity, 237, 257

conflict: across race, 132–34, 142–68, 180; meaning the end of relationship, 132, 231–32

Constructing the Self, Constructing America, 61

The Cultural Creatives, 244–46, 254

cultural loss, 21–26, 44, 66

Cushman, Phillip, 61, 68

De Gruy Leary, Joy, xvii, xviii, 69
devil's advocate, 17–18, 224
dialogue, suggestions for: with people of color, 221–25; with white people about race, 219–21
disconnection, 4, 129–31, 134–35, 138–39, 176, 194–95, 225, 242, 249

ethnicity over race, 3, 20–26, 104, 106
equal protection under the law, 13–19
evolution, 30, 69, 131, 172, 174

Frankenberg, Ruth, 10, 27–28

Gladwell, Malcolm, 246
Gottfred, Katie, 102–6, 118, 121–22, 124, 181–83, 185, 187, 215–16
guilt, xiii–xvi, 4, 25, 45–49, 74–77, 98–99, 144, 168, 193–94; adverse consequences of, 37–39, 42, 45, 236

Haney Lopez, Ian, 70
healthy sense of self, xvi, 46, 49, 87, 226–34
heart, as organ of perception, 253
The Heart of Whiteness, 209
Hecate, 5–6, 11, 36, 46, 86, 111, 114, 143, 168, 173, 190, 194, 200, 240
Hillman, James, 136–37
historical memory, 247, 258–60
hooks, bell, 54, 180–81, 189, 194–95
hopefulness, 243
Howard, Gary, 47
Hurricane Katrina, 15–16, 175

individualism, 10, 29, 63, 73, 250–52, 255
Individuation process, 250–51
institutional racism, 8–9, 14, 47
interconnection, 208, 249–53
internalized racism, 174, 181, 193, 207, 240
interracial dating, 30

intersection of race and class, 10, 114, 203, 244
The Invention of the White Race, 54–61
isolation, 65, 128–30, 135, 238, 242, 250

Jensen, Robert, 171, 209
Jung, Carl, 113, 250

Kendall, Frances, vi, 4
Killian, Gloria, 204
Kivel, Paul, 209

Lipsitz, George, 120
Loewen, James, 259

McIntosh, Peggy, 11, 119, 126, 150
Meade, Michael, 88–91, 125–26, 130, 134–37, 178, 183–84, 262
media, 15–17, 126–27, 172, 210–11, 260
mentoring white people, 85, 101, 147, 234–40, 257
misattribution of color terms to humans, 55–56, 136–37
models of how to be white, 36–37, 46–50
modern worldview, 66–68, 75, 114, 245, 248–50
Morrison, Toni, 63, 181
Mosaic Multicultural Foundation, 88, 185, 213
multiplicity, 247–49, 263
Mun Wah, Lee, 93–94, 115, 118–19, 125–26, 131–32, 135, 144, 159–68, 187

Obama, Barack, 9, 16, 28, 172, 178
Obidah, Jennifer, 45, 98–101, 117–20, 124–26, 132–34, 144–52, 187–88, 191–92, 223
obligation, 247, 253–54, 263
Oliver, Kelly, 50–51, 247
Omi, Michael, 22
Ozawa v. United States, 72

passion, 247, 251–53, 263
percepticide, 134, 255
Perez, Amanda, 106–7, 109–10, 186, 188–90
pity, 45
Project Return, 91, 136, 174, 176
Putnam, Robert, 129, 250, 253

race: classification systems, 69–71; early use of term, 55–56; is not real, 9–10, 19–20, 46 neutrality, 8, 10, 12, 14–15, 18, 211
racism: definitions of, 8–9; practiced responses to, 216–19; seen as in the past, 14–19
Radical White Identity, xvi, 48–49, 233–34. *See also* AWARE-LA
Ray, Paul, 244–45
reconciliation, 247, 260–63
Roberts, Robert, 91–93, 98, 115–16, 118–19, 132, 136, 174–77, 180, 232
Rodriguez, Luis, 88, 116–18, 120, 125–27, 183–85, 190
Roediger, David, 14, 79n42
Rule of 150, 246

savior complex, 39–41, 236
segregation, xii, 9, 91–92, 200–202, 250, 259
Singley, Bernestine, 169, 209
"Statement on Race," American Anthropological Association, 9–10
Sundown Towns, 259
superiority complex, 39, 41–44, 191–92
systemic white supremacy, viii, 7, 9

Tarnas, Richard, 66–67, 131–32
Tatum, Beverly Daniel, 8, 36, 47, 149, 151, 168, 209, 230
Teel, Karen, 45, 98–102, 120, 124, 132–33, 144–52, 174, 188, 191–92, 232
Thandeka, 193
Thompson, Becky, 77, 98

The Tipping Point, 246
transcending race, 3, 12, 28–31
trauma, xvii, 4, 31–32, 50, 135, 163, 167, 173, 175, 179–80, 189, 231–32, 260, 262–63

United States v. Thind, 72
Uprooting Racism, 209

vigilance, 247, 254–56, 263
Virginia Codes, 59, 70

We Can't Teach What We Don't Know, 47
When Race Becomes Real, 209
white culture, 1–12, 20, 90, 103–4, 115–18, 127, 129–34, 137, 147, 241–43, 247–52
White Like Me: Reflections on Race from a Privileged Son, 209
Whiteness: in American literature, 63–64, 180–81; legal, 70–73; as related to Western and modern, 67–68, 75, 114–17, 190, 242; shifting nature of, 9–12, 138n3; symbolic meanings of, 136–37, 262–63. *See also* American as a new identity; conflict; disconnection; isolation; white culture
white privilege, xiii, xv–xvi, 11, 16, 117, 119–28, 138, 151, 154–61, 166, 191–92, 205, 208–10, 215, 224, 235, 238
White Privilege Conference, 213–14
Why Are All the Black Kids Sitting Together in the Cafeteria?, 8, 149, 209
Winant, Howard, 22
Wise, Tim, 16, 209
witnessing communities, 200, 233–39, 257–58

Zinn, Howard, 74

About the Author

Shelly Tochluk is an educator with a background in psychology, and she spent ten years as a researcher, counselor, and teacher in California's public schools. She now trains teachers to work with Los Angeles' diverse school population as the Chair of the Education Department at Mount St. Mary's College.

Shelly's personal dedication to confront issues of race developed first through her participation with UCLA's NCAA Division-I All-American Track and Field 4X400 meter relay team and later through her inner-city teaching experiences. Shelly currently serves on the leadership team of AWARE-LA (Alliance of White Anti-Racists Everywhere-Los Angeles). She also co-created a workshop series that leads white people into a deeper understanding of their personal relationship to race, white privilege, and systemic racism. Shelly has presented at the White Privilege Conference, National Conference on Race and Ethnicity in Higher Education, Southeastern Conference on Cross-Cultural Issues in Counseling and Education, the Association of Independent Schools-New England, and the YWCA National Conference, and is committed to speaking at community forums whenever possible to highlight issues of white racial identity.